Teaching Miller's
Death of a Salesman

Approaches to Teaching
World Literature

Joseph Gibaldi, series editor

For a complete listing of titles,
see the last pages of this book.

Approaches to Teaching Miller's *Death of a Salesman*

Edited by

Matthew C. Roudané

The Modern Language Association of America
New York   1995

For information about obtaining permission to reprint material from
MLA book publications, send your request by mail (see address below),
e-mail (permissions@mla.org), or fax (212 477-9863).

Library of Congress Cataloging-in-Publication Data

Approaches to teaching Miller's Death of a salesman /
edited by Matthew C. Roudané.
p.   cm. — (Approaches to teaching world literature; 52)
Includes index.
ISBN 0-87352-727-5 (cloth) — ISBN 0-87352-728-3 (pbk.)
1. Miller, Arthur, 1915-   Death of a Salesman. 2. Miller, Arthur, 1915-   —Study
and teaching. I. Roudané, Matthew Charles, 1953-   II. Series:
Approaches to teaching world literature ; 52.
PS3525.I5156D432   1995
812'.52—dc20   94-32025
ISSN 1059-1133

Cover illustration of the paperback edition: photograph of the original Broadway
production of *Death of a Salesman*, starring Lee J. Cobb and Mildred Dunnock
Photo © Eileen Darby

Second printing 1998. Set in Caledonia. Printed on recycled paper

Published by The Modern Language Association of America
10 Astor Place, New York, New York 10003-6981

For
Charles and Orient

CONTENTS

PREFACE TO THE SERIES

In *The Art of Teaching* Gilbert Highet wrote, "Bad teaching wastes a great deal of effort, and spoils many lives which might have been full of energy and happiness." All too many teachers have failed in their work, Highet argued, simply "because they have not thought about it." We hope that the Approaches to Teaching World Literature series, sponsored by the Modern Language Association's Publications Committee, will not only improve the craft—as well as the art—of teaching but also encourage serious and continuing discussion of the aims and methods of teaching literature.

The principal objective of the series is to collect within each volume different points of view on teaching a specific literary work, a literary tradition, or a writer widely taught at the undergraduate level. The preparation of each volume begins with a wide-ranging survey of instructors, thus enabling us to include in the volume the philosophies and approaches, thoughts and methods of scores of experienced teachers. The result is a sourcebook of material, information, and ideas on teaching the subject of the volume to undergraduates.

The series is intended to serve nonspecialists as well as specialists, inexperienced as well as experienced teachers, graduate students who wish to learn effective ways of teaching as well as senior professors who wish to compare their own approaches with the approaches of colleagues in other schools. Of course, no volume in the series can ever substitute for erudition, intelligence, creativity, and sensitivity in teaching. We hope merely that each book will point readers in useful directions; at most each will offer only a first step in the long journey to successful teaching.

Joseph Gibaldi
Series Editor

PREFACE TO THE VOLUME

If one were to hazard a guess as to what American play is most studied at the university level, it might not be too fanciful to suggest Arthur Miller's *Death of a Salesman*. The play remains what Walter Benjamin would call a "cultural treasure." Such is the case, I suspect, because within the psycho-drama of the Loman family lies a tragic mixture of pity and fear that stirs primal emotions. On one level, the play seems indebted to *The Poetics* and Hellenic heroism, but on a deeper level the play transcends the wonderful tyranny of Aristotle: *Death of a Salesman* is classically traditional and, at the same time, it subverts classicism with its surprisingly postmodernist textures. Moreover, the play presents various enabling fables which define "the myth of the American dream" to such an extent that many students (if not teachers) assume, on an a priori level, that the principles Willy Loman values—initiative, hard work, family, freedom, consumerism, economic salvation, competition, the frontier, and so on—animate American cultural poetics.

Teaching the play well is thus exceedingly challenging precisely because its text and subtext replicate a model of community and of citizenship to which most Americans—no matter what their race, gender, or ideology—respond. Defining the nature of such a response, however, immediately challenges claims that Miller presents a monologic vision of human experi-ence. After all, the contributors to this volume implicitly ask, what exactly is Miller representing? For the rhetorical critic, the play invites an explora-tion of the effects of language and the ways in which language persuades and emotionally affects us. The structuralist or semiotician is drawn to the linguistic richness of the play and the ways in which the social conditions of Miller's work generate meaning. For feminists, the playwright creates a grammar of space that marginalizes Linda Loman and, by extension, all women, who seem banished to the periphery of a patriarchal world. For the universalist, *Death of a Salesman* seems beyond philosophical limits, a play to which all—social constructionists, Jungians, Marxists—react. For the mythopoeic critic, it embodies a rich matrix of archetypal patterns. The list goes on. No wonder some students have ambivalent feelings about the play. For the serious student, it embodies a constellation of conflicting views, the contents of which are explored in the following essays.

Locating Miller's intellectual position in the context of the action that unfolds onstage is particularly important. The play seems so simple (while Miller privileges language, his is an idiolect of clichés), seems so wedded to American culture (family, employment, making ends meet), yet *Salesman* may be analyzed from so many cultural and critical perspectives. Hence the contributors to this volume discuss the value of reexamining both the principles that Miller reifies on the stage and the ways in which teacher-scholars may interpret Miller's paradigm of the social contract.

This volume took shape from several principal sources. First, following the editorial model of the series, I prepared a questionnaire to gauge the way in which my colleagues teach *Death of a Salesman* and, with the help of the MLA staff, mailed more than two hundred survey forms to faculty members in both English and theater departments. After evaluating the returned surveys and proposals, I singled out instructors whose approaches seemed, collectively, to cover a healthy range of pedagogical concerns and invited them to submit essays. I designed part 1, "Materials," to address the major ideas discussed within the contributors' essays and the survey responses. This part highlights primary and secondary text options, reviews selected Miller scholarship, and raises several important issues that were not discussed in the essays or questionnaires but seem helpful to anyone teaching Arthur Miller. *Approaches to Teaching* Death of a Salesman thus serves, I hope, as a stimulating and practical resource for nonspecialists teaching the play to undergraduates and perhaps also for specialists in graduate seminars.

I would like to thank all survey participants and the members of the MLA Publications Committee. Adrienne Ward and Sonia Kane, assistant acquisitions editors for the MLA, were extremely helpful. Special thanks go to Joseph Gibaldi, general editor of the series, whose invaluable assistance, patience, and judgment throughout every phase of developing this volume made the editorial process a pleasure. I wish to thank, too, the many anonymous outside readers whose evaluations and suggestions for revisions, from my original proposal through the final review, helped shape the volume. Thanks to Erin Sledd Holmes, Mariane Schaum, and Elizabeth Day for their editorial help. Finally, thanks to Susan Ashley, again.

Matthew C. Roudané
Georgia State University

Part One

MATERIALS

Editions

Teachers who include *Death of a Salesman* in their courses have several texts from which to choose, each with its own advantages and limitations. Although there is no official standard edition, many scholars regard *Arthur Miller's Collected Plays*, volume 1, as the nearest thing to such an edition. Indeed, *Collected Plays* emerges as an authoritative volume, providing a reasonable sampling of Miller's early work and giving readers some sense of the technical versatility and range of the playwright's aesthetic and moral imagination. *Collected Plays*, which many survey participants use, allows teachers and students to see Miller's experiments with realism, naturalism, and expressionism and to track the evolution of his career. In addition to *Death of a Salesman*, the *Collected Plays* edition includes *All My Sons* (1947), *The Crucible* (1953), *A Memory of Two Mondays* (1955), and *A View from the Bridge* (produced 1955; first published as one-act play, 1955; revised two-act version, 1957). *Collected Plays* also contains Miller's own introduction, an introduction that many feel captures vividly the playwright's dramatic theories, social commitment, and moral seriousness. In fact, after reading Miller's introduction, one comes away with a clear awareness of the playwright's technique, his use of psychology and time, his sense of "the fundamental nature of theater, its historic function" (3), and the way in which he regards the creative process itself.

Many teachers and students prefer as their standard edition the Viking Penguin paperback, which is simply entitled *Death of a Salesman*. Indeed, contributors use this edition for all citations in the essays that follow. Despite cosmetic changes to the cover, this slender volume has long been a text of choice. The least expensive edition now available, the Viking Penguin volume contains only the playscript itself and is textually reliable. The simplicity of this edition, according to one respondent, makes the play less imposing than *Collected Plays* for students reading Miller for the first time.

Several other available editions include critical introductions, selected theater reviews, critical essays, essays by Miller, chronologies, and other addenda that may make them particularly useful for upper-division courses in drama and graduate seminars on Miller. (Since few respondents report using acting versions of the play, I do not include them here.) Many teachers still order, for instance, *Arthur Miller*: Death of a Salesman: *Text and Criticism*, edited by Gerald Weales. Part of the Viking Critical Library Series, this volume has numerous scholarly features. The volume contains a chronology of important dates and Weales's informative introduction, one that takes into account the play's impact on the critical establishment ever since Willy Loman "died the death of a salesman on the stage of the Morosco Theatre on February 10, 1949"; Willy stands as a major literary figure, Weales suggests, who comes "back to elicit sympathy, evoke pity, provoke anger, stir up controversy, ask for judicial appraisal" (vii). Students will find particularly fascinating in this edition the reproductions of typescript pages of *Salesman* on which Miller was working a month before the first rehearsal, complete with his penciled-in revisions. The following two thirds of the volume contains criticism of the play, including some of Miller's own well-known and influential theater essays: "Tragedy and the Common Man," "The 'Salesman' Has a Birthday," "The American Theater," "Introduction to *Collected Plays*," and "Morality and Modern Drama." Readers will also discover an excerpt from Jo Mielziner's *Designing for the Theatre*, "Designing a Play: *Death of a Salesman*." Mielziner—famous for working with Elia Kazan on, among many other productions, Tennessee Williams's *A Streetcar Named Desire*—was largely responsible for the innovative sets and lighting for the original staging of *Salesman*. Many students also find it refreshing to read selected theater reviews of the Broadway premiere, which convey the excitement generated on the night of 10 February 1949 by the cast: Lee J. Cobb (Willy), Mildred Dunnock (Linda), Arthur Kennedy (Biff), and Cameron Mitchell (Happy). This volume contains seven reviews. Readers will also find eight critical essays, some of which are notable for their harsh assessments of *Salesman* (especially Joseph A. Hynes's critique). Next are five "general essays" on Miller's theater, followed by a section entitled "Analogues," which contains Eudora Welty's "Death of a Traveling Salesman" and Tennessee Williams's *The Last of My Solid Gold Watches*, among other pieces. The Viking Critical Library edition closes with a section appropriate to the teaching of the play, "Topics for Discussion and Papers," compiled by C. P. Noyes and Malcolm Cowley, and a useful if dated bibliography including fifty entries.

The *Portable Arthur Miller*, like *Collected Plays*, offers students and teachers a broad view of Miller's dramatic oeuvre as well as selections from Miller's nondramatic writings. Edited by Harold Clurman, this volume contains—along with *Death of a Salesman—The Crucible, Incident at Vichy*, and *The Price*. Complementing the play scripts and Clurman's informative introduction and biographical notes are the two versions of *The Misfits* ("the original story" and "a cinema novel" version); two short stories, "Fame" and "Fitter's Night"; excerpts from *In Russia* (1969), Miller's reportage on the Soviet Union, complete with photographs by his coauthor, his wife, Inge Morath; and "Lines from California," a Miller poem. The bibliography that wraps up the 592-page volume, like the one in the Viking Critical Library edition, is dated but nonetheless informative. It lists all plays through *The Price*, Miller's lesser-known radio plays, his fiction, his articles (through 1969), and selected interviews with Miller (through 1966). The Clurman volume, unlike Weales's, contains no secondary bibliography.

One of the few plays that have helped define American literary canonicity, *Death of a Salesman* is widely anthologized. Instructors and students will have little difficulty locating the play, as it is reprinted in at least a half dozen anthologies.

For a more comprehensive sense of Miller's theater, students and scholars should consult volume 2 of *Collected Plays*, which contains an introduction by the playwright as well as the dramas *The Misfits* (1961), *After the Fall* (1964), *Incident at Vichy* (1965), *The Price* (1968), *The Creation of the World and Other Business* (1973), and the teleplay *Playing for Time* (1981).

The playwright's more recent work includes *Everybody Wins* (1990), his first screenplay since *The Misfits*. The published version of *Everybody Wins* contains an informative preface by Miller, "On Screenwriting and Language." Many of the thematic and cultural ideas he presents in *Death of a Salesman* are noticeable in such plays as *The Ride Down Mt. Morgan* (1991), *The Last Yankee* (1994), and *Broken Glass* (1994). The published edition of *The Last Yankee* features his essay "About Theatre Language," a lengthy reflection on the state of American theater in which Miller also writes intelligently about Chekhov, Ibsen, Strindberg, Yeats, Eliot, O'Neill, Odets, Williams, and Beckett and analyzes selected plays from his own oeuvre.

Readings for Students and Teachers

A healthy amount of scholarship awaits students and teachers engaged in serious research on Arthur Miller. I highlight only books, collections of critical essays, and selected bibliographies devoted to Miller. Readers may find additional information in the thousands of articles published on the man and his work, but space limitations preclude an account of those articles and of the many collections of critical essays that may include one or two pieces on Miller. Readers may wish to consult the *MLA Bibliography*; *Modern Drama*, which publishes an annual bibliography in each June issue; and such sources as *American Drama*, the *Journal of American Drama and Theatre*, the *Journal of Dramatic Theory and Criticism*, *Theatre Journal*, *Studies in American Drama, 1945–Present*, the *Michigan Quarterly Review*, and other journals that often include essays on Miller. Nonetheless, the following survey of the major statements on Miller provides a critical point of departure.

Bibliographies and Checklists

Several bibliographies and checklists remain available: those by Martha Turnquist Eissenstat, Tetsumaro Hayashi, Harriet Ungar, and George H. Jensen immediately come to mind. Also helpful are Robert A. Martin's "Bibliography of Works (1936–1977) by Arthur Miller" and Charles A. Carpenter's "Studies of Arthur Miller's Drama: A Selective International Bibliography, 1966–1979." Carpenter covers many foreign-language entries not found elsewhere. Teachers directing theses and dissertations may wish to consult Hayashi's *Arthur Miller and Tennessee Williams: Research Opportunities and Dissertations Abstracts.* This reference work includes abstracts of all dissertations on Miller through 1980 and, equally important, gives professors ideas regarding new research opportunities for graduate students and themselves. Useful, too, is a dissertation by Dwain E. Manske, which includes a catalog of the Arthur Miller Collection at the University of Texas at Austin.

While the preceding entries retain their usefulness, they have been superseded by the meticulous work of John H. Ferres, whose *Arthur Miller: A Reference Guide* remains crucial to researching Miller. Although it was published back in 1979, as of this writing it still stands as the most comprehensive Miller bibliography and hence the resource to which scholars should perhaps turn first. Ferres includes primary and secondary Miller sources from 1944 through 1978. He covers critical books and essays, theater reviews, book reviews, interviews, bibliographies, selected accounts of Miller's public life, and dissertations. His annotations are precise.

C. W. E. Bigsby's *File on Miller*, part of Methuen's Writer-Files series, contains a chronology and a list of Miller's stage, radio, and television plays, films and operas, and nondramatic writings. After a summary of each work, Bigsby includes excerpts of reactions at the time of production or publication. This handy guide concludes with a selected primary and secondary bibliography.

Three outstanding bibliographic essays that give readers a much more detailed account of the extant Miller scholarship are by James J. Martine, Alvin Goldfarb, and June Schlueter. Martine's essay introduces the volume he edited, *Critical Essays on Arthur Miller*, and remains a thorough and balanced review of the relevant criticism. Goldfarb's appears in Philip C. Kolin's valuable *American Playwrights since 1945: A Guide to Scholarship, Criticism, and Performance.* Readers will find Goldfarb's "Production History" very helpful, especially regarding his account of the major revivals of *Death of a Salesman.* Clearly, Martine's and Goldfarb's essays are as valuable as they are authoritative, but perhaps the most thorough bibliographic essay is Schlueter's, which appears in Matthew C. Roudané's *American Dramatists: Contemporary Authors Bibliographical Series.* Schlueter provides detailed primary and secondary bibliographies as well as a lengthy discussion of the Miller interviews, all the books, collections of critical essays, bibliographies, and major reviews, articles, and book sections devoted to Miller through most of 1988.

Biographical Dimensions

Since there is no biography on Miller to date, his autobiography, *Timebends: A Life*, becomes a significant text for gaining insights about the person behind the art. If the autobiography, which nearly all respondents say they recommend to students, lacks objectivity, the book plainly gives us the most thorough, even poignant, account of Miller's life. His story seems as reflective as it is detailed, from early stories about his parents and family to memories of his marriage to Marilyn Monroe, from his "impregnable naivete" (278) regarding his introduction to Hollywood to his felt awareness, voiced throughout the last portions of the book, of how richly ironic his life has been. He also traces his life in a language that reads like fiction, not fact. Philosophical in tone, with little regard for the actual chronology of his life experiences, *Timebends* reads rather like a novel—and perfectly suits the playwright's narrative: Miller bends time, honorably, resulting in a satisfying autobiography.

Many teachers note that they put the book Salesman *in Beijing*, Miller's own account of directing the play in China, on library reserve. It helps students understand the play's universality, many teachers feel, because the inherent drama of *Death of a Salesman* transcends translation concerns and cultural differences. Staged in a language and culture as distant from the Lomans' as students might imagine, the Beijing production nonetheless engaged the Chinese audience. As Miller observes throughout his account, the Chinese were transfixed by the plight of the Loman family, even though salesmanship as we know it—and all the cultural assumptions those in the United States may make about the sales profession—simply was not part of, to use Stephen Greenblatt's terms, the "circulation of social energy" in Chinese culture at the time. As Miller explains:

> What still remained in great doubt was whether [the Chinese] could mount *Salesman* without outside help, and this finally led them to insist I come to China to direct it. Naturally, I was astonished at the idea at first—how could one hope to direct a cast without being able to talk to them? Worse yet, because it was more than thirty years since China had known even a rudimentary civilization, how could I hope to create on stage the realities of a kind of life that had no existence in Chinese memories? (vii)

The book records the answers to such questions.

Robert A. Martin's edition of *The Theater Essays of Arthur Miller* remains essential reading for Miller scholars. This enormously useful volume is cited in nearly all the survey responses. If *Timebends: A Life* appears personal, intimate by nature, the theater essays give a more public, formal indication of Miller's dramatic strategies and ideas. The volume contains fourteen essays and three interviews. "Collectively," suggests Martin, "Arthur Miller's essays on drama and the theater may well represent the single most important statement of critical principles to appear in England and America by a major playwright since the Prefaces of George Bernard Shaw" (xvi). Further, Martin's textured introduction authoritatively traces the playwright's career, particularly in the context of his major themes and their relation to a broader cultural mythology.

Many of the critical studies noted in this introduction include brief biographical sketches that, considered together, give a portrait of Miller's life. Benjamin Nelson's *Arthur Miller: Portrait of a Playwright*; C. W. E. Bigsby's *A Critical Introduction to Twentieth-Century American Drama*, volume 2, as well as his *Modern American Drama: 1945–1990*; and June Schlueter and James K. Flanagan's *Arthur Miller* are particularly rich in their documenting of connections between the artist's life and work.

For yet another perspective on Miller's life and artistry, one that complements *Timebends*, Salesman *in Beijing*, and *Theater Essays*, readers may wish to consider the many interviews Miller has granted. Indeed, by examining his conversations with various interviewers, teachers and students will find a rewarding four-decade forum on Miller's response to *Death of a Salesman*, his other plays, and the state of American theater in general. Richard I. Evans's *Psychology and Arthur Miller* emerges as a book-length dialogue that Evans, a psychologist, conducted with Miller. Thirty-five of the most significant interviews are collected in Matthew C. Roudané's *Conversations with Arthur Miller*. Miller on Miller becomes more than an informal talk, for the interviews reveal his dramatic and aesthetic theories, his concern for language and structure, and his preoccupation with various sociopolitical issues. Each interview contains its own unique set of responses, but collectively they form a coherent narrative. Ever engaged with the personal and the public functions of drama, Miller continually discusses the role of tragedy and fate and their influence on what Miller calls "the common man."

The Instructor's Library

Critical Studies

Teachers will have little difficulty finding critical studies on Miller. In *Arthur Miller*, Dennis Welland considers the dramatist in the context of American literary history and in terms of the mythic traces of American romanticism and realism that, for Welland, seem inscribed in Miller's artistry. Robert Hogan's comfortably brief *Arthur Miller*, part of the Pamphlets on American Writers series once published by the University of Minnesota Press, considers Miller's preoccupation with tragedy and the way in which the tragic dominates his stage. Like Welland and Hogan, Sheila Huftel, in *Arthur Miller: The Burning Glass*, explores the crisis of conscience that afflicts

Miller's heroes, but in greater detail. Edward Murray's *Arthur Miller: Dramatist* explicates all the plays up to and including *Incident at Vichy*; this book yields few critical insights and lacks a critical introduction, which so often helps teachers during lecture preparations. Leonard Moss's *Arthur Miller* provides instructors with many valuable topics: biographical background, chronology, bibliography, and a 1979 interview Moss conducted with Miller. A Twayne publication, Moss's study differs from much other scholarship by concentrating on the psychological and metaphysical, rather than the social and political, dimensions of Miller's theater. Teachers may also wish to consult James Goode's *The Story of* The Misfits, which concerns the filming of the movie, and C. J. Partridge's *Death of a Salesman*, a booklet designed for students in British schools. In retrospect, Welland's book emerges as perhaps the most balanced and sensitive of the studies to appear in the 1960s.

Ronald Hayman's *Arthur Miller*, which highlights Miller's convictions regarding the social contract, is a reliable study. Hayman views Miller within an international context. Benjamin Nelson's *Arthur Miller: Portrait of a Playwright* remains a good source for scholars, in part because he draws together biographical as well as dramaturgical elements while discussing the existentialist quality of Miller's theater. Sidney H. White's thin pamphlet, *Guide to Arthur Miller*, focuses mainly on *Death of a Salesman*; readers may also wish to consult I. Altena and A. M. Aylwin's pamphlet *Notes on Arthur Miller's* Death of a Salesman. Dennis Welland, author of the 1961 study of Miller, returned to the playwright in *Miller: A Study of His Plays* (1979), which he revised and expanded four years later under the title *Miller: The Playwright*. Welland's analyses of the plays through *The Archbishop's Ceiling* and *Fame* are consistently illuminating, and readers will find his chronology and listing of American and British premieres of Miller's films and plays a handy resource in this solid book. For a compact study, some may wish to consult Karl Harshbarger's *The Burning Jungle: An Analysis of Arthur Miller's* Death of a Salesman. Harshbarger discusses the play as modern tragedy, its style and structure, and its social dimensions as a critique of the American dream myth.

Neil Carson's *Arthur Miller*, part of the Grove Press Modern Dramatists Series, begins with a biographically centered introduction and covers the plays through *The Creation of the World and Other Business* and *Playing for Time*. Carson ends his well-conceived study with an interpretation of Miller's major contributions to American literature: his use of language, his social commitment, and his religious vision. N. Bhaskara Panikkar's *Individual Morality and Social Happiness in Arthur Miller* considers Miller's theater in the context of various cultural codes, while Santosh K. Bhatia's *Arthur Miller: Social Drama as Tragedy* analyzes six Miller plays, including *Salesman*, suggesting that economics and tragedy seem central to Miller's unified tragic vision. Written by scholars from India, these two books present Miller within a largely philosophical context and from a trans-cultural vantage point.

June Schlueter and James K. Flanagan's *Arthur Miller*, part of the Ungar Literature and Life series, is a rewarding study (Flanagan contributes the forty-page biographical chapter; Schlueter considers the plays through *Danger! Memory* [*I Can't Remember Anything* and *Clara*]). Schlueter's analyses, particularly of the late plays, are notable for their quality of thought. Schlueter discusses Miller's dramatic innovations, social commitment, and the ways in which his private experiences influence his theatrical work. "Willy Loman," argues Schlueter, "may not have had the capacity or strength to see himself, but for two generations he has been responsible for our seeing ourselves through him" (66).

Bernard F. Dukore's Death of a Salesman *and* The Crucible: *Text and Performance* persuasively discusses the importance of moving from text to social context, from the play as literature to the theater as live spectacle. While in the "Text" half of the book Dukore discusses language, American myths, dramatic structure, and tragedy, in part 2, "Performance," he broadens our perspective with a less-discussed but equally vital element of the play: its virtual performance. Of notable importance are Dukore's comparisons of the original 1949 production with five others, from the London premiere on 28 July 1949, starring Paul Muni, to the Broadway revival on 29 March 1984, starring Dustin Hoffman. While his discussion of *The Crucible* may not be of central interest, Dukore's treatment is informative.

Collections of Critical Essays

Some fourteen collections of critical essays on Miller's theater have been published. While eight of the volumes address Miller's corpus, five concentrate solely on *Death of a Salesman* and a sixth on *Salesman* and Williams's *A Streetcar Named Desire*.

John D. Hurrell's *Two American Tragedies: Reviews and Criticism of* Death of a Salesman *and* A Streetcar Named Desire contains two dozen entries, including Miller's "Tragedy and the Common Man" and "On Social Plays," reprinted essays that respondents say they often assign to their students. Further, there are twelve reviews and essays on *Salesman*, and teachers may still find the suggested topics for student research valuable for undergraduates.

I have already mentioned Weales's volume on *Death of a Salesman*, which many use in the classroom because of the editor's thoughtful introduction and chronology that complement the play script. The volume may also be used, however, as a solid collection of essays, as the contents of part 2 suggest: five of Miller's theater essays; twenty-one reviews and essays; and four literary analogues by Eudora Welty, Tennessee Williams, and others.

Sensible topics for classroom discussion and papers, as well as a bibliography, close this volume.

Walter J. Meserve's *The Merrill Studies in* Death of a Salesman, with its many foreign reviews, brings an international perspective to the play. Meserve arranges the ten essays under such rubrics as "Social Problem," "Tragedy," "Characters," and "Style."

Helen Wickham Koon edited *Twentieth Century Interpretations of* Death of a Salesman, which includes ten previously published essays. Hers is an informative introduction because she draws on Miller's life and production concerns, as well as on the more standard issues of family, character, and tragedy.

Harold Bloom has edited several collections on Miller in his Modern Critical Views, Modern Critical Interpretations, and Major Literary Characters series. His *Arthur Miller's* Death of a Salesman contains ten essays, including contributions from Esther Merle Jackson, Brian Parker, Ruby Cohn, C. W. E. Bigsby, and others. The essays themselves are exemplary. While Bloom's introduction may be adequate for nonspecialists, however, Miller scholars will find his argument, like his bibliographies and chronology, sketchy, thin, and less than satisfying. Bloom's *Willy Loman* reprints ten essays whose central goal is to analyze Miller's most famous protagonist. Bloom also provides an introduction and a section called "Analysis of Character" that are fresh and insightful. The bibliography, while thin, at least appears slightly updated as compared with those of Bloom's other volumes on Miller. In many respects, this book emerges as the most rewarding of all the Bloom collections devoted to Arthur Miller.

In addition to the preceding volumes focusing on *Death of a Salesman*, there are eight other collections whose critical emphases include, but are not limited to, Miller's masterpiece. Robert W. Corrigan's *Arthur Miller: A Collection of Critical Essays* features nine essays by Herbert Blau, Harold Clurman, Gerald Weales, and others. Corrigan's introduction provides a thoughtful assessment of the playwright's achievement and is complemented by a chronology and selective bibliography.

Often cited in the survey was James J. Martine's *Critical Essays on Arthur Miller*. Indeed, Martine's meticulous bibliographic essay that serves as the volume's introduction remains essential reading for those teaching or researching Miller. In addition to Martine's illuminating introduction, the volume contains fourteen theater reviews, sixteen critical essays, and Martine's own interview with the playwright. The detailed footnotes and index only add to the volume's solid reputation.

Robert A. Martin's *Arthur Miller: New Perspectives* contains fourteen essays; overviews by Kenneth Rowe (one of Miller's creative writing professors at the University of Michigan during the late 1930s), Ruby Cohn, and others; and analyses of particular plays, with Enoch Brater discussing *Death of a Salesman.* Like his introduction to *The Theater Essays of Arthur Miller*, Martin's introduction to this collection provides a brief but authoritative overview. Martin seems particularly insightful when pointing out the shifts in Miller's themes as they relate to his conception of the primal family unit.

The other Harold Bloom volumes devoted to Miller may be of secondary interest. *Arthur Miller* and *Arthur Miller's All My Sons* include useful material, although much if not all of it appears elsewhere, and Bloom recycles his introductions: they appear essentially identical in all the Chelsea House volumes, with minor revisions inserted to suit each book. The following three collections also may be of tangential interest: Weales's The Crucible: *Text and Criticism*; John H. Ferres's *Twentieth Century Interpretations of The Crucible*; and Dorothy Parker's *Essays on Modern American Drama: Williams, Miller, Albee, and Shepard.* The Parker volume draws exclusively from material previously published in the journal *Modern Drama.* If these volumes fill a secondary role, they nonetheless will add a wealth of information to teachers' and students' understanding of *Death of a Salesman.*

Of all the available books, collections, chapters in books, and so on, C. W. E. Bigsby's *A Critical Introduction to Twentieth-Century American Drama* may be viewed as one of the most important sources in any instructor's library. All three volumes provide an impressive examination of the evolution of American theater—and Bigsby alludes to Miller throughout—but fully one third of volume 2 is devoted exclusively to Miller and was cited by the majority of respondents as essential reading. In this volume Bigsby—who helped found the Arthur Miller Centre for American Studies in East Anglia, Great Britain—explores both biographical and aesthetic concerns while surveying Miller's contributions. Bigsby also edited a nonacademic festschrift for Miller's seventy-fifth birthday, entitled *Arthur Miller and Company.* Tributes from other writers; dialogues between Bigsby and Miller; reactions to each play by directors, critics, designers, and actors make up this curious volume. Its best contributions are Miller's remarks on the power of dramatic language.

Bigsby's *Modern American Drama, 1945–1990* features a surprisingly fresh and erudite reconsideration of Miller's career. His real achievement, Bigsby suggests, "is as a writer whose plays have proved so responsive to the shifting pressure of the social world and whose characters embody that desperate desire for dignity and meaning which is the source of their wayward energy, their affecting irony and their baffled humanity" (125). This book, like Bigsby's others, is essential reading.

David Savran's *Communists, Cowboys, and Queers: The Politics of Masculinity in the Work of Arthur Miller and Tennessee Williams* provides an innovative reading of Miller's theater through a consideration of the "authoritative Cold War masculinity for which Miller's protagonists yearn" (41).

Steven R. Centola has edited two volumes on Miller: *Arthur Miller in*

Conversation, which features Centola's lengthy interviews with the play-wright, and *The Achievement of Arthur Miller: New Essays*, a collection of critical essays by Jan Balakian, C. W. E. Bigsby, Robert A. Martin, Brenda Murphy, Matthew C. Roudané, Gerald Weales, and June Schlueter, among others.

Finally, scholars should be aware of several forthcoming books on the playwright that promise to make important contributions to the field. Enoch Brater's *The Stages of Arthur Miller*—much like his *Why Beckett*—is a narrative about Miller and his work accompanied by some 125 photographs. Robert A. Martin's Death of a Salesman: *The End of the American Dream*, part of Twayne's Masterwork series, is a book-length analysis of the play. Divided into such chapters as "Historical Context," "Critical Reception," and "A Reading," Martin's book may well be the most detailed interpretation of the play to date. If the audience for both Brater's and Martin's books is the general, well-informed reader, undoubtedly these studies will appeal to specialists, too. C. W. E. Bigsby is editing a collection of critical essays on Miller, *The Cambridge Companion to Arthur Miller*, that will cover the playwright's entire career. Bigsby and Don B. Wilmeth are coordinating *The Cambridge History of American Theatre and Drama*, a three-volume history that will certainly include a detailed consideration of Arthur Miller.

Text and Performance

Theatricians have long argued, and rightly so, that in few ways can a play script re-present the talismanic quality inscribed in a live performance. Reading a text, they claim, cannot recapture the kinetic energy of a Lee J. Cobb and a Mildred Dunnock, a George C. Scott and a Teresa Wright, or a Dustin Hoffman and a Kate Reid. While this point seems true enough, teachers can nevertheless address important performance considerations while teaching the play in the classroom—whether stressing the play as dramatic literature or as live spectacle. For teachers particularly concerned with questions of text and performance, John L. Styan's excellent three-volume study *Modern Drama in Theory and Practice* seems essential. Further, although many scholarly books on Miller analyze the text-performance dialectic, two stand out for their emphasis on the play as a performing text, on its very theatricality: Neil Carson's *Arthur Miller* and Bernard Dukore's Death of a Salesman *and* The Crucible: *Text and Performance*. Both Carson and Dukore pay careful attention to the technical roles played by direction, scenography, and acting and to the ways in which performance elements aurally, intellectually, and emotionally influence our comprehension of the theatrical moment.

Introducing such theatrical factors to students' reading of the play broadens their awareness of the text-performance dialectic. Many respondents to the

MLA survey say that, in an effort to stage a model of mimesis, they ask students to read parts or to act out scenes. Several essays in this volume—those by Thomas P. Adler and Susan C. Haedicke, for instance—outline the pedagogical value of a performance approach. Many teachers use recordings and video productions as a way to harmonize the text-performance dialectic in their classes, but readers of this volume will find specific strategies for making such aids even more valuable.

Further Selected Readings

The following studies are a mere sampling of further possible readings to complement the more-obvious recommendations in the section "Instructor's Library." Many of these books were cited in the questionnaire as valuable readings, sources that may feature chapters or sections on *Death of a Salesman* or on Miller's theater in general. Others address Miller only minimally but raise important literary, theatrical, and ideological questions that place the Miller corpus in a larger perspective. Some are landmark studies that have long been standard reading, while others represent the more specialized interests of individual professors. I categorize all these works under general rubrics, although many if not all of the listed books overlap in the substance of their critical discussions. Other important titles not mentioned here appear in various essays later in this volume.

Language and Psychology

All scholars and teachers of *Death of a Salesman* must come to terms with Miller's language, an idiolect that appears as clichéd as it is eloquent. Intelligent studies concerned with such ideas are Theodor W. Adorno's *The Jargon of Authenticity*, Wayne C. Booth's *The Company We Keep: An Ethics of Fiction*, Ruby Cohn's *Dialogue in American Drama*, Gareth L. Evans's *The Language of Modern Drama*, and John Mander's *The Writer and Commitment*. Perhaps Cohn best represents the curious power of the playwright's idiotext. "Miller uses an appropriately informal syntax and many casual repetitions to suggest an all-American quality," writes Cohn. The play, she reminds us, "is larger than Willy Loman, and a variety of dialogue contrasts with his platitudes." Willy's platitudes are "relieved by Charley's cynical urban idiom, Uncle Ben's rugged phrases, Linda's sententious or sentimental outbursts, Happy's wise guy banter, Biff's lyricism about nature, and, most important of all, the range of Willy Loman's clichés" (71).

Like all classics of the stage and literature, *Death of a Salesman* accommodates metaphysical speculation and invites a psychological approach. To a large degree, many teachers indicate, language reveals the psychology of Linda Loman and her family. Such diverse studies as Anthony S. Abbott's *The Vital Lie: Reality and Illusion in Modern Drama*, Sigmund

Freud's *Civilization and Its Discontents*, Jacques Lacan's *The Language of the Self: The Function of Language in Psychoanalysis*, and Jean-François Lyotard's *The Postmodern Condition: A Report on Knowledge* are noted by several contributors as valuable supplemental readings. So, too, are the following: David W. Seivers's *Freud on Broadway: A History of Psychoanalysis and the American Drama* and Robert B. Sharpe's *Irony in the Drama: An Essay on Impersonation, Shock, and Catharsis*, both of which in many ways anticipated a book already mentioned, Evans's *Psychology and Arthur Miller*.

American Myths and the Family

Many if not all analyses of the play necessarily confront the animating principle engendered in the myth of the American dream and its relation to the family, one's work, and one's sense of self-validation. The following titles represent but a few of the numerous studies addressing such concerns. For a rethinking of male hierarchical structures and feminist perspectives, readers may wish to consult June Schlueter's *Feminist Rereadings of Modern American Drama*, a collection of critical essays that includes Gayle Austin's feminist analysis of the play. Participants in the MLA survey about *Salesman* often cited the following titles as being helpful: Bert N. Adams's *The American Family: A Sociological Interpretation*, Michele Barrett and Mary McIntosh's *The Anti-social Family*, Daniel Bell's *The Coming of Post-industrial Society: A Venture in Social Forecasting*, Murray Bowen's *Family Therapy in Clinical Practice*, Louis Broussard's *American Drama: Contemporary Allegory from Eugene O'Neill to Tennessee Williams*, Harold Clurman's *The Fervent Years: The Story of the Group Theater and the Thirties*, Peter Conn's *Literature in America: An Illustrated History*, Jacques Donzelot's *The Policing of Families*, John Kenneth Galbraith's *The New Industrial State*, Joseph Golden's *The Death of Tinker Bell: The American Theatre in the Twentieth Century*, Thomas Allen Greenfield's *Work and the Work Ethic in American Drama, 1920–1970*, Delores Hayden's *Redesigning the American Dream: The Future of Housing, Work, and Family Life*, Christopher Lasch's two books *Haven in a Heartless World: The Family Besieged* and *The Culture of Narcissism*, Peggy Noonan's *What I Saw at the Revolution: A Political Life in the Reagan Era*, Thomas E. Porter's *Myth and Modern American Drama*, Tom Scanlan's *Family, Drama, and American Dreams*, and Edward Shorter's *The Making of the Modern Family*. Since several contributors call attention to the Loman family's history, Monica McGoldrick and Randy Gerson's *Genograms in Family Assessment* might also be relevant. Finally, of particular interest is Tony Manocchio and William Petitt's "case study" of the Lomans in their book *Families under Stress: A Psychological Interpretation*. Other helpful titles used by the contributors appear in the list of works cited at the end of this book.

A Tragic Vision

If *Death of a Salesman* lacks the structural and aesthetic criteria of pure Hellenic tragedy, the play has nevertheless invited teachers to consider its tragic qualities. Further, ever since Miller's provocative—and not always convincing—"Tragedy and the Common Man" appeared in the *New York Times* soon after *Death of a Salesman* opened, many scholars have investigated Miller's modified Aristotelian tragic vision and the ways it both fails and triumphs mimetically. The following titles are only some of the many studies whose arguments involve the tragic mode. The list appropriately begins with Aristotle's *The Poetics* and, among many other suitable choices, Nietzsche's *The Birth of Tragedy* but quickly extends to various modern treatments of what defines the tragic. Other recommended books include Maxwell Anderson's *The Essence of Tragedy*, Normand Berlin's *The Secret Cause: A Discussion of Tragedy*, Larry D. Bouchard's *Tragic Method and Tragic Theology: Evil in Contemporary Drama and Religious Thought*, G. F. W. Hegel's *The Philosophy of Fine Art*, Robert B. Heilman's *Tragedy and Melodrama: Versions of Experience* and *The Iceman, the Arsonist, and the Troubled Agent: Tragedy and Melodrama on the Modern Stage*, Walter Kaufmann's *Tragedy and Philosophy*, Murray Krieger's *The Tragic Vision: The Confrontation of Extremity*, Mitchell A. Leaska's *The Voice of Tragedy*, Clifford Leech's *Tragedy*, Elder Olson's *Tragedy and the Theory of Drama*, John Orr's *Tragic Drama and Modern Society: Studies and Literary Theory of Drama from 1870 to the Present*, D. D. Raphael's *The Paradox of Tragedy*, Richard B. Sewall's *The Vision of Tragedy*, George Steiner's *The Death of Tragedy*, Jean-Pierre Vernant's *The Origins of Greek Thought*, Dan Vogel's *The Three Masks of American Tragedy*, John von Szeliski's *Tragedy and Fear: Why Modern Tragic Drama Fails*, George Wellwarth's *Modern Drama and the Death of God*, and, among many others, Raymond Williams's *Modern Tragedy*.

Public Issues, Private Tensions

"Miller is a playwright," Bigsby observes, "who has consistently sought to translate the social world into private anxieties and to trace the connection between personal availabilities and public betrayals" (*Critical Introduction* 2: 136). Indeed, for nearly a half century Miller has taken pride in citing the civic function of the theater and the way in which the spectacle influences the private tensions of the individual. As for Sophocles and Ibsen, Miller believes in the ideographic impact that the struggle of a Willy Loman or Kate Procter (or Oedipus or Nora) exerts on the body politic. Not surprisingly, then, many excellent studies address the public-private dimension of Miller's theater. To begin, see Phillip Gelb's "*Death of a Salesman*: A Symposium," a dialogue between Miller and six interviewers. Other useful studies include Thomas P. Adler's *Mirror on the Stage: The Pulitzer Prize as an Approach to American Drama*, Eric Bentley's *What Is Theatre?* and *The Playwright as Thinker*, C. W. E. Bigsby's *Confrontation and Commitment: A Study of Contemporary American Drama, 1959–1966*, Robert Brustein's *Who Needs Theatre: Dramatic Opinions*, Edmond M. Gagey's *Revolution in American Drama*, Robert Corrigan's *The Theatre in Search of a Fix*, Lewis W. Falb's *American Drama in Paris, 1945–1970: A Study of Its Critical Reception*, A. P. Foulkes's *Literature and Propaganda*, Morris Freedman's two books *The Moral Impulse: Modern Drama from Ibsen to the Present* and *American Drama in Social Context*, Martin Gottfried's *A Theater Divided: The Postwar American Stage*, Jean Gould's *Modern American Playwrights*, Allan Lewis's *The Contemporary Theatre: The Significant Playwrights of Our Time* and *American Plays and Playwrights of the Contemporary Theatre*, Gerald Weales's *The Jumping-Off Place: American Drama in the 1960s*, Raymond Williams's *Drama from Ibsen to Brecht*, and Robert Neal Wilson's *The Writer as Social Seer*. Another relevant collection of critical essays containing work on Miller is *Public Issues, Private Tensions: Contemporary American Drama*, edited by Matthew C. Roudané. Other sources of some interest are Julie Adam's *Versions of Heroism in Modern American Drama*; *Contemporary American Theatre*, edited by Bruce King; and Gerald M. Berkowitz's *American Drama of the Twentieth Century*.

Dramatic Innovations

Theatergoers at the original Broadway staging of *Salesman* were struck by Jo Mielziner's set, Elia Kazan's directing, and the way in which their collaborative efforts brought to life Miller's theatrical and ideological concerns. Many of the following books, while noting Miller's indebtedness to the past traditions, elucidate his innovative uses of the stage; others offer insights on dramatic invention in general: Herbert Blau's *The Audience*, William Demastes's *Beyond Naturalism: A New Realism in American Theatre*, Keir Elam's *The Semiotics of Theatre and Drama*, Martin Esslin's *The Field of Drama: How the Signs of Drama Create Meaning on Stage and Screen*, John Gassner's *Form and Idea in Modern Theatre*, Elia Kazan's *A Life*, Frederick Lumley's *New Trends in Twentieth-Century Drama*, Jo Mielziner's *Designing for the Theatre: A Memoir and a Portfolio*, Brenda Murphy's *American Realism and American Drama, 1880–1940*, Edward Murray's *The Cinematic Imagination: Writers and the Motion Pictures*, Philip Rahv's *Literature and the Sixth Sense*.

Those interested in the playwright's use of time—both theatrically and psychologically—may wish to consult Patricia R. Schroeder's *The Presence of the Past in Modern American Drama*. J. L. Styan's three-volume work *Modern Drama in Theory and Practice* is authoritative, particularly his overviews on realism and naturalism and his arguments concerning the text-performance question.

In addition to using the standard literary and theatrical studies noted, a number of teachers supplement their lectures by assigning historical and cultural studies. I mention only those book-length works that surfaced with some regularity in the survey. Many of them address issues that interest Miller in *Death of a Salesman*: economics, the individual, the social contract, American history, the family, tragedy and psychology, among others.

For general overviews of the American work ethic and history, some teachers assign Max Weber's *The Protestant Ethic and the Spirit of Capitalism*, which concerns the origins of the American work ethic and capitalism. Also useful are David Riesman's *The Lonely Crowd: A Study of the Changing American Character* and *Individualism Reconsidered*, Dale Carnegie's *How to Win Friends and Influence People*, Henry Steele Commager's *The American Mind*, and Russell H. Conwell's *Acres of Diamonds*. Published in the early to middle twentieth century, these works recapture the social and intellectual milieu that most likely influenced audience if not scholarly responses to the play.

Courses

If American drama occupies a precarious position in the university curriculum (especially in English departments), *Death of a Salesman* remains one of our few dramas that has been overwhelmingly valorized, and canonized, in our nation's literary history. It is therefore not surprising to find that the play is taught in a wide variety of literature courses, from Introduction to Drama to Major American Writers. Respondents also note that they often include the play in their more specialized upper-level elective seminars, courses such as The Pleasures of Tragedy or Work and Community (which George Newton team-teaches as an interdisciplinary seminar). Some professors mention that they include the play in their composition courses, others find a place for the Lomans in their American literature survey courses, and still others use the text in comparative literature classes and in courses linking philosophy and literature. My colleague Dabney Hart uses *Salesman* in her business writing classes, a required course for accounting majors at our university.

Although the implications relative to the play's canonical status remain debatable, clearly *Death of a Salesman* stands as one of the few plays that consistently finds its way into the mainstream curriculum of American literature courses. Surely there are many reasons for its wide inclusion, but according to teachers of the play, students whose majors have little or no connection with literature react to the plight of the Lomans. The Loman family psychohistory embodies a struggle to which students of various cultural, social, ethnic, and economic backgrounds respond. Despite the nonrealism of the play and despite whatever lack of formal literary, theatrical, or cultural "education" students may bring to their first college course including *Salesman*, they do have personal experiences that give them a starting point for a critical examination of the play. As James Hurt suggests in his essay, most readers and spectators seem to agree that the story of the Lomans is exemplary of American experience of the period over which it extends. Or as Alexander G. Gonzalez points out, in a remark echoed by many other respondents, "Most of my students are sophomores whose social background is primarily blue-collar—so the middle-class notion of the American dream is in various ways an integral part of their lives, whether it be what they aspire to or what they rebel against." For students as for those teaching the play, then, *Death of a Salesman* seems to be one of the exemplary dramatic texts of American literature.

Part Two

APPROACHES

Introduction

In this portion of the volume, two major pedagogical issues emerge in the discussion of *Death of a Salesman*: the play, on careful examination, appears rather flawed yet, despite itself, may be the quintessential American drama. The tension generated between formal deficiencies one may detect in the text and the emotional power of the performance, however, creates a rich set of pedagogical questions that produce deeper, more complex questions. If the play captures something truthful about contemporary American experience—particularly in its display of American linguistic cadence, focus on the family (dis)unity, versions of the American dream myth, the relation between business and one's self-validation, questions of representation and gender—few scholars seem to agree on what issues shape the American experience since 1945 or define the play's "quintessentialism." Herein lies the power of Miller's masterpiece. Indeed, the play's implicit ambiguities—its very indeterminacy, its multivalent textures—make locating its essential dramatic and literary power challenging for those on both sides of the lectern. For the plight of the Lomans raises important aesthetic and cultural issues that, as the following essays confirm, invite students and teachers to test multivocal cultural attitudes regarding literary and cultural essentialism.

In "Prologue: Arthur Miller and the Modern Stage," Susan Harris Smith considers the traditional critical view—that *Death of a Salesman* is the quintessential American play—only to show her students how an audience may dismantle the play's dominant hierarchical structures to reveal the impossibility of defining American essentialism. Hers emerges as a provocative essay, in part because she asks her students to rethink "traditional" experience as represented by the Lomans, demonstrating that perhaps the deeper value systems underpinning the Lomans' world—and by extension much of American cultural poetics—are as illusory and destructive as Willy's words and deeds.

The four essays in the following section, "Text and Performance," provide suggestions for understanding Miller's major techniques and themes. The text-performance question spotlights the difficult issue of teaching a literary work that was created first and foremost for the stage. Nevertheless, Alexander G. Gonzalez demonstrates the value of paying careful attention to an element of drama that, according to Roman Ingarden in *The Literary Work of Art*, most distinguishes a play from a novel or poem: the didascalia, or stage directions. Hence Gonzalez explicates for his students the lengthy stage directions that preface the opening scene. Miller's stage notes establish, Gonzalez observes, the central themes that will be enacted in the play script itself.

Susan C. Haedicke, Thomas P. Adler, and Barbara Lounsberry also chart specific methods for understanding the relation between text and performance. Haedicke systematically points out the theatrical elements in the play. These elements enable her to respond to one of her student's quips: "Willy deserved what he got. He was a loser." She approaches the play in a method that closely resembles attendance at a production. Her theatrically based lectures first establish a theoretical framework and a consideration of visual aspects of the play; she then uses actual performance in class as an interpretive technique. Adler concentrates on the scenery and how that setting embeds theatrical and social meaning in the play. Adler discusses the scenic design and its relation to textual authority, the memory structure of the play and music cues, realism and expressionism, questions of narrativity and, finally, questions of closure.

Lounsberry brings the "Text and Performance" section to an end by exploring one of Adler's points in some specificity: the use of expressionism that is such an integral part of the play's structural design. For Lounsberry, "the balance between expressionistic and realistic moments in *Death of a Salesman* is both its essence and its highest achievement." Considering musical motifs, sets, lighting, characters, and costume, Lounsberry teaches her students about "the interpenetration of outer and inner forces within the human psyche."

The essays in the "Critical Concerns" section of the volume explore ideas that have been debated ever since Willy Loman appeared, as well as some newer topics, such as feminist approaches to the play. Topics discussed in the essays include the role of modern heroes and their anti-Hellenic stature, questions of guilt and shame, the individual's reconciliation of blame with notions of honor, the ways in which a culture that sacramentalizes business contributes to the Loman's condition, and the play's depiction of a world in which women are marginalized. Employing a Burkean analysis of the play, Martin J. Jacobi explains to his students the relevance of rhetorical criticism as a way to appreciate Miller; by considering the dramatist's intentions and effects, Jacobi concludes, perhaps students themselves can change and, in turn, perhaps improve the culture in which they live. The play, Jacobi suggests, becomes part of our cultural equipment for living.

William W. Demastes discusses dramatic form, especially definitions of realism and, more precisely, the ways in which Miller reinvents our traditional notions of the realistic image. "What Miller presents," Demastes concludes, turns into a "distortion of the conventional, objective vision of time," but it is a distortion that students must see as being realistic from Willy Loman's point of view. As Demastes suggests, "the distortion does not fly into some surreal flight of fancy; it is still concrete" and most real for Willy.

The essays by Stephen Barker and Linda Kintz employ current critical theory in their arguments. Barker considers ancient dialogues concerning versions of the tragic and combines them with recent poststructuralist and psychoanalytic theories. The approach makes sense, Barker notes, because the theories considered complement what he sees as the essence of the play:

the "crisis of authenticity." Kintz, too, suggests ways in which we can make theory more relevant to our students. She examines the staging of "social space" and the ways in which individuals regard themselves as subjects. In an essay that complements Susan Harris Smith's, Kintz contends, finally, that Willy Loman's struggle is not a universal one but that of "a white man falling out of the middle class."

The ideas voiced by Smith and Kintz are also considered in Jan Balakian's essay. Through the male gaze, Balakian suggests, Miller "accurately depict[s] a postwar American culture that subordinated women." Accordingly, the play asks us to question whether the dichotomized image of woman as either mother or whore is a desirable cultural value. Balakian makes a connection between the pervasive male point of view in the play and Miller's critical look at capitalism and the American myth of success. Her essay, using a student debate, points to the complex role of Linda Loman, whom Balakian sees as both marginalized and indomitable.

The "American Myths" section includes essays that address some of the most important class-discussion issues that inevitably arise in teaching *Death of a Salesman*. Paula Marantz Cohen locates the play in the context of the transition from industrialism to postindustrialism in Western society. The advantage of this approach, Cohen observes, is that it draws students' attention more to the status of technology than to the effects of capitalism, a shift that "renders certain conventional ideological arguments less relevant." The play anticipated by decades, Cohen says, the shape of "society's evolution" and thus appears to her students as a paradigm for their own individual concerns in a postmodernist cosmos.

James Hurt traces four generations of Loman family psychohistory, noting that these generations "seem to suggest four stages in the history of American individualism." The family tree Hurt uses in the classroom helps students historicize the play and aids them in drawing their own conclusions about what Hurt calls the American experience.

If teaching theory to our students remains one of our most formidable tasks, many of the essays here discuss strategies for incorporating current performance theories in discussions of the play. Defining specific methodologies, Barker and Kintz point toward sensible ways to make the theoretic concrete for students and teachers. June Schlueter, too, employs theory in her classroom. She tells her students to concentrate on the recurring monologue that Willy Loman conducts with himself as well as on the Loman family history; the students are then in a good position to deconstruct the orthodoxies inscribed in the play while Schlueter guides them through central concerns of postmodernism. She shows that even freshmen can grasp how authors of texts—even the students themselves—construct "meaning."

Ruby Cohn's "Coda" brings this volume to a fitting close by surveying the role of the salesman in American drama from Eugene O'Neill to David Mamet. By comparing Willy Loman with O'Neill's Hickey and with Mamet's salesmen in *Glengarry Glen Ross*, Cohn frames *Salesman* in the context of the American dramatic imagination, noting that, when compared with Hickey and Ricky Roma, Willy Loman emerges as "the vulnerable middle-man." Cohn concludes, "Miller's Willy Loman advises his beloved son Biff, 'And don't undersell yourself.' For all his lies, clichés, and contradictions, that is exactly what Willy does during his vivid stage life, but Miller's play prices him out of the market."

The variety and intelligence of the essays in *Approaches to Teaching Death of a Salesman* define the serious commitments to and the collective efforts of scholar-teachers who have, despite other professional commitments, set aside the necessary time and energy to teach the play well. I believe all who contributed to this volume have played an important part, as Joseph Gibaldi suggests in his preface to the series, in the "serious and continuing discussion of the aims and methods of teaching literature."

PROLOGUE:
ARTHUR MILLER AND THE MODERN STAGE

Contextualizing *Death of a Salesman* as an American Play

Susan Harris Smith

Arthur Miller's *Death of a Salesman* frequently is described as the quintessential modern American play. This assertion is a good point of entry for an examination of the play's themes and structure as well as for an inquiry into the problem of American essentialism.

I teach *Death of a Salesman* at the University of Pittsburgh in an upper-division American drama class that is open to all students and in which the students write a weekly paper. I have constructed this course around several issues: the dominance of the white male experience as the "American" experience and of the white male playwright in the dramatic canon; the concomitant marginalization of women and of racial and ethnic minorities; the articulation and impact of the idea of the American dream on American culture and drama; the search for an individual identity as well as a place in the American landscape; and the dramaturgical strategies modern playwrights use to position the audience and to explore the issues.

To this end, students begin the course by "placing" themselves as Americans in terms of two questions: What is America? What is an American? (Students who are not Americans place themselves in relation to their image or experience of America.) I ask the students to consider, from a wholly personal perspective, the issues that inevitably arise in the initial discussion and that will recur as thematic concerns in the plays and essays they will be reading: America as a geographical, concrete reality (the land, the cities, the boundaries of which students are or are not conscious); America as a political construct (a democratic republic with all the conflict inherent in the paradox); America as the embodiment of abstractions and values (freedoms, rights, dreams); America as a country taken from native peoples, reimagined and remade by waves of immigrants; America as a mythic place (a new Eden to the Puritans, a hoard of wealth to gold rushers, etc.); America as the site of the American dream of unrestrained individualism and assured material success; the quintessential American as . . . who? the farmer? the pioneer? the cowboy? the businessman?

After the initial discussion periods and before they read any plays, the students read some traditional, seminal definitions of Americanism: Ralph Waldo Emerson's "Self-Reliance"; St. Jean de Crèvecoeur's "What Is an American?"; James Truslow Adams's "The American Dream," from *The Epic of America*; Henry Steele Commager's "Who Is Loyal to America?"; A. Bartlett Giamatti's "Baseball and the American Character"; Benjamin Franklin's "The Way to Wealth"; Horace M. Kallen's *Individualism: An American Way of Life*; Andrew Carnegie's *The Empire of Business*; and "How to Become a Millionaire," from Richard Nelson's play *The Return of Pinocchio*.

When I begin the course by asking students to name American playwrights, they usually can name only white males. The University of Pittsburgh library neatly demonstrates the problem as it pertains to gender. In a representative collection of forty-five anthologies of American drama compiled between 1918 and 1986, eleven include no plays by women at all, and fourteen include only one. Of the 740 plays total, only 90 are by women, and many of them are one-acts or date back to the regional movement of the twenties and thirties. That the American experience is understood to be the province of the white male is an assumption inextricably linked to a phallocentric, white-dominated theater system.

If a course reflects the dominant hierarchy, it should do so self-consciously and self-reflexively. To this end, I have constructed a syllabus that deliberately reflects the gender and racial bias in the American dramatic canon. The play readings are divided into six sections: White Males on the Inside, White Males on the Outside, The Black Male Experience, The Indian Experience, Men at War—Vietnam, and Urban Cowboys. The selections change from term to term but usually include works by Clifford Odets, Eugene O'Neill, Tennessee Williams, Arthur Miller, Edward Albee, Jack Gelber, Lorraine Hansberry, LeRoi Jones, Hanay Geiogamah, David Rabe, Sam Shepard, and David Mamet.

Along with each play, the students read one or two relevant or provocative essays that I have chosen to stimulate arguments and debate. For instance, with Albee's *The American Dream*, they read Philip Wylie's "Common Women"; with Gelber's *The Connection*, Norman Mailer's "The White Negro"; and with Kopit's *Indians*, Jane Tompkins's " 'Indians': Textualism, Morality, and the Problem of History." With *Death of a Salesman*, the students read

Richard Parker's "America the Beautiful," from *The Myth of the Middle Class*; "Reflections on the American Identity," from Erik Erikson's *Childhood and Society*; "Dream or Rat Race Success in the Twentieth Century," from John Cawelti's *Apostles of the Self-Made Man*, and Erving Goffman on the dream as self-delusion, in a section of his book *Frame Analysis* (111–16).

Traditionally, most University of Pittsburgh students come from blue-collar and middle-management families in which the mother stays home and the father struggles to "make it." Under present economic constraints, the pattern has been modified to include working mothers, but the image of the mother at home persists as the dominant and desirable cultural value for most students. As a consequence, the students respond strongly to the obvious thematic concerns of *Salesman*, usually feeling torn between Willy's corrupted Franklinian urges and Biff's poorly realized Jeffersonian ones. Harsh moralists and absolutists, the students have already condemned Tom for abandoning his family in *The Glass Menagerie*; Emersonian individualism strikes many students as mere selfish arrogance.

Despite the thematic structure of the course, I try first to direct students to the play's dramaturgical strategies. Because students have a tendency to read for the "story" and to respond to the play as if it were a novel, I ask them to assess Miller's dramaturgical strategies as ways of manipulating and positioning the audience into a consideration and reconsideration of the arguments. I want them to resist reducing *Death of a Salesman*, or any other play, to a limp, linear narrative just as I want them to explore their impulse to make a "realistic" play out of an experimental one. My students' discovery of the ways in which dominant forms of dramatic discourse (melodrama, naturalism, realism) hold sway over their expectations prompts them to become more analytical readers of plays. To this end, we spend some time on Miller's expressionistic devices. By placing the audience in "the inside of his head" (the original title of the play), Miller aligns the audience with Willy and seems therefore to be privileging Willy's own take on his predicament. The move outside in the Requiem, of course, sets up the audience as judge for the unresolved argument among Biff, Happy, Linda, and Charley. As the students become aware of the positioning and repositioning of the audience vis-à-vis Willy, they can renegotiate their judgmental stance.

As in most modern and contemporary plays, time and space are fundamental considerations in *Death of a Salesman*. There are three temporal modalities created by Miller's "time bends" in the play: the historical time (1949); the fragments of a remembered time, seventeen years ago, that intervene with striking immediacy for Willy; and a new sense of time, a nonsequential conflation of past and present created by the play and shared by Willy and the audience. The episodic, fragmented structure points to the relativity of time and connects neatly with Miller's similar fragmenting of place. The juxtaposition of the burning, angry, distorted city with the dreamlike, transparent house is the frame for the action, which in turn frames other sites of action (Howard's office, Charley's office, the hotel room, the restaurant); examining these scenic choices opens the way for discussion of Miller's play-within-play layering of temporal and spatial memories.

Like a Chinese box opening up to reveal more boxes within, the play's dramaturgy itself explores the structure and interconnectedness of place with memory. This consideration is important for the course as a whole because it ties into the creation of America as a place with a concrete, geographical reality and a strong mythic presence. In *Death of a Salesman*, of course, the frontier conquered by Willy's pioneering father and the jungles penetrated by Ben, as well as the salesman's territory controlled by Dave Singleman and Willy Loman, are such mythic constructs. Plays that the students read later in the term, such as Sam Shepard's *True West*, also use the mythic-past-versus-disappointing-present to explore the problem of an American male identity.

The connection between fluctuating time and space and the various musical interventions (the father's flute, The Woman's hot jazz, Ben's sinister music), the projections of leaves, the open playing area, and the transparent walls are all part of a complex dramaturgical matrix that I ask the students to assess. Connected to this matrix is the audience's knowledge that Ben is dead, a point that most students initially overlook. The one figure who moves between past and present in Willy's head is a figure of death as well as the embodiment of an unrealistic dream. Miller deliberately weighs the argument against Ben; there is no ambiguity about opportunism, cheating, or cruelty as "success incarnate." Ben does not appear at the Requiem, as he might have if Miller had thought his position worth debating.

As a transition from dramaturgical strategies to the themes of the play, we also consider the critical but peripheral role of the women in the play. I ask the students to consider the possibility that there is something essentially human in Willy's aspirations, something that transcends the contingencies of gender. But the marginalization of all the women in the play suggests that within this dramatic frame, at least, there is not. By this point in the course, the students have arrived at the conclusion that to be an American is to be a white male. The youth of the country, the violence by which men made it "ours," and the wilderness that had to be taken and tamed all support the contention that the paradigmatic experience of being American is male. The dominant image of the hero in American fiction as a restless adventurer on a quest, usually westward, fleeing traditional social restraints embodied by the domestic woman, is recapitulated in much American drama.

These tensions are manifest in *Death of a Salesman*: Willy's desire to be on the road, like his father and like Ben, and to die while traveling is in direct opposition to his impulse to build a home, embodied by the domestic Linda. The interesting thing about Willy is that his best side is his nurturing one. Biff, if not Linda, sees that Willy is drawn to building, to consecrating a home, to establishing a garden, to caring for his family. Thus Miller apparently has set up a simple binary opposition between male and female, boy and adult, wild and domesticated, an easy conclusion that is undermined by the Requiem.

The plays we read later in the course—specifically those by Shepard, Rabe, and Mamet—focus on gender-specific violence. The violence between men is foregrounded and open, but the violence to women is distorted, concealed, partially obscured by odd dramaturgical maneuvers. *Death of a Salesman* partially prepares the way for the displacement of women in the contemporary plays. Though I do not directly expose students in this course to feminist theory, they do become aware of the differences among various dramaturgical strategies.

Willy's repeated interruption of Linda's speech, for instance, anticipates similar silencings of women by men in Mamet's plays. In describing Linda as sharing Willy's dream but lacking the temperament to push for it, Miller initially suggests that she is a lesser person. The audience is not allowed into her character, which Miller defines as being one of "iron repression" (*Salesman* 12). Linda, unlike all the men in the play, offers no philosophy, no opinion on how life ought to be lived. Her passive, attentive domesticity places her in direct subordination to Willy, Biff, and Happy. She does not talk about herself, only about the men, and she is reduced to tears on several occasions.

Unlike the men, who move freely from site to site, the women (Linda, The Woman, and the pickups) are confined to specific and symbolic places. Happy's description of the first pickup as a "strudel" with "binoculars" (100) anticipates Mamet's male characters who can describe women only as "holes" and similar vulgar epithets. The depiction of woman as object, as "the Other," rather than as subject, a fully actualized equal, is an American cultural problem reified in American drama. We spend some time on this point so that students can connect it later with the intersections of sexism, racism, and imperialism that are the subjects of Kopit's *Indians* and Rabe's *The Basic Training of Pavlo Hummel* and *Sticks and Bones*.

Finally, we consider the "American" quality of the play and the limits to which that approach can be pushed. The drama is no exception to the desire for an indigenous Americanism that courses through American cultural history. Vagaries and abstractions about what it means to be American have dominated the critical discourse, and the students are no less given to confusion than the critics are. Recently, poststructuralism has decentered received notions of an American character and challenged the idea that American culture (or any other culture) is homogeneous. The desire to appropriate certain texts as quintessentially American persists, however, so I encourage students to consider the powerful appeal of *Death of a Salesman* as an American play. The play is, after all, also a modern play in that it uses expressionistic devices, lacks closure, argues for redemptive change, and redefines classical tragedy.

At this juncture, I ask the students to assess the impact of capitalism on their lives. In particular, I want them to consider the importance of work in the culture; Willy's entire identity, for instance, is tied up in his image of what the ideal salesman should be. Americans are peculiar in that they define themselves not by who they are but by what they do. True, Biff is caught in the paradigmatic myth of the adolescent male escaping from the east to the rural west for self-realization in a "world elsewhere." In Biff, at least, Miller seems to suggest that there may be some spiritual transcendence and redemption for the Adamic man who freely redefines himself in an open wilderness. But Miller's focus is on Willy and how he ought to have lived meaningfully in an urban, business-driven context. Howard shows the dehumanizing effects of business, but Charley has heart. Understanding the situation in the present necessitates a return to the past and to the tradition of pioneering entrepreneurship.

We discuss the American family tree Miller has constructed, from Willy's pioneer heritage to Happy's corporate scrambling. Because most of the students tend to cling to the promise of material success despite the empirical evidence of their own fathers' lack of it, I use Stephen J. Rose's *The American Profile Poster*, which graphically foregrounds the radical pyramidal structure of American wealth, as an antidote to illusion. We also explore the larger issue of the American dream itself as possibly a driving delusion that many Americans actively participate in and promote. Erving Goffman's analysis of the dream as a form of self-deception is particularly useful in getting students to consider Miller's dramaturgical strategies as having a direct relation to his thematic intentions.

For their paper, I usually ask the students to focus on the Requiem and to consider each of the final positions offered by the characters. I ask them to weigh Charley's dream speech against Biff's appraisal. I also ask them to consider the implications of Linda's having the last words in the play and to analyze the degree to which they read those words as melodramatic or ironic. Here, again, is another place in which the students, swept up in their familiarity with traditional melodramatic patterns, which offer satisfying closure to a problem, have to confront the albeit muted modernist lack of resolution. The plot may have closed with Willy's death, but the problems stirred up by the debates about success and personal fulfillment remain ambiguous. The students, as members of a challenged audience, are required to reach their own conclusions and take a position. Willy's "head," the house, is gone; only the flute and the city are left in sharp juxtaposition. I urge the students to make their final judgment not merely in terms of what the characters say but also in terms of the closing image. "Attention must be paid" to the ambiguities that make Miller's classic a play without easy solutions to the problem of what it means to be a successful American male.

TEXT AND PERFORMANCE

Utilizing the Initial Stage Directions in *Death of a Salesman*

Alexander G. Gonzalez

I teach *Death of a Salesman* in an Introduction to Literature course. Most of my students are young (as opposed to older, "nontraditional") sophomores whose social background is primarily blue-collar, so the middle-class notion of the American dream is in various ways an integral part of their lives, whether it be what they aspire to or what they rebel against. When I teach the play, however, I do not begin with a discussion of the American dream; rather, treating the play as great literature—as well as superb drama—I pursue a minute analysis of the lengthy preliminary stage directions (11–12). I do not neglect to indicate that a director may choose to ignore or modify Miller's directions, but since my students only read the play, this concern is of little import to them, as they may, unfortunately, never see the play performed.

In the opening class I place great emphasis on that narrated commentary— the first such directions that many of my students have ever read—remembering that, beyond the title, these words are essentially the first ones they see when they sit down to read the play. In many ways these dense initial lines are prose poetry, rich in symbolism and deep in significance; I proceed line by line, addressing each concept as I would in analyzing a poem and with the same respect. These lines are of great importance in establishing the play's underlying themes. I find their discussion tremendously useful in promoting an understanding of the more complex forms of those themes that arise later on.

In the first two lines we see that the flute is associated with "grass and trees and the horizon." Why? Eventually most students will make the connection: that the flute is one of the simplest, most "natural," and most easily crafted of instruments. This association, of course, leads to some discussion of Willy's father and of Willy's repressed inner nature; it also acts as a preparation for Willy's seed-planting attempt at the play's end. The word *horizon*, moreover, suggests the limitlessness associated with the American dream in the time of our youth: anything is possible when no boundaries are recognized. Further, the horizon represents the openness that is the antithesis of the urban environment hemming in the Loman residence.

In the third line we find the phrase "the Salesman's house." Why not "Willy Loman's house"? The point to make here, naturally, is that Willy has become his occupation. That is, he doesn't merely work as a salesman; he *is* a Salesman, with a capital S. He is what he does, is defined by what he does. A seemingly obvious part of the next sentence often needs to be identified for some students: what are the "towering, angular shapes . . . surrounding it on all sides"? These enveloping, suffocating high-rise buildings with all their straight lines and aesthetic drabness represent the annihilation of the natural world in a once-green neighborhood. The "angry glow of orange" is the concomitant pollution that discolors the natural "blue light of the sky," the only patch of which significantly hovers over the Loman house, and when we then read of "a solid *vault* of apartment houses" (emphasis added), the suggestion of entombment, of living death, is strong indeed. Once again we are reminded of the hopelessness of Willy's attempt to plant seeds in a place that the sun cannot effectively reach.

I read the phrase "dream rising out of reality" as a metaphor for the entire play. At this point I usually lay the groundwork for the forthcoming discussion of the connection between dreams and reality, dreams and lies, and the American dream and the average man and woman.

The lines that follow become increasingly concrete and begin to focus on the Loman house itself as represented on the stage. I draw attention to the specified dearth of "fixtures." Since most of my students have no background in modern drama, either studied or performed, I explain that a relatively uncluttered set allows the members of the audience to see clearly the occurrences in each room; that the play emphasizes the imaginings of Willy's mind over the absolute realism of the moment; and that, again on a functional level, the actors must have the facility of stepping through walls at various points in the play. Moreover, the lack of realistic clutter forces us to focus on the objects that we *are* permitted to see; the bareness of the boys' bedroom, for example, draws all the more attention to Biff's athletic trophy, which stands "[o]n a shelf over the bed." Clearly, we are being prepared for the all-important role that athleticism plays in young Biff's everyday life and for the central part it plays in shaping the older Biff's character and values. We learn next that "[a] window opens onto the apartment house at the side": here I usually reemphasize points I have already made about entombment and the absence of natural things. I also make comparisons with the setting in Melville's "Bartleby the Scrivener" (which they have studied earlier in the semester)—particularly its walls, partitions, and general sense of the tomb. Realizing the spiritually isolated condition of human beings thus surrounded by mortar and brick always inspires lively discussion. Despite the humorous purpose of such television shows as *The Honeymooners* and *Barney Miller*, my students readily admit to feeling mildly claustrophobic when watching them, because of the closed-in nature of the sets: the "view" out the window is of bricks. I also draw attention to the ironic use of the verb *opens* in the above direction from *Salesman*, for the view is markedly closed.

The third paragraph of the directions seems to me entirely functional. The dormer window is mentioned to establish the character of buildings that were once designed with some sort of aesthetic sense, again in sharp contrast to the nearly identical and certainly impersonal structures that now crowd in on all sides. Similarly, that the stairway up from the kitchen "curves" distinguishes it from the straight lines that characterize newer apartment buildings. Some students tend to overanalyze these lines after they have so painstakingly interpreted the two previous paragraphs. Often they see the dormer window as symbolizing a place where Biff has probably always been able to get away from the pressures placed on him by his father, a place where Biff can detach himself from his ugly neighborhood and dream about his future. I gently discourage such analyses by pointing out that nothing later in the play supports such a reading—that young Biff is consistently shown as an active rather than contemplative boy.

A connection to the sparse furnishings originally mentioned in Miller's second paragraph is made at the start of the fourth. This is probably the better place to make some explanations about modern theater and the evolution of the set as a device to facilitate meaningful action and to act as a reflection of such aspects of a character as thoughts, moods, and even consciousness. The skeletal, "partially transparent" makeup of the Loman home also prevents us from forgetting those looming, sterile apartment buildings. The remainder of the paragraph is dedicated to the functional task of explaining the set's logic as it relates to the "imaginings" of Willy's mind and the action "in the present." Many students do not know what a stage's "apron" is, so some explanation is usually required, not just a definition but a discussion of the apron's role relative to the rest of the stage.

What follows, in the fifth paragraph, is the students' first real exposure to the character Willy Loman. It is, of course, important to discuss how much we can learn about him before he even speaks. Once again he is described as "the Salesman," but this time the connection is infinitely more substantial because of the heavy "large sample cases" he carries with him. The flute plays on but, symbolically, is not heard by the exhausted Salesman; that is, the spirit of his father lives on in Willy but unbeknownst to him.

This is a good place to discuss the virtues of the making of things, as opposed to the insubstantial and spiritually draining liabilities inherent in the mere selling of what some other person—more probably some machine—has mass produced. We learn Willy's age—sixty—and for the first time are likely to feel pity for a man who is thus occupied at this stage of his life. The physical pain involved—the thankful letting down of his "burden," the "soreness of his palms"—must be visualized and appreciated. The "word-sigh" that follows completes the portrait of Willy, whose even heavier spiritual burdens he carries everywhere with him. Some students analyze his two heavy valises as symbolizing Willy's guilt: one for the way Biff has turned out, the other for Willy's betrayal of Linda. This seems to me a fair and plausible interpretation.

Linda, the subject of the sixth and final paragraph, receives more direct, far less symbolic, treatment. We learn several essential pieces of information about her character. That she has developed "an iron repression of her exceptions to Willy's behavior" immediately indicates two important facets of her nature: that she has, in fact, resented aspects of her husband's personality—having gone as far as fearfully discouraging him from going with his brother to Alaska—and that she has since subsumed her own wants and needs to the furthering of Willy's now-conservative dreams, which she has adopted wholesale. Her own recessive, enabling way has helped solidify their position in life: stability bought at the cost of natural inclinations and aptitudes, dreams having replaced reality. She "lacks the temperament" to have any longer a positive effect on him; she can now merely patch him up emotionally so that he can continue to endure in his stupefied state.

These final two paragraphs provide strong indications of the nature of their relationship: Willy, spiritually isolated and exhausted, is virtually neurasthenic; Linda, even with all her "admiration" of her hardworking husband, cannot provide the sustenance he needs and remains something of a tangential force in his life—intimately close to him but not directly touching or influencing him. She suffers with him but is incapable of relieving his suffering, which is beyond hope of alleviation. In these skeletal views of their relationship, their house, and their neighborhood, Miller has given us a remarkably effective outline of the play's deepest concerns and most significant themes. A careful analysis of their content establishes a firm basis from which to branch out into the play's more particular complexities and prepares us for an informed interpretation of those complexities, reminding us that *Death of a Salesman* is not only great drama but great literature as well.

Celebrating Stylistic Contradictions:
Death of a Salesman
from a Theatrical Perspective

Susan C. Haedicke

To begin with the assertion that on the stage *Death of a Salesman* has the power to capture the imagination of generations of theatergoers despite the weaknesses in the dramatic text seems to be stating the obvious (see Bloom, *Modern Critical Views* 1). Yet I must begin at that point, for it is precisely Miller's theatrical viability that directed new insights into teaching the play. My early teaching experiences with the text of *Salesman* met with resistance from students who easily recognized that the play does not read well, but the first time I showed the television production based on the Broadway revival with Dustin Hoffman, they were enthralled. At the end they did not jump up without a thought to what they had seen but sat silently for what seemed like several minutes until each one began to offer perceptive and involved reactions. Even later in the day, I overheard my students talking animatedly about the play to others not in the class, and one student came up to me saying incredulously, "Hey, that was really good. Do you know any more *movies* like that?"

Seeing a production, even on video instead of onstage, stimulated the students in a way that reading and analysis had not. That experience helped me formulate a pedagogical approach by which the students examine the play with a method that more closely resembles attendance at a performance than it does traditional literary analysis. What they do is to focus on how a particular scene fits into the structure of the play as a whole and interweaves character, theme, and previous action (so important in this play) to present a coherent and theatrically powerful moment. The students thus see the dramatic action in addition to reading the words as a literary text. This approach highlights, even celebrates, rather than minimizes, the contradictions in the play because it focuses on Miller's synthesis of realism and expressionism as it helps students understand what these terms mean not only as literary movements but also as theatrical conventions. When examined theatrically, these differences in style are immediately apparent, as are the difficulties and limitations of judging one by the standards of the other. To say that *Death of a Salesman* has synthesized realism and expressionism thus necessitates the acceptance of a play that, though fraught with contradictions, has transcended the limitations of each style while retaining its appeal. What the theatergoer perceives as Miller's brilliance and originality are also the source of the literary critic's problems with the play. To students approaching the play from a theatrical vantage point, these problems, however, begin to offer interpretive possibilities for production choices that can be handled in a variety of ways. The students gradually learn to look for "producible interpretations," a term coined by Judith Milhous and Robert Hume (3), rather than for one "correct" meaning.

While several scholars have explored the dramatic integration of realism and expressionism to aid in a literary analysis of the play, they have not examined this synthesis as the source of the play's theatrical viability. Raymond Williams touches on the blending of the two styles when he writes, "*Death of a Salesman* is an expressionist reconstruction of naturalist substance, and the result is not hybrid but a powerful particular form" (Bloom, *Modern Critical Views* 12). John Styan suggests that Miller unites a logically motivated, if somewhat mundane, story with expressionistic stylistic conventions and thus transcends realism while retaining many of its characteristics to create a play that exceeds the possibilities of either technique alone (3: 118). Helene Wickham Koon concurs as she writes, "Miller's ability to reconcile two normally antithetical types of expression into a coherent entity gives him the advantages of both" (11). And Leah Hadomi uses this realistic-expressionistic synthesis, which she asserts exists both thematically and structurally, as the basis of her analysis of the play's dramatic rhythm. Building on the work of these scholars, I help the students explore how the performability of the play arises from this blending of these contradictory styles, a point one may easily miss when reading the play. This onstage viability and its achievement form the core of my pedagogical approach.

As I learned how to teach the students to read the play theatrically, I found the need to begin with the video version less pressing, and, in fact, some students objected to its limitations and melodrama. This reaction is hardly surprising. Referring to an earlier filmed version, Miller, in the introduction to his *Collected Plays*, points out that while the play appears to be cinematic in structure, it "failed as a motion picture" because

> the dramatic tension of Willy's memories was destroyed by transferring him literally, to the locales he had only imagined in the play. . . . The screen is time-bound and earth-bound compared to the stage, if only because of its preponderant emphasis on the visual image, which, however rapidly it may be changed before our eyes, still *displaces* its predecessor.   (26–27; emphasis added)

I now make the video starring Dustin Hoffman available to students after the initial discussion. Here they see firsthand how particular directorial choices influence the play.

Since I encourage my students to see the dramatic action while they read the words of the literary text, I focus on the visual aspects of the play first. After becoming acquainted with Miller's scenic vision of, as the playwright himself puts it, "suggestion scenery, just enough to help each person build his own scenery in his imagination" (Roudané, *Conversations* 11), the students design their own set, according to the stage directions and the early scenes. Often someone volunteers to be our artist and draws the floor plan on the board (or, if the room is large enough, on the floor), and the class directs bits of scenes to see if the design works. Today's students are accustomed to expressionistic scenic techniques, so they have little trouble designing a skeletal house with bedrooms on platforms of differing heights overshadowed by huge apartment buildings that can fade from sight during Willy's excursions into the past. Slightly more troublesome are the backyard and locations away from the house, but at least one student comes up with an idea that closely resembles Jo Mielziner's flexible forestage in the original production.

Once the class agrees on the basic floor plan, we contrast the use of realistic set pieces—the refrigerator, selected pieces of furniture, and props—with an expressionistic set where walls can appear and disappear, where the roof is open to the sky and the overbearing apartment buildings, and where the action occurring in different places can be seen simultaneously by the audience. The advantages of a set that transcends the limits of realism become immediately apparent. We explore how the design as a whole—in particular, the high-rise apartments towering over the seemingly fragile house in the present—visually highlights the idea of being trapped, "walled in," especially when contrasted with the openness of the backyard in the past. We also examine how the few practicable set pieces acquire a significance impossible in a realistic setting. The refrigerator (as often pointed out, a symbol for Willy himself) in a kitchen with no other appliances not only becomes the focus of attention but visually implies isolation and displacement.

This stylized set design, which also makes possible simultaneous staging, provides a multifaceted perspective of the action shown from several vantage points at once. The first example of this usage occurs early in act 1 when the audience can see Linda in her bedroom worrying about her husband, Biff and Happy in their room discussing their father's problem, and Willy as the source of their concern mumbling to himself in the kitchen. Later in act 1, the spatial juxtaposition of the forestage action (Willy giving the gift of stockings to The Woman in the hotel) with the background action (Linda sitting at the kitchen table mending her torn stockings) not only adds poignancy to the scene but visually underscores Willy's misplaced ethics. Each of these actions is, on its own, realistic, yet their simultaneous presentation, especially since one is from the past and one from the present, provides an exciting use of an expressionistic theatrical convention that reinforces what Miller labels "the concurrency of past and present" (Introduction 26). It is precisely the visual juxtaposition of these two images, obvious in performance, that shifts a moment so transparent and heavy-handed on the page to one so significant, multileveled in meaning, and theatrically exciting on the stage. Miller, in the introduction to his *Collected Plays*, insists that such a flexible set, with the house always visible onstage, increases the dramatic tension between the "now and then" (26). While Willy loses his awareness of the actual world as his hallucinations force themselves into his consciousness, the audience sees both worlds simultaneously. For Enoch Brater, the scenic design signifies even more: "in a very basic sense, the set *is* Miller's play" ("Miller's Realism" 119). The set metaphorically presents the dramatic issues as it encourages movement "from literal to emblematic realism" (121).

To reinforce the visual juxtaposition, Miller repeats dramatic rhythms to connect past and present. Exciting and complex examples of this repetition reverberate throughout act 2 (as I discuss later), but an early example occurs in the first excursion into Willy's memories. In the first dream sequence, Willy rapidly shifts from confidence in his own potential for success as a salesman to acknowledgment that people laugh at him (36). This theatrical moment is so pointed on the stage in part because it rhythmically repeats an earlier extreme and rapid shift. Soon after Willy's unexpected late-night return, he rails to Linda against his son's laziness and seconds later proudly boasts, "There's one thing about Biff—he's not lazy" (16). These rhythms, which resonate in performance, are difficult to perceive when one merely reads the text, so to aid our theatrical approach, the class frequently conducts oral readings of various scenes. Listening to the play also highlights interpretive possibilities as vocal intonations and emphases change the meaning of a scene. How Linda responds to Willy's realization that he imagined he was driving the 1928 Chevy from the past, for example, may color their relationship for the rest of the play.

Designing the set and listening to repeated rhythms help clarify how the shifts between the play's levels of reality—the actual world of the present and the hallucinatory world of Willy's mind—are rendered in theatrical conventions. We explore how Miller prepares the audience for the first shift into Willy's dream world: the hallucination that begins during Biff and Happy's conversation in the bedroom as their father putters in the kitchen below. Early foreshadowing of this shift relies on subtle gestural elements to alert the audience to Willy's excursions into the dream world. Willy, explaining to Linda why he arrived home unexpectedly, nostalgically describes how he "opened the windshield" to enjoy the day but found himself "dreamin' again," nearly "goin' off the road" (14). The gestural element of his speech demands a slow rhythm and perhaps a physical disorientation, both of which underscore the words spoken. The action implied in the words intensifies a little later in the scene as Willy reminisces about Biff's popularity in high school, but Linda pulls him back into the present with the announcement that she bought a new kind of American cheese. The volume, pace, and rhythm of Willy's response and an accompanying physical gesture, probably a jerk, reveal Willy's abrupt return to the actual world. When Linda joyfully suggests a Sunday drive in the country with the windshield open, a startled

Willy realizes that he had earlier imagined he was driving the 1928 Chevy of Biff's high school days—the only hallucination he acknowledges. Miller accompanies this acknowledgment with an aural theatrical sign: a few chords of flute music heard in the distance.[1] The preparation is now complete, and the audience is ready to move with Willy into the past as changes in the set, notably the disappearance of the apartment buildings, signal the shift to Willy's mind.

This blending of a realistic casual structure with an expressionistic episodic one (evident in the shifts between the play's levels of reality) encourages the students to struggle with the idea that the play is a paradox encompassing contradictory styles. The expressionistic form of the play is a result of Willy's seesawing between the real world and his dream world, but the actual scenes enacted on the stage are realistic. If this realistic storyline is disengaged from the play, it can be narrated as causally related incidents based on logically motivated actions. The students easily see, however, that this approach does not do justice to the play, because the plot becomes trivial and predictable. The structural elements of expressionism—an episodic construction with thematically connected scenes juxtaposed to reveal, for example, Willy's misconceptions about success and the American dream—are equally disappointing when extracted from the play, because they force it into the mold of thesis drama, even propaganda. Miller has written a play that is not truly episodic, since one scene flows into the next without a clear break; nor is it truly realistic, since the structure follows the twists and turns of Willy's mind more than it does the actual events. Only in the acceptance of the contradictory coexistence of realism and expressionism in one work can the brilliance of the play be appreciated. The expressionistic conventions, much more evident in performance than in the written text, raise the mundane story to a universal and significant plane, but the realistic conventions keep the audience attendant on the action in the story.

This dichotomy is reflected also in the characters: the people in Willy's world are paradoxes. They are individuals with distinct personalities; at the same time they are types, representatives of a social attitude. Willy stands at the heart of the contradiction as a character who is both realistic and expressionistic. An audience not only empathizes with Willy as an individual, a small man beaten down by the forces of society as he struggles to raise a family and achieve some measure of success, but also distances itself and views Willy as the archetypal middle-class American citizen—the salesman—battered by the conflict of self-delusions and accomplishments. So while Willy retains his identity as an aging man verging on senility and full of idiosyncratic quirks, he simultaneously becomes everyman, representing the failure of the American dream.

Miller underscores this dichotomy in Willy's character in the final confrontation between father and son. All theatrical conventions in this scene—except for the peripheral presence of Ben at the end, luring Willy toward what the salesman views as the best solution—seem to portray Willy as a realistic character who cannot grow and cannot learn, and while he may arouse our sympathy, he ultimately disappoints us with his lack of depth. This interpretation, however, neglects the subtle expressionistic devices used in this masterful scene, which, both thematically and rhythmically, represents a microcosm of the play as a whole. The action in the confrontation not only echoes but also highlights Willy's earlier equation of success and popularity. In his expressionistic mode, Willy cannot change, cannot understand the truth of his failures that Biff forces on him. He is unable to face this realization not because he is stupid or inadequate but because it would destroy his expressionistic function, his social attitude. He can, however, recognize that Biff loves him, and he can understand that the "spite" (129–31), which he is convinced destroyed his son's promise, has disappeared. This enlightenment causes the father to revert to the past and associate love with success. In the happier days when Biff idolized his father, the boy seemed unbeatable, so in the present Willy's realization that his son still "likes" him activates the same response. Instead of accepting Biff for what he is, Willy again dreams that his son will be "magnificent" (133). The result, disappointing when viewed realistically, brilliantly employs expressionistic techniques to underscore the inevitability of his suicide and to accomplish Miller's goal to create "not a mounting line of tension, nor a gradually narrowing cone of intensifying suspense, but a bloc, a single chord presented as such at the outset, within which all the strains and melodies would already be contained" (Miller, Introduction 24). That Willy never changes, never really understands his situation or himself—a crucial factor in any evaluation of Willy as a realistic character—loses its significance when he is evaluated as an expressionistic one; in the latter interpretation, his individuality is not as important as what he represents: an everyman fighting with his life to preserve his dignity. To an actor performing the role of Willy Loman, the contradiction in character presents a definite challenge. The actor who is able to acknowledge Willy's individuality yet simultaneously to emphasize his universality and to present the character as an expressionistic type ennobles the small man in a unique situation.

Looking at other characters in the play, notably Charley, as expressionistic types representing counterpoints to Willy helps explain their apparent inconsistencies as well. Charley, the straightforward, no-nonsense businessman who throughout the play speaks in clipped sentences without emotion, suddenly seems to change in the Requiem with his poetic speech, which begins, "Nobody dast blame this man" (138). This eulogy sums up the failure of the American dream for the middle-class American as represented by Willy Loman and thus must be set apart from the rest of the dialogue. The speaker of these words should shift into a different style of language than previously used, because the words, not the character, must be heard. It is logical for

Charley to deliver this summation because throughout the play he has provided commentary on Willy's actions and ideas. Through his function, Charley thus remains a consistent character even as he sounds different.

Death of a Salesman leaves the audience with a strong impression of the failure of the American dream on a personal and social level, but exactly what that dream is or why Willy failed is vague. I do not encourage my students to discover the "one true meaning" of the play, however. Instead, I ask them to imagine producible interpretations and to explore which ideas are communicable onstage and how those ideas influence character and plot. Orm Overland, in an article on Miller's dramatic form, points out that Eric Bentley, perhaps toying with the idea of producible interpretations, recognized that the key scene of the play shifts from the interview in Howard's office to Willy's memory of the Boston hotel incident when the "meaning" of the play shifts from social commentary to psychological insights. When one reads the play, Overland continues, the "balance [between the social and the psychological motivations] is restored," but in production the hotel scene overshadows the interview (4). My asking students whether they agree that the scenes with The Woman must dominate a production leads to a close examination of the interview and the abortive dinner in the restaurant: two key scenes that seem to be pointing in different directions in terms of theme but that rhythmically parallel each other, thus presenting a multifaceted impression of the failure of both Willy and the American dream.

The interview scene begins with the expectant hope for a better life as represented by a desk job, a hope heightened by the optimism in the opening scene of act 2, a conversation between Willy and Linda. The action intensifies in Howard's office as Willy attempts to achieve some measure of success. When the beaten salesman yells at his employer and is consequently dismissed, the drama inadvertently contrasts a personal ethic with the cold rules of business. The past then forces itself into the present as Willy tries to discover where his life went wrong. This pattern of expectant hope, actual attempts to achieve success, words of anger, and resultant failure recurs in the restaurant. Like the interview, this scene begins with a prologue to set the tone, but unlike the optimistic interchange between Willy and his wife, here we see Happy's sleazy tactic with women; the contrast is striking as we witness the product of Willy's fathering. With Biff enters the hope, not for a better life but for better understanding and acceptance. As in the interview, the action intensifies when Biff tries to communicate honestly with his father, whose grasp on the present is rapidly slipping as images from the past keep intruding on his consciousness. The angry words again mark the moment of dismissal, after which the boys desert their father and the memory that has haunted Willy from the beginning of the play bursts into the present. In both scenes, Miller expertly unites the causal structure of realism with an expressionistic convention of rhythmic repetition.

An additional parallel pattern, between the restaurant scene and the hotel scene, contributes yet another level of the realism-expressionism synthesis: the hotel incident in the dream world rhythmically echoes the restaurant incident in the actual world. In the present, the lechery between Happy and his "babe" precedes Biff's rejection of his father when Willy does not live up to his son's ideal—understanding and acceptance of the truth. Willy's memory of the Boston hotel repeats this pattern: the suggested lust, this time between Willy and The Woman, is followed by Biff's rejection of his father when he realizes that his role model has fallen short of his ideal. To accept the affair as the sole cause of Biff's, and ultimately Willy's, failure trivializes the script, so exploring the rhythmic parallels of these two scenes, experienced on several levels in performance, helps the students move beyond that easy solution. They see the interweaving of the past and the present visually and hear it rhythmically, and they understand how Miller uses form expressionistically to highlight his themes.

The students learn to see a play that functions simultaneously on several levels. While they may not agree on whether a production of *Death of a Salesman* should condemn the American system or expose the torments of one man, they recognize that the play paradoxically embraces these contradictions and that one interpretation is not more valid than the other. They also begin to see which character traits, speeches, images, and scenes a director needs to emphasize to encourage an audience to see the play in a particular way. This pedagogical approach encourages even the most reticent student to contribute to class discussion because it emphasizes multiplicity of interpretations rather than a single correct one. The students thus finish their work on *Death of a Salesman* with the seeds of an understanding that may ultimately grow into a coherent and theatrically exciting production or an insightful and complex analysis.

NOTE

[1] For an examination of the use of music in *Salesman*, see Brater, "Miller's Realism" 124–26.

Miller's Mindscape: A Scenic Approach to *Death of a Salesman*

Thomas P. Adler

As the theater critic and director Robert Brustein has written, "When the lights go up on a play, you are entering a designer's world, and it is the designer's images that plant themselves indelibly on the edge of your mind" ("Designs" 27). Most of us, as teachers of dramatic literature, probably tell our students that a play seen onstage affects us emotionally before it engages us intellectually, which is to say that a play communicates through visual signs and symbols as well as (or perhaps as much as) through verbal ones. Nevertheless, I suspect that the visual dynamics tend more often than not to be relegated to asides in many classrooms, where ideas seem the thing to catch the attention of students. Miller's *Death of a Salesman*, however, forces us to pay more than lip service to this equality of visual elements with verbal, since so much of the play's structure and meaning are tied to its deservedly famous setting.

Yet precisely how might one "teach the scenery," and to what end? In what ways does attention to elements of stage design help us understand how a playwright creates meaning? Few instructors would want to pursue all the avenues suggested below with a single class, as the appropriateness of each depends on the level of the students' sophistication as well as on the context in which the work is taught (Introduction to Theater, Modern Drama, Great American Works, or American Drama, for instance). To focus on the scenic design of *Salesman* means raising with our students questions about the textual authority of set descriptions; about the relation between the memory structure of the play and music cues; about the interplay of realism and expressionism; about the formal connections between certain dramaturgical devices and the limited point of view in fiction; about narrativity in drama; and about the play's coda, what Miller calls the Requiem, and how it effects closure in *Salesman*.

Of all the set designs for the American theater, Jo Mielziner's for *Salesman* may well have the greatest familiarity among readers. Two of Mielziner's conceptual drawings form the centerpiece of his *Designing for the Theatre* (146–47), which also includes his extensive diary about working on the original production from initial discussions to opening night; furthermore, production photographs frequently appear in anthologies and critical studies, most recently as the only visual of its kind in Peter Conn's *Literature in America: An Illustrated History* (471). The genesis of this set, the collaborative process of imagining that led to its creation, was complex. In an interview Miller comments, "[Y]ou can play *Death of a Salesman* the way I first wrote it, without any setting at all" (Roudané, *Conversations* 341). Despite praising

Mielziner as "a genius" and the *Salesman* realization as "his greatest set," Miller later claimed that the impetus for the now-famous design was already specified in the earliest draft of his play script: "three rooms on as many levels . . . was indeed my original concept set out in my stage directions which called for three platforms" (Salesman *in Beijing* 6). This comment implies that the text was not in need of fundamental alteration to fit a later design concept.

Yet in *Timebends: A Life* the playwright admits that Mielziner fleshed out his setting, "stretching reality in parallel with the script . . . by balancing on the edges of the ordinary bounds of verisimilitude" (188). The element of the setting that Mielziner specifically credits himself for is what he terms its "major visual symbol" (25); the play's initial director, Elia Kazan, confirms that " 'the spectral house' . . . was urged on us by the scenic designer . . . it was the single most important contribution. . . . Both Miller and I were praised for what Jo had conceived" (361). What is indisputable is that in this instance the designer's work came to assume the same authority as the text, for, as Kazan further indicates, "Art [Miller later] rewrote his stage direction for the book based on Jo's design" (362). When we teach the play, we embrace the set descriptions as Miller's own, devoting to them the same attention that we would in analyzing and interpreting the function of narrative passages describing place in a novel.

The assumption underlying the overall structure, as well as the characterization of the central figure in *Salesman*, is Miller's understanding of the mind as unlimited spatially and temporally, an assumption that finds expression in Mielziner's set design. In the introduction to his *Collected Plays*, the dramatist reports that the image from which *Salesman* sprang "was of an enormous face the height of the proscenium arch which would appear and then open up, and we would see the inside of a man's head" (23). Though this elementary notion for a stage drop was wisely jettisoned, the concept of getting inside, of seeing things from the interior, came to control the play's form, "which . . . would literally be the process of Willy Loman's way of mind" (23–24): past and present, truth and fiction, dream and fact would coexist simultaneously in "a mobile concurrency" (26) creating a qualitatively new reality.

As Mielziner attests, however, the playwright left to the artist the problem of discovering the means to accomplish the interweaving of then and now, here and there, when Miller wrote at the end of his script, " 'The scenic solution to this production will have to be an imaginative and simple one. I don't know the answer, but the designer must work out something which makes the script flow easily' " (Mielziner 24). Miller was aware that hiatuses that might be disorienting for a reader must be made easily understandable to an audience. As described in the published play text, Mielziner found his solution for avoiding potentially disorienting jumps and effecting necessary transitions in time and place through devising the house's "imaginary wall-lines," the scrims of overpowering apartment houses and idyllic spring-green leaves, and the "apron, curving beyond the forestage into the orchestra. . . . [that is] the locale of all Willy's imaginings" (12)—all aided by lighting and music. The stage apron thus becomes the mind, "the inside of [Willy's] head." Since the apron serves also as the location of all the various scenes that occur away from the Loman house and yard, the stage set establishes the mix of objective reality with subjective perception that Miller desired.

For by no means is all of *Salesman* interior (unlike Miller's later play *After the Fall*, for which Mielziner designed a set using mainly platforms and ramps). Only six segments actually occur within Willy's mind, two in the first act and four in the second. Although these segments dramatize past events, Miller prefers that they not be considered flashbacks (Introduction 26), evidently because such an attitude would deemphasize the link between the now and the then. For purposes of teaching the play, one might usefully see them instead as memory sequences—a device that most students know from Tennessee Williams's *The Glass Menagerie* (1945) and that Miller himself employs throughout *A View from the Bridge* (1954).

Granted, not all of *Salesman* is remembrance of things past, and therefore it may not be strictly appropriate to say of it, as Williams does of *Menagerie*, "the play is memory" (23). Nevertheless, Miller's unacknowledged debt to that earlier work—for which Mielziner also created a set using transparent scrims, to usher in what came to be called an "age of gauze" in stage design— may be even greater than the influence Miller attributes to Williams's *A Streetcar Named Desire* (1947). In *Timebends* Miller points to that work, whose original set was likewise designed by Mielziner, as having provided not just an example of "fluidity in the form" but also a revelation about "words and their liberation, the joy of the writer in writing them, the radiant eloquence of its composition" (182). The specific link between memory and music, however, belongs to *Menagerie*; as Williams's narrator says in the opening scene, "In memory everything seems to happen to music. That explains the fiddle in the wings" (23).

Music is associated with each of the interior sequences in *Salesman*, although as the play proceeds an ironic counterpoint may be increasingly established between sound and image. Usually accompanied by the scrim of leaves that serves as "an easily recognized symbol of the springtime of [Willy's] life" (Mielziner 35), the music throughout (with some exceptions) is almost invariably that of "a flute. It is small and fine, telling of grass and trees and the horizon" (11). The nostalgic melody, then, recalls the country and the garden (both literal and mythic); it speaks of freedom and expansiveness and possibility in much the same way that, in one of the work's most memorable scenic moments, Willy's touchingly pathetic attempt to plant the seeds by moonlight speaks of restriction and loss. The handling of the first memory sequence (27–41) sets the pattern for the remaining five: as it begins, the surrounding apartments fade from view while the leaves, accompanied by music, cover the entire set—in something akin to a cinematic dissolve. As it ends, the process reverses itself.

A few isolated moments outside the memory sequences are even more expressionistic in their use of scenic elements to objectify Willy's inner experience, and at these moments the influence of *Streetcar* on *Salesman* may be strongest. The major instances include Willy's vision of Biff apotheosized in "a golden pool of light" and the ominous "gas heater begin[ning] to glow through the kitchen wall . . . a blue flame beneath red coils" (68) near the end of act 1; "the light on [Howard's] chair grow[ing] very bright and strange. . . . animating it" (82) as Willy hallucinates that Howard's father, Frank, once again occupies it; and, most like *Streetcar*, the disorientation represented by "sounds, faces, voices . . . swarming in upon him and . . . music . . . ris[ing] in intensity, almost to an unbearable scream" (136) as Willy moves toward suicide.

Although Miller somewhat overstates the evidence when he judges that there was "more innovation [and] conscious use of . . . formal experimentation in the theatre going into *Death of a Salesman* than any other American play I could think of" (Roudané, *Conversations* 337)—he seems to have forgotten, for instance, the expressionism of Eugene O'Neill, John Howard Lawson, and Elmer Rice and the theatricalism of Thornton Wilder—his technique moves far beyond what he deemed a severely limiting naturalism ("a picture of life . . . uninterpreted by the artist's visible hand" [337]) and even broadens considerably the notion of what stage realism can accommodate without becoming some other "ism."

Miller claims, further, that he did not employ the "expressionistic elements" in *Salesman* to create "coldness, objectivity, and a highly styled sort of play" that would demonstrate a social thesis (as German expressionism and its disciples had); rather, he "employed expressionism . . . always to create a subjective truth, and this play, which was so manifestly 'written,' seemed as though nobody had written it at all but that it had simply 'happened'" (Roudané, *Conversations* 39). *Salesman* was thus intended—as reflected and embodied in Mielziner's stage setting—to be for its audience simultaneously illusionistic, making them forget that they are in a theater watching a play, and nonillusionistic, making them ignore the conventions of realism yet observe how these conventions are being manipulated and even violated. But as Kazan suggests, once the media of film and television can achieve a level of naturalism the stage never could, a decrease in the attempt at theatrical realism may mean an increase in art (364–65).

The crucial distinction, nevertheless, between realistic-illusionistic drama and nonrealistic-nonillusionistic drama resides in whether the playwright has maintained the imaginary "fourth wall" between stage and auditorium or allowed a crossing over of the boundary between actor-character and audience. To use Roman Ingarden's terms, it is a distinction between a "closed" and an "open" theater (383–84), between the spectators' assuming "an aesthetic attitude" by suspending disbelief and disregarding the fictive nature of what they see onstage (that is, by making believe that they are not making believe) and the spectators' being consciously reminded that they are an audience watching actors who are aware of being observed. The various ways in which Miller manipulates the audience's expectation that Willy will assume the role of narrator, as well as the flexibility and lack of rigidity with which Mielziner treats the notion of the putative fourth wall, contribute to the difficulty of pinning any easy, all-encompassing descriptor on the formal structure of *Salesman*.

As spectators, we have become conditioned to think that whenever a play's action occurs within the confines of a proscenium stage but its characters move freely to an apron forestage (or vice versa), we may conclude that the play is nonillusionistic because a complicity recognizing the presence of the other has been established between actor and audience. This conclusion is not, however, precisely what Miller—as interpreted through Mielziner—intends in *Salesman*. True, as Willy first prepares to go out onto the forestage that is his mind, he "is gradually addressing—physically—a point offstage, speaking through the wall of the kitchen" (28); the point to which he directly addresses his words, though, is never specified as the audience. In essence, Willy—who is coming unhinged—confesses aloud (or rationalizes) his past actions to himself in what Miller in the *Collected Plays* subtitles "Certain Private Conversations in Two Acts" (1: 129). To employ Gerald Prince's designation, Willy is his own "narratee," not "intend[ing] the narration to be for anyone other than himself" (18). At this point in the play, then, all that Mielziner has done is to move the imaginary fourth wall out from the proscenium and reposition it in front of the apron forestage. For Miller does not intend that Willy be construed as a traditional stage narrator—certainly not in the way we view Wilder's Stage Manager in *Our Town* or Williams's Tom Wingfield, both of whom set the physical scene, control the passage of time, and ruminate on the meaning of the action. Consequently, in contrast with the scenes reenacted from the past in *Menagerie*, those in *Salesman* always seem to the viewer more subjective and solipsistic than objective and distanced.

Rather than be termed narration, Willy's memory sequences (which, as noted above, Mielziner usually signals through leaf scrim and music) might better be considered as acted-out soliloquies or dramatized monologues. Seen in that light, the memory sequences in *Salesman* resemble most closely the stream-of-consciousness and first-person-limited point of view that are the hallmarks of modernist fiction. Indeed, as Martin Esslin suggests, "the dividing line between a dramatic text and narrative fiction become[s] . . . tenuous" (25) in those instances when one or the other of the two genres assumes the form of the dramatic monologue. And so Miller's play, in its handling of stage space and character, implies certain ideological or philosophical stances: experience is relative, reality is pluralistic rather than unitary, and moral judgments are ambiguous.

Our understanding, and that of our students, about how *Death of a Salesman* works scenically perhaps makes the biggest difference when we come to read the play's coda—what Miller calls the Requiem. Now, for the first time during action supposedly occurring in the present, the actors "all move toward the audience, through the wall-line of the kitchen" (136), a boundary they had always respected before except in the retrospective sequences. When Linda says in the curtain line, "We're free" (139), one thing from which the audience is now "free" is the subjective perspective of Willy. We have moved out of Miller's mindscape. Here Linda refers literally, of course, to having made the last payment on the house mortgage and thus finally being clear of debt. Ironically, to acquire what is promised by the system, these characters have unwittingly helped it flourish by their unquestioning acquiescence to its rules—which in turn, over the years, have imprisoned them in a cycle of indebtedness, of earning and paying. And the house, once achieved, no longer fulfills the dream of pastoral life in a garden. Equally ironic, Biff will never be "free" of responsibility for Willy's death, since his father, held accountable for failing to be the moral authority the son demands, died so that Biff might live and prosper materially.

On one level, the Requiem is a meditation on the meaning of Willy's life and death and on the lives of the survivors; furthermore, it is perhaps a dramaturgically necessary element, designed to restore the play's focus on Willy, since so much of the latter half of act 2 centers on the process of the individuation and evolving self-awareness—however belated—of the second protagonist, Biff. On another level, the Requiem is a mediation between the play and the spectators, and it could be argued that only during this coda or epilogue does the imaginary fourth wall evaporate and *Salesman* become nonillusionistic; here, finally, an awareness of the audience's presence is implied, and their powers of seeing themselves as spectators at an "open" rather than a "closed" dramatic experience are deliberately called into use.

The scenic image at the end of the Requiem replicates that of the play's beginning. Like brother Ben's glistening diamonds and the apparently all-too-real insurance money that is linked linguistically to those gems, the Edenic state hinted at by the delicate leaf scrim was never anything more than an illusory patina over the urban economic jungle, promising a time of possibility that, if it ever did exist, is now irretrievable. One could no more escape back to it than to "the old island that flowered once for Dutch sailors' eyes—a fresh, green breast of the new world" or to "the green light at the end of Daisy's dock. . . . that year by year recedes before us" in *The Great Gatsby* (182)—and indeed the final paragraphs of F. Scott Fitzgerald's novel, familiar to many students, and the last moments of Miller's drama make interesting glosses to each other. The potentiality for Biff's ever becoming the kind of man he desires to be, through a Thoreauvian retreat from society, has become severely circumscribed with the passage of time. What Mielziner's closing scenic image of the enveloping apartments impresses on audiences is that, whether by choice or not, we have been wrenched free of the garden, condemned to live in the world of getting and keeping, of what Willy sees as the ruinous competition that is the dark underside of his and our America's dream of success, the souring of the romance of capitalism for the little man.

"The Woods Are Burning": Expressionism in *Death of a Salesman*

Barbara Lounsberry

> I had always been attracted and repelled by the
> brilliance of German expressionism after World War I,
> and one aim in *Salesman* was to employ its quite
> marvelous shorthand for humane, "felt"
> characterizations rather than for purposes of
> demonstration for which the Germans had used it.
> —Arthur Miller, introduction to *Collected Plays*

The tones of a flute, "small and fine," opened the original production of *Death of a Salesman*. The curtain rose on a small, "fragile-seeming" transparent house surrounded by an angry glow of orange (11). Beyond were the dark and menacing towers of encroaching buildings. As the play unfolded, the astonished audience saw characters walk through wall lines. It saw a gas heater begin to glow threateningly and white light grow on an office chair until the light itself became a living presence.

The balance between expressionistic and realistic moments in *Death of a Salesman* is both its essence and its highest achievement. Through this delicate balance, Miller found a form to dramatize the intermingling of individual psychology and social forces, which is one of his greatest themes. He could also demonstrate his complex notions of human time. Since the original Elia Kazan production, many others—including the acclaimed Volker Schlondorff version, starring Dustin Hoffman, which is often shown today in schools—have diluted or discarded many of the expressionistic devices that made the 1949 *Salesman* so startling: the musical motifs, the terrifying orange and red glows, the menacing towers, even the fragile transparent house itself. Such tipping of the scales toward greater realism is often done deliberately to shift the focus away from Willy Loman. It is done to place greater emphasis on the role of Linda Loman, or on Biff and Happy Loman.[1] While these emphases are viable production choices, teachers and directors ignore the expressionism in *Death of a Salesman* at a price. That price is the opportunity to showcase expressionism at one of its highest levels of achievement. That price is the audience's lost recognition of the intertwining of the personal and the social.

Expressionism: A Brief History

Death of a Salesman represents both a summation and an extension of German expressionism. The term *expressionism* itself is of French origin, first popularly used in France around 1901 to distinguish the painting of van Gogh, Gauguin, and others from the works of the impressionists, who tried to capture objects as seen in a certain light at a specific moment in time (Brockett and Findlay 269–70). Expressionists, in contrast, tried to stress strong inner feelings about objects and to present life as modified or distorted by the painter's own inner vision of reality. Thus, while impressionists employed the eye, expressionists accentuated the mind.

Expressionism as a term entered German usage in 1910 or 1911. Among the many influences on expressionist drama were the free-verse forms of Walt Whitman, the works of Freud and Jung on the unconscious mind, and the drama of Heinrich von Kleist and Georg Büchner. Büchner's *Woyzeck* was first staged in Germany in 1913. Another strong influence was Goethe's *Faust*, part 2, which dramatized the search for spiritual fulfillment. This play received its first full-scale production in 1911.

More immediate influences, however, were probably the plays of Frank Wedekind and the Swedish dramatist August Strindberg. A cycle of Wedekind's plays was produced by Max Reinhardt in 1911. Strindberg's *To Damascus*, parts 1, 2, and 3 (published 1898–1904), are dream—or nightmare—dramas depicting the psychological and spiritual agonies of a personal quest. In his explanatory note for *A Dream Play* (published in 1902 and produced in 1907), Strindberg writes, "Everything can happen. . . . Time and space do not exist. . . . The characters split, double, redouble, evaporate, condense, scatter, and converge" (19).

German expressionists were involved in a political and philosophical movement as well as in an aesthetic revolution. Most were opposed to realism and naturalism because they glorified science, which the expressionists associated with industrialism and technology, tools of the materialist society they sought to change. In contrast, they criticized the neoromantics for their flight from contemporary social problems.

Death of a Salesman may be seen as a summation of both the early and late stages of German expressionism. Reinhard Johannes Sorge's 1912 play *The Beggar*, often called the first true expressionist drama, is typical of the movement's early stage. Until about 1915 the primary emphasis of German expressionism was on the conflict between older and younger generations and between established conventions and new values as seen from a highly subjective point of view. Sorge's Poet-Beggar was on an ecstatic quest for spiritual fulfillment. Like Miller's early work, such plays were often dramas about families as well as about the individual.

As World War I unfolded, expressionism became more and more pessimistic. German dramatists increasingly abandoned personal concerns in order to warn the public of impending universal catastrophe and to plead for reformation of individuals and society. For a time at the end of the war, it seemed as if the expressionists' vision of a transformed culture might be achieved. The communes established in many cities were soon suppressed, however, and the severity of the Versailles Treaty led to bitterness and the belief that humanity was beyond salvation.

This war and postwar disillusionment is seen in the works of George Kaiser and Ernst Toller. Toller's *Transfiguration* (1918), subtitled *A Man's Wrestling*, alternates between realistic scenes and dream visions. It shows reality through the eyes of a sensitive patriot. Toller's *Man and the Masses* (1921) also alternates realistic scenes with dream visions.

Since the goals of expressionism were idealistic—nothing less than the transformation of individuals and society—it is not surprising that the movement ended in disenchantment. The anti-German sentiment following the war explains why expressionism remained essentially a German phenomenon. Nevertheless, a number of American playwrights borrowed techniques from the German drama. In *The Emperor Jones* (1921), Eugene O'Neill used sound effects and symbolic scenes to project the racial memories of a modern African American.[2] In *The Hairy Ape* (1922), he again created symbolic scenes, along with distorted, grotesque characters and settings, to suggest the disharmony between nature and civilization. In Elmer Rice's *The Adding Machine* (1923), the walls close in and the floor spins as Rice presents both a psychological and social study of a brutalized human being: Mr. Zero.[3] In George S. Kaufman and Marc Connelly's zany dream play *Beggar on Horseback* (1924), an American capitalist has a telephone attached to his chest while his vulgar wife appears with a rocking chair stuck to her bottom. The American Marxist playwright John Howard Lawson employed crude and garish vaudevillian backdrops; burlesque stereotypes of Jews, African Americans, and city slickers; brassy saxophone music; and song-and-dance routines to depict racial prejudice, jingoism, class warfare, and other social problems in his 1925 drama *Processional*. Elements of expressionism also appear in the plays of Thornton Wilder and Tennessee Williams.

As Oscar Brockett and Robert Findlay write, "Perhaps the ultimate heirs of expressionism are those playwrights of the present day who, rebelling against materialism and hypocrisy, seek to discomfit the enemy with allegorical stories told through caricature, distortion, and a vision of regenerated man" (283). Arthur Miller's interests center on many of these themes; it is thus not surprising that he was drawn, early and enduringly, to the works of the German expressionists. In "The Shadows of the Gods," Miller admits that he read the Greeks and the German expressionists at the same time. "I was struck by the similarity of their dramatic means in one respect," he noted. "[T]hey are designed to present the hidden forces, not the characteristics of the human beings playing out those forces on the stage" (*Theater Essays* 181).

In his 1966 *Paris Review* interview, Miller revealed his reaction to the bitter disillusionment of expressionism's final phase:

> I know that I was very moved in many ways by German expressionism when I was in school; yet there too something was perverse in it to

me. It was the end of man, there are no people in it any more; that
was especially true of the real German stuff: it's the bitter end of the
world where man is a voice of his class function, and that's it.[4] . . .
And yet, at the same time, I learned a great deal from it. I used
elements of it that were fused into *Death of a Salesman*.

(Theater Essays 272)

As the epigraph to this article suggests, what Miller learned from the
expressionists was their "quite marvelous shorthand" for presenting hidden
forces. Miller extends expressionism by applying its techniques to create
"felt" human character at the same time that he is presenting social types.
Willy Loman is a salesman. To this degree Miller pays homage to the German
allegorical tradition, but Miller employs the techniques of expressionism to
make Willy a particular human being as well. The Lomans are round, not
flat, characters. There are people in Miller's plays, not class functions.

In *Death of a Salesman* Miller also solves the most difficult problem faced
by the German expressionists: how to avoid the purely aberrational while
using a subjective approach to reveal and comment on objective reality.
German expressionism, particularly in its final stages, tends to be associated
in the public mind with aberrant or nightmare visions. Miller's delicately
balanced expressionism allowed him to present a psyche in the process of
deterioration, but one that appears to audiences as far more representative
than aberrant. As Miller explains in the introduction to his *Collected Plays*,
"Indeed, [Willy's] terror springs from his never-lost awareness of time and
place" (27).

One way to diminish expressionism's aberrational taint was to employ its
techniques to reveal Ibsenesque cause and effect; to reveal, for example,
the relationship between past sins and present actions. German expressionism was such a message-centered drama that it was usually organized according to idea, theme, or motif rather than on cause-and-effect relations
among incidents. In *Death of a Salesman* Miller demonstrates that expressionism can be employed in the service of cause and effect.

The Expressionistic Devices in Death of a Salesman

Musical Motifs

From the opening flute notes to their final reprise, Miller's musical themes
express the competing influences in Willy Loman's mind. Once established,
the themes need only be sounded to evoke certain time frames, emotions,
and values. The first sounds of the drama, the flute notes "small and fine,"
represent the grass, trees, and horizon—objects of Willy's (and Biff's) longing
that are tellingly absent from the overshadowed home on which the curtain
rises. This melody plays on as Willy makes his first appearance, although,

as Miller tells us, "[h]e hears but is not aware of it" (12). Through this music we are thus given our first sense of Willy's estrangement not only from nature itself but from his own deepest nature.

As act 1 unfolds, the flute is linked to Willy's father, who, we are told, made flutes and sold them during the family's early wanderings. The father's theme, "a high, rollicking tune," is differentiated from the small and fine melody of the natural landscape (49). This distinction is fitting, for the father is a salesman as well as an explorer; he embodies the conflicting values that are destroying his son's life.

The father's tune shares a family likeness with Ben's "idyllic" (133) music. This false theme, like Ben himself, is associated finally with death. Ben's theme is first sounded, after all, only after Willy expresses his exhaustion (44). It is heard again after Willy is fired in act 2. This time the music precedes Ben's entrance. It is heard in the distance, then closer, just as Willy's thoughts of suicide, once repressed, now come closer at the loss of his job. And Willy's first words to Ben when he finally appears are the ambiguous "how did you do it?" (84). When Ben's idyllic melody plays for the third and final time it is in "accents of dread" (133), for Ben reinforces Willy's wrongheaded thought of suicide to bankroll Biff.

The father's and Ben's themes, representing selling (out) and abandonment, are thus in opposition to the small and fine theme of nature that begins and ends the play. A whistling motif elaborates this essential conflict. Whistling is often done by those contentedly at work. It frequently also accompanies outdoor activities. A whistler in an office would be a distraction. Biff Loman likes to whistle, thus reinforcing his ties to nature rather than to the business environment. But Happy seeks to stifle Biff's true voice:

> HAPPY.   . . . Bob Harrison said you were tops, and then you go and do some damn fool thing like whistling whole songs in the elevator like a comedian.
> BIFF, *against Happy.*   So what? I like to whistle sometimes.
> HAPPY.   You don't raise a guy to a responsible job who whistles in the elevator!   (60)

This conversation reverberates ironically when Howard Wagner plays Willy a recording of his daughter whistling "Roll out the Barrel" just before Willy asks for an advance and a New York job (77). Whistling, presumably, is all right if you are the boss or the boss's daughter, but not if you are an employee. The barrel will not be rolled out for Willy or Biff Loman.

Willy's conflicting desires to work in sales and to do outdoor, independent work are complicated by another longing, that of sexual desire, which is expressed through the "raw, sensuous music" that accompanies The Woman's appearances on stage (116, 37). It is this music of sexual desire, I suggest, that "insinuates itself" as the first leaves cover the house in act 1.[5] It is heard just before Willy—reliving a past conversation—offers this ironic warning to Biff: "Just wanna be careful with those girls, Biff, that's all. Don't make any promises. No promises of any kind" (27).

This raw theme of sexual desire contrasts with Linda Loman's theme: the maternal hum of a soft lullaby that becomes a "desperate but monotonous" hum at the end of act 1 (69). Linda's monotonous drone, in turn, contrasts with the "gay and bright" music, the boys' theme, which opens act 2. This theme is associated with the "great times" (127) Willy remembers with his sons—before his adultery is discovered. Like the high, rollicking theme of Willy's father and like Ben's idyllic melody, this gay and bright music is ultimately associated with the false dream of materialistic success. The boys' theme is first heard when Willy tells Ben that he and the boys will get rich in Brooklyn (87). It sounds again when Willy implores Ben, "[H]ow do we get back to all the great times?" (127).

In his final moments of life, Willy Loman is shown struggling with his furies: "sounds, faces, voices, seem to be swarming in upon him" (136). Suddenly, however, the "faint and high" music enters, representing the false dreams of all the "low" men. This false tune ends Willy's struggle with his competing voices. It drowns out the other voices, rising in intensity "almost to an unbearable scream" as Willy rushes off in pursuit.

And just as the travail of *Moby-Dick* ends with the ongoing flow of the waves, nature, in the form of the flute's small and fine refrain, persists—despite the tragedy we have witnessed.

Sets

In the introduction to his *Collected Plays*, Miller acknowledges that the first image of *Salesman* that occurred to him was of an enormous face the height of the proscenium arch; the face would appear and then open up. "We would see the inside of a man's head," he explains. "In fact, *The Inside of His Head* was the first title. It was conceived half in laughter, for the inside of his head was a mass of contradictions" (23). By the time Miller had completed *Salesman*, however, he had found a more subtle correlative for the giant head: a transparent setting. "The entire setting is wholly, or, in some places, partially transparent," Miller insists in his set description (11). By substituting a transparent setting for a bisected head, Miller invited the audience to examine the social context as well as the individual organism. Productions that eschew transparent scenery eschew the nuances of this invitation.

The transparent lines of the Loman home allow the audience physically to sense the city pressures that are destroying Willy. "We are aware of towering, angular shapes behind [Willy's house], surrounding it on all sides. . . . The roof-line of the house is one-dimensional; under and over it we see the apartment buildings" (11–12). Wherever Willy Loman looks are these encroaching buildings, and wherever we look as well.

Willy's subjective vision is expressed also in the home's furnishings, which are deliberately partial. The furnishings indicated are only those of importance to Willy Loman. That Willy's kitchen has a table with three chairs instead of four reveals both Linda Loman's unequal status in the family and Willy's obsession with his boys. At the end of act 1, Willy goes to his small refrigerator for life-sustaining milk (cf. Brecht's parallel use of milk in *Galileo*). Later, however, we learn that this repository of nourishment, like Willy himself, has broken down. That Willy Loman's bedroom contains only a bed, a straight chair, and a shelf holding Biff's silver athletic trophy also telegraphs much about the man and his family. Linda Loman has no object of her own in her bedroom. Willy Loman also travels light. He has nothing of substance to sustain him. His vanity is devoted to adolescent competition.

Chairs ultimately become surrogates for people in *Death of a Salesman* as first a kitchen chair becomes Biff in Willy's conflicted mind (28) and then an office chair becomes Willy's deceased boss, Frank Wagner (82). In, perhaps, a subtle bow to Georg Kaiser's *Gas I* and *Gas II*, Miller's gas heater glows when Willy thinks of death. The scrim that veils the primping Woman and the screen hiding the restaurant where two women will be seduced suggest Willy Loman's repression of sexuality.

Lighting

Expressionism has done more than any other movement to develop the expressive powers of stage lighting. The German expressionists used light to create a strong sense of mood and to isolate characters in a void. By contrasting light and shadow, and by employing extreme side, overhead, and rear lighting angles, they established the nightmarish atmosphere in which many of their plays took place.

The original Kazan *Salesman* made use of more lights than were used even in Broadway musicals (*Timebends* 190). At the end of act 1, Biff comes downstage "into a golden pool of light" as Willy recalls the day of the city baseball championship when Biff was "[l]ike a young God. Hercules—something like that. And the sun, the sun all around him." The pool of light both establishes the moment as one of Willy's memories and suggests how he has inflated the past, given it mythic dimension. The lighting also functions to instill a sense of irony in the audience, for the golden light glows on undiminished as Willy exclaims, "A star like that, magnificent, can never really fade away!" We know that Biff's star faded, even before it had a chance to shine, and even as Willy speaks these words, the light on him begins to fade (68). That Willy's thoughts turn immediately from this golden vision of his son to his own suicide is indicated by the "blue flame" of the gas heater that begins immediately to glow through the wall—a foreshadowing of Willy's desire to gild his son through his own demise. Productions that omit either the golden pool of light or the glowing gas heater withhold this foreshadowing of Willy's final deed.

Similarly, productions that omit the lights on the empty chairs miss the chance to reveal the potency of Willy's fantasies. Perhaps even more important, the gas heater's flame at the end of act 1 recalls the "angry glow of orange" surrounding Willy's house at the play's beginning (11). Both join with the "red glow" rising from the hotel room and the restaurant to give a felt sense of Willy's twice articulated cry: "The woods are burning! . . . There's a big blaze going on all around" (41, 107). Without these sensory clues, audiences may fail to appreciate the desperation of Willy's state.

Characters and Costumes

Miller employs expressionistic technique when he allows his characters to split into younger versions of themselves to represent Willy's memories. Young Biff's letter sweater and football signal his age reversion, yet they also move in the direction of social type. The Woman also is an expressionistic type, the play's only generic character other than the marvelously individualized salesman.

Miller's greatest expressionistic creations, however, are Ben and Willy Loman. In his *Paris Review* interview, Miller acknowledged that he purposely refused to give Ben any character, "because for Willy he *has* no character—which is, psychologically, expressionist because so many memories come back with a simple tag on them: somebody represents a threat to you, or a promise" (*Theater Essays* 272). Clearly Ben represents a promise to Willy Loman. It is the promise of material success, but it is also the promise of death.[6] We might consider Uncle Ben to be the ghost of Ben, for we learn that Ben has recently died in Africa. Since Miller never discloses the cause of Ben's death, he may be a suicide himself. His idyllic melody, as I have noted, becomes finally a death march. In Willy's last moments, the contrapuntal voices of Linda and Ben vie with each other, but Willy moves inexorably toward Ben. Alluding to Africa, and perhaps also to the River Styx, Ben looks at his watch and says, "The boat. We'll be late" as he moves slowly into the darkness (135).

Willy Loman, needless to say, is Miller's brilliant demonstration that expressionistic techniques can express inner as well as outer forces, that expressionism can be used to create "felt," humane character. The music, setting, and lighting of *Salesman* all function to express the world inside Willy Loman's head, a world in which social and personal values meet and merge and struggle for integration. As Miller writes in the introduction to his *Collected Plays*:

[The play's] expressionistic elements were consciously used as such, but since the approach to Willy Loman's characterization was consistently and rigorously subjective, the audience would not ever be aware—if I could help it—that they were witnessing the use of a technique which had until then created only coldness, objectivity, and a highly styled sort of play.   (39)

In 1983, when Miller arrived in Beijing to direct the first Chinese production of *Death of a Salesman,* he was pleased to find that the Chinese had created a mirror image of the original transparent set. Seeing this set, and observing that the kitchen was furnished with only a refrigerator, table, and two (not even three) chairs, Miller felt "a wonderful boost" to his morale (Salesman *in Beijing* 3–4). Teachers and directors might offer a similar boost by giving full weight to the expressionistic moments in *Death of a Salesman.* For directors, achieving such moments may be technically demanding, but they should not be abandoned simply because they are challenging.[7] Similarly, the expressionistic devices should not be considered too obvious for postmodern taste. In truth, the expressionism in *Salesman* is not intrusive. Its very refinement of German expressionism lies in its subtlety, in its delicate balance with the realistic moments in the drama. This ever-shifting tension between realism and expressionism allows us to feel the interpenetration of outer and inner forces within the human psyche. The expressionistic devices also elevate Willy's suffering, for they place it in the context of the natural order. To excise the expressionism is to diminish the rich chord that is Miller's drama.

NOTES

[1] Miller himself has acknowledged his disappointment that "the self-realization of the older son, Biff, is not a weightier counterbalance to Willy's disaster in the audience's mind" (*Theater Essays* 14).

[2] In scene 1, a native tom-tom begins "at a rate exactly corresponding to normal pulse beat—72 to the minute" (20) and continues at a gradually accelerating rate to the end of the play.

[3] Few have noted the parallels between Rice's *The Adding Machine* and *Death of a Salesman.* In each play, a low(ly) man is discharged from his position after long service, and in each a machine usurps the man. In Rice's play it is a giant adding machine; in *Salesman* it is a dictaphone. Both plays feature building walls that close in, and both have graveyard scenes and a protagonist haunted by adulterous thoughts. Harold Clurman, in fact, listed *The Adding Machine* as an antecedent to *Salesman* in his review of Miller's play (*Lies* 68.)

[4] Miller has noted that in *Gas I* and *Gas II* George Kaiser placed a human figure against the image of industrial society "but without the slightest attempt to characterize the man except as a representative of one or the other of the social classes vying for control of the machine" (*Theater Essays* 75).

[5]A parallel to Eve's betrayal in the Garden of Eden is here implied. Miller's interest in the Genesis story is demonstrated by his 1972 and 1974 works *The Creation of the World and Other Business* and *Up from Paradise*.

[6]In his 1987 autobiography, *Timebends: A Life*, Miller reports that Elia Kazan's wife, Molly, repeatedly pressed him to eliminate Uncle Ben and all the scenes of the past as unnecessary in the strictest sense. "It was," he writes, "an amazing example of the 'nothing-but' psychoanalytical reductionist method of peeling away experience only as far as its quickly recognizable conventional paradoxes, in the misconceived belief that color, tone, and even longing in themselves do not change fate" (334).

[7]Miller brought the original musical score to Beijing. It was taped and played on an antiquated Chinese tape recorder, which Miller perpetually feared would break down. His efforts to reproduce the original lighting effects were hampered by lack of sufficient equipment.

The Dramatist as Salesman: A Rhetorical Analysis of Miller's Intentions and Effects

Martin J. Jacobi

Every student at my university is required to take a literature course at the sophomore level, and by far the most popular course is Contemporary British and American Literature, the course in which *Death of a Salesman* is taught. A typical class includes students from many different majors, with varying levels of interest in and knowledge of literature. Their attitudes and abilities help shape the way I teach the course, but whether I teach these students or upper-division and graduate-level English majors, my teaching of Miller's play also reflects my bias toward rhetorical criticism. In this essay I show how I apply rhetorical criticism to Miller's play; my orientation derives primarily from Kenneth Burke and, secondarily, from Wayne Booth. Both, while good Aristotelians, offer methods of and uses for literary analysis that Aristotle does not.

People sometimes see literature as a kind of substitute for the games of childhood, lacking relevance to their adult lives and responsibilities. I try to convince my students that reading literary works carefully is not only pleasurable but practical, that literature, like anything else they read or view, does things to them and for them, can help them or hurt them. And I want them to see—although I do not address this issue here—how the ability to discern intentions and effects in a literary work can help them read critically other and perhaps less benign forms of persuasive discourse.

I will provide first a brief rationale for my particular approach, then a description of a methodology of rhetorical criticism, and finally an application of this methodology to Miller's play.

The Nature of Rhetorical Criticism

Rhetorical criticism begins, as all good criticism should, with a close analysis of the text. It differs from other critical approaches in that it aims to determine what the work is doing to and for the reader. It employs what New Criticism has called the intentional and the affective fallacies to achieve these ends. Some rhetorical critics, such as Edward P. J. Corbett, Oscar G. Brockett, and Donald C. Bryant, limit their analyses of authorial intentions and audience effects to the text itself. Others "move back and forth between the work and the author and the audience, with glances, if need be, at external documents for supplementary or confirmatory evidence" (Corbett xxviii). Burke, for instance, takes the position that a critic should "use all that is there to use" ("Philosophy" 23).

Some of the available materials, Burke argues, are an artist's engrossments. Artists necessarily write about what engrosses them, and "nothing more deeply engrosses a man than his *burdens*" ("Philosophy" 17). Literary works are strategies that "size up situations, name their structure and outstanding ingredients, and name them in a way that contains an attitude towards them" (1); the artist, in writing, develops a strategy to diminish or even remove these burdens. Burke allows that a reader need not know an author's particular burdens to appreciate the work, but he does say that learning what the work is doing for the author helps clarify what it may do for—and to—the reader. Along these lines, Booth suggests the useful tactic of analyzing the "implied author" as a means of understanding effects on audiences (*Rhetoric* 71–76; *Company* 174–79, 221–23).

The rhetorical critic, then, analyzes the text itself, the author, and the effects, and considers whether to adopt, adapt, or reject the text's argument. *A Doll House*, for instance, takes a stance on sexism, *Othello* on trust and jealousy, and *Antigone* on the relation of the individual to civil law. *Death of a Salesman* takes a stance on the relation of the individual to business, and it asks of my sophomores at least that they reconsider their understanding of and preparation for the pursuit of the American dream.

As students work through a rhetorical analysis, they come to see the "practical" applications of reading as well as the effects their reading has on them. As a result, they read closely to learn what these texts can offer them, and they thereby grant to their reading of literary works at least some of the seriousness they grant to primary texts in their major fields. Of course, the close analysis also improves their ability to see and so be pleased by the aesthetic qualities of the play—that is, by the skill with which the plot is contrived, the characters developed, and the language arranged. One student has even said that rhetorical criticism "tricks" readers into appreciating the aesthetic aspect of literature. I would prefer a more honorific verb, but given the predisposition of many business and engineering majors, it makes good rhetorical sense to take up the practical aspects before the "literary."

A Methodology for Rhetorical Criticism

Used to its full extent, Burke's methodology is rich and complex; used partially, it is easy to manage and still helpful to students. The two aspects of his methodology most useful for sophomores not majoring in English are the pentad and ratios and the dream-chart-prayer triad.

The pentad is a means for looking at a text from every angle. It originally consisted of five terms—*act, agent, scene, agency,* and *purpose*—although some time after this original formulation Burke added a sixth term, *attitude,* which he describes as an incipient action and which may also be thought of as an agent's intention. (In my sophomore class I apply attitude in this way.) Ratios are the relations between terms; for instance, an act-scene ratio considers the way an act is affected by the scene in which it takes place.

Burke uses *dream, chart,* and *prayer* to explain three emphases he sees in artistic creation. Dream is the self-expressive, subconscious articulation of what engrosses the artist; it provides the impetus for artistic creativity but is not "adjusted" for real life and real audiences. Chart is the adjustment of dream, its "socialization," its translation into what audiences are able and willing to understand. Prayer is the persuasive emphasis, going beyond the mimesis of chart to induce the audience into accepting the artist's vision. Dream emphasizes authors and intentions in its examination of the symbolic action of a literary work and might be examined through psychoanalytic, biographical, and historical criticism; chart emphasizes the text itself, using a New Critical close examination; and prayer emphasizes audiences and effects and might be examined through reader-response criticism as well as through feminist, Marxist, and other types of sociological criticism. As can be seen, this triad considers the three elements that in my introduction I list as the domain of the rhetorical critic: the text, the author, and the effects on the audience. To talk about these elements in a sophomore class, I employ the less idiosyncratic terms of textual analysis (chart), ethical criticism (dream), and affective criticism (prayer).

I ask students to apply the pentad to each element of the triad, which means they have available fifteen initial descriptions (see appendix) plus the numerous ratios. Students begin with a textual analysis, trying to understand the play "as in itself it really is." Next, they consider what they know and can find out about the implied author as well as the public, historical author. I am less concerned, however, with having these students learn about the historical Miller—that is, less interested in the psychoanalytic criticism that would look for Miller's real-life "burdens"—than in getting them to consider what sort of person the implied author must be to perform the symbolic action that *Salesman* represents. That is, I ask them to consider, in Booth's terms, the ethical nature of the author with whom they are "keeping company" when they read the play; I also ask them to consider the nature of the ethical universe they are being asked to inhabit, if only for the duration of their reading. This ethical criticism, as I illustrate, provides another way of considering the ambiguities of the play as they are realized through the textual analysis; it also provides a useful bridge to the final part of the students' job, that of affective criticism. In this last stage, students consider the "messages" of the play—not only what it suggests to be the appropriate act for Willy but also what it suggests to be appropriate ways for the audience to act.

A *Rhetorical Reading of* Death of a Salesman

Before offering my rhetorical analysis of *Death of a Salesman*, I should mention one more piece of background material. I organize my sophomore-level class loosely around two issues: the broad literary movement from Romanticism to realism to naturalism and the nature of tragedy and the tragic hero. Before the course syllabus reaches Miller's play, the class has had ample instruction, illustrations, and analyses, thereby having developed a context in which to answer a central question concerning Miller's play: whether it is tragedy or pathos, whether Willy destroys himself or is destroyed by a modern business and social world he does not understand.

Textual Analysis

A close analysis of Willy and the other *agents* does not answer this question but does help focus it. Willy is confused about his life and about himself. He doubts himself, doubts the skills of salesmanship he had convinced himself he possessed, and even doubts the validity of his vision of the American dream. He illustrates a basic confusion through his frequent self-contradictions— about the worth of automobiles, refrigerators, and whipped cheese; about the appropriate professional response to whistling, banter and joking, and physical appearance. Ben's apparition indicates that, at least subconsciously, Willy doubts the correctness of his decision to turn his brother down and remain in New York. Biff underscores Willy's sense of confusion when he says of Willy, "He never knew who he was" (138). Willy, it can be said, lacks this self-awareness also on a more fundamental level. He can barely remember his father; his mother, as he tells Ben, "died a long time ago" (46); and Ben himself apparently had not played much of a role in Willy's life. Willy thus possesses hereditary proclivities for a successful life outside the New England sales force—as evidenced in his father's and brother's successes, in his ability to work with his hands, and in his love of the outdoors—but he has always lacked familial guidance in their use.

Instead, and by default, he comes under other "paternal" influence. One is that of Dave Singleman, whose success he cannot emulate. Possibly he cannot because times and conditions have changed—that is, the *scene* has changed since Singleman was a young salesman. Such a scenic reason for the impossibility of success argues against tragedy and for naturalism. A correlative reason for failure might be that Willy simply is not equipped to succeed in such an environment: like O'Neill's Yank, he finds himself out of his element, whereas Singleman and Howard Wagner are like the functional New Yorkers who continually best Yank. This reason as well implies naturalism rather than tragedy.

Linda, curiously, is also a paternalistic influence on Willy. While Singleman provides Willy with a model, it is Linda who shapes him to it. When Ben offers him an alternative career, she pushes him to keep the one he already has. When he questions his ability as a salesman, she always compliments him. And when he brings home meager or no earnings, she still compliments him. That is, while lacking malevolent intent, she misdirects a hapless Willy as thoroughly as Iago misdirects Othello.

A scene-agent ratio provides another angle on Willy's character. Like Oedipus's Thebes, Willy's land is dead, sterile, and ruined. As the opening stage setting announces, the Loman house exists within a "vault of apartment houses" (11); later we learn that the wooded area around the house has long since been cut down and that the yard is no longer capable of sustaining any sort of vegetation. The house, as Willy tells Linda, will soon itself be barren, since their children are childless. Has this devastation been caused by Willy's bad acts, as Oedipus has caused the devastation in his city? (Oedipus also is troubled with not knowing who he is, and of course that play has also generated a considerable body of criticism on the question of its tragic status.) Or, rather, is the devastation simply a scenic given, a condition that Willy has not caused and can neither change nor control?

In sum, these indicators all suggest that Willy lacks the basic defenses one needs to avoid disaster. If Willy is completely manipulated—by his wife and others, by his society's bankrupt dreams, by the forces of his universe— he could never have escaped his doom. He would be, in Burke's sense, no agent at all: it would have to be said that he does not act but is moved, pushed about by the events of his life rather than contending with them. George Jean Nathan accurately observes that the play's effects are comparable to "the experience we suffer in contemplating on the highways a run-over and killed dog" (Schlueter and Flanagan 63).

The class's discussions of agent and scene affect their consideration of what Burke sees as the central critical issue of a work: its *action*. Has Willy acted in such a way as to bring on himself a catastrophic end, or has he not truly acted at all? An analysis of Willy's putative intention suggests victimization rather than tragic status.

One way of explaining his intention is to say that, like Othello, Willy realizes his affront to higher justice and so takes his life in retribution; few students, though, wish to argue for this depiction of Willy as a traditional tragic figure. Another way of explaining his intention is to say that Willy, old and tired and defeated, simply gives up; such an explanation makes him a pathetic victim of forces beyond his control. A third way of explaining his intention, and of mitigating the pathos of the previous reading, is to say that he courageously, albeit foolishly, kills himself to better his sons' condition in the world. He wants his boys—especially Biff—to succeed, but his attempt fails if success is measured financially, because the insurance company probably will not pay. But, more significant, even if the insurance company were to pay on the policy, Willy has learned nothing and gains nothing for his boys. As Biff says of his father at the play's end, "He had the wrong dreams. All, all, wrong" (138): Willy would have Biff and Happy integrated into the very system that destroyed him. In addition, while it is possible to say that Biff's acceptance of himself and his own place in the world indicates a success, this growth does not result from any conscious action by Willy. Rather, Biff learns through Willy's self-destruction.

Whatever the nature of the act, the analysis of it determines the angle of analysis for textual agency and purpose. I want to assume for the time being that Willy is capable of action, that he does have tragic potential, in considering the last two pentadic terms. Later, I reconsider this assumption.

Willy's *agency* can be seen in part as his flawed perspective on life, his belief in the ideal of a back-slapping salesman who can sell anything simply by force of character and who lives in the best of all possible economic systems. Willy increasingly comes to realize not only that he will never be promoted to management but that he has become unable to provide for himself and his wife. A more adequate agency would disallow such failures and would be more resilient in the face of the failures that do occur. Willy's bankrupt agency, by contrast, proves unable to sustain him in his darkest moments. In this context, it is fitting that the immediate agency for his suicide is not the rubber hose and the gas but his car, his means of livelihood as a traveling salesman.

Such an analysis of agency casts *purpose* in a pessimistic light, in that Willy "purposes" to escape what he no longer feels able to contend with and what he has not come to understand to the extent that a fully tragic protagonist should. Less pessimistically, his purpose might be to give his family a good, fresh start, so that he foolishly, albeit bravely, sacrifices himself for his sons. Regarding the question of Willy's status as either tragic hero or naturalistic victim, however, it is interesting that he purposes to achieve his sons' success by presenting himself as the victim of an accident.

The textual analysis provides students with good reasons to argue that Willy is a defenseless victim, even a pathetic one; it also provides good reasons to argue that he is a tragic figure. That is, a textual analysis does not resolve, but only sharpens, this basic ambiguity of the play. Managed well, textual analysis turns students toward the author of the play and so toward an ethical analysis, for possible answers.

Ethical Analysis

As I have already suggested, this aspect of the triad approaches psychoanalysis and historiography and as such is of limited value unless one knows a
good deal about the life and times of Arthur Miller as well as about the
particulars of psychoanalysis. A course can ask students to learn some of the
former, at least, and research-based assignments can ask students to consider
Miller's personal life at the time he wrote and staged the play: his family
condition, his personal relationships, his political beliefs, and so on. For
instance, of what significance might it be that Miller-as-agent said that he
hated living in hotels—certainly a problem for a traveling salesman? What
about the importance of manual labor when one considers that Miller built,
by himself, the place in which he wrote *Death of a Salesman*? And what
should be made of Miller's statement that he is "a confirmed and deliberate
radical" (Roudané, *Conversations* 17) and of his having written other plays
with the same theme, the theme of our need to examine ourselves and our
relations to society? (These pieces of information, and much more about
Miller, appear in Roudané, *Conversations*.) Students may also consider Daniel Walden's remark that *Death of a Salesman* represents a conflict between
Miller's Jewish heritage and the American present (195). Instructors might
also ask students to consider the historical scene for the play—post–World
War II America, with special emphasis on its economic prosperity and seeming social uniformity—as well as the increasing technologization, impersonal-
ity, and economic and political centralization the country has since
undergone. And as regards act: What to make of an author who writes and
ushers into production a play that questions some of the basic beliefs of his
own society as well as the livelihood of his father and brother?

One also ought to consider, of course, the import behind the ambiguity
regarding tragedy and naturalism that Miller built into the play. What does
a focus on this agency tell us? For instance, what can we say of an author
who sees the world in terms of tragedy or in terms of pessimistic naturalism,
and what can we say about the question and implications of the tragedy-
versus-naturalism issue if we know that Miller has written repeatedly about
his play as a tragedy? What do we conclude about an author whose dramatic
scene questions whether humans have free will and presents the breakdown
of stable societal definitions?

Along these lines, June Schlueter and James Flanagan note that Miller's
statement about the tragic hero being one who lays down his life to preserve
his dignity is couched exclusively in terms of commitment; it leaves unstated
Willy's relationship to "a commonly agreed-upon moral structure that dic-
tates the principles to which commitments are made and by which their
admirability and rightness might be assessed. [Miller] mentions nothing of
the tragic hero's self-awareness, nothing of the recognition—always too
late—that precedes disaster" (62). Conversely, Walden notes that in the

early sketch "In Memoriam" (which serves as the basis for Willy seventeen years later) Miller came to appreciate "the heroism of those who know, at least, how to endure [hope's] absence" (190). In sum, students might well ask why Miller makes the statements he does about the nature of the tragic hero and why he has chosen to complicate the play in such a way. (To look at agency differently, what might we say of the play when we know that the author chose the particular set design at least in part because he felt that his first play's failure was due to an overelaborate set?)

The analysis of purpose is perhaps the most problematic under the aspect of ethical criticism. It is best described as, in Burke's terms, a "ritual of rebirth," by which Burke means that the author tries to adjust his perspectives to the world's or the world's to his but in either event wishes to be "born" into a new, more favorable condition ("Philosophy" 103–13; see also Burke, *Rhetoric* 3–13). On one level, the argument behind Burke's position is almost self-evident: dramatists, like all other people, have problems—with family members, with social or economic group members, even with their own ideas, tendencies, desires, and weaknesses. On another level, the argument holds that dramatists tend to use these problems as subject matter for their plays—both because they naturally tend to write about their obsessions and because in writing about their problems they might find a means of working through these problems. Employing an agent-purpose ratio, one can echo Miller's question in *The Man Who Had All the Luck*: can we control our own fates, or are we "jellyfish moving with the tide" (Mottram 26)? Apparently, one of Miller's purposes in writing drama is to explore the issues that lie at the root of the tragedy-naturalism distinction.

Affective Analysis

Ethical analysis both amplifies and is amplified by textual analysis; similarly, affective analysis both amplifies and is amplified by these other analyses. Students have already seen how knowledge of the author helps them understand the text and how knowledge of the text helps them "predict" the public author and even, to some extent, the biographical one. In this last stage of the analysis, I ask them to focus on what they can identify as equipment for living a better life; the purpose of this affective analysis is to identify what they might call the play's moral and to consider its utility for their own lives.

Students achieve their purpose, of course, by the act of reading and responding to a play that portrays the devastating results of a certain standard American attitude toward family, society, business, and the self. They achieve these purposes through the agency of their critical reading skills—primarily their ability to read the play, but also their ability to read and critique their own attitudes about family, society, business, and themselves. They thus consider the moral in the context of their own scene: a scene that is immediately a sophomore literature course; a scene that is less immediately a land-grant university where they are pursuing a major which, if not in the business college, is most probably oriented toward business; a scene that is more generally the American capitalistic society which celebrates the values that lead to Willy's destruction. Finally, in this self-analysis of agent they also examine their attitude toward the careers for which they are preparing and that they will pursue in a business world not substantially different from Willy's.

A good way to begin the affective analysis is to ask students to offer their choices for the moral of the play. (Burke suggests such a strategy in "Literature as Equipment for Living.") Some that bridge a number of possible approaches include such commonplace aphorisms as "Know thyself (and thy limitations)," "He who hesitates is lost," and "Admit mistakes and move on." Students also contend that the play warns against losing control over one's life, a warning that some students rephrase, in narrower, economic terms, as "Be your own boss or be destroyed." A student with Marxist tendencies might see the play as reinforcing the law of economic determinism, while one who is interested in gender issues might see it as warning against falling prey to paternalism. (In this context, see August's discussion of Willy in " 'Modern Men'; or, Men's Studies in the 80s." August identifies Willy as exemplifying his belief that males as well as females are victimized, that males are in fact "the principal victims of patriarchal society" [588]). Since the purpose of analysis is not to determine a final reading but, rather, to examine the possibilities, the class considers any number of alternatives.

Once again, the tragedy-naturalism ambiguity aids analysis. The case for Willy as naturalistic victim helps students explain many problems in their own lives. Remembering that some conditions and events are outside their control (for instance, their gender, race, and parentage) can help them be healthy and happy. Pushing too far the emphasis on a naturalistic scene is unrealistic, however, given that people do act as if they believe they can control their own fortunes and lives. For affective analysis the tragic vision is thus the more realistic—at least insofar as students perceive their capability for tragic action. For instance, students consider how professional choices are not literally beyond a person's control, how they must know their own limitations and goals and know whether and how those factors affect their jobs. Willy, they see, fails to examine the experiences he undergoes and the advice he receives. Instead, he falls prey to the human tendency to ignore hard realities or to blame them on others, the tendency to treat symptoms rather than causes—that is, the tendency to ignore the inadequacy of his perspective. In *Permanence and Change* Burke refers to barnyard chickens that learn to recognize the ring of a bell as a food signal and so come running one last time when that same bell is used to invite them not to eat dinner but to be it. Students consider that it might be difficult to jettison a career and all the training that goes into it, but doing so might be necessary to avoid Willy's fate. Willy's abdication of self-determination, his failure to realize and respond to changing conditions, warns students against forgetting that they do possess free will and ought not to cede it to other people or things or ideas; his fate tells students to examine critically and repeatedly the principles by which they live their lives and to change those principles when they are not working satisfactorily.

Affective criticism should also indicate that the agency one uses to become a happy and productive member of society is a means, not an end that is necessarily important in itself. As Burke might say, the question is not "What is good for business?" but "What is business good for?" Willy could have been a carpenter or a mason or an outdoorsperson of some kind and been much happier, but he thinks (as does Happy) that such work is good only as a hobby. Willy is wrong to say that Charley is not a man simply because he is not good with his hands (44), just as Charley would be wrong if he were to say that Willy's failure as a salesman makes him unmanly. The play encourages students to reflect on their career choices and, more specifically, on the professional attitudes that they are developing.

As the class works through an affective analysis of *Death of a Salesman*, I encourage discussion about questions that are peripheral to the play but central to its use as equipment for living. A good pair of early questions are, Do you know people like Willy? and Have you heard of or met people like Howard Wagner? Students are liable to recount tales of an uncle who was fired just before he was eligible for a pension or of a boss who wanted them to cut corners. Specific questions that point to the moral issues of the play include the following: Is Howard Wagner "wrong" to treat Willy as he does? What alternatives does he have? Is Willy "wrong" to do what he does with The Woman? What sorts of things—what agencies—do businesspeople use or do that the students or "society in general" find to be "wrong"? What does *wrong* mean in these contexts? What do *we* mean by *wrong*?

An important follow-up question is, How might Biff make a living now that he "knows who he is"? Can we imagine that he could work in sales— if not in New York then perhaps in Denver or Santa Fe or Laramie? How would he operate, as distinct from his father's method or from Howard Wagner's? This issue is broad, but it is certainly one of the most important topics for students to consider. Biff is the one who learns from Willy's disaster; if the students also have learned something from Willy, then their thoughts on this question are also thoughts about how they will operate in their careers. That is, they can consider the question "What is business good for?" Near the conclusion of my available time for the play, I try to make sure that students address the larger issues concerning the purpose people have in working. I want them to consider their reasons for pursuing their perception of success. I want them to consider how work and success are means rather than ends, and I want them to consider the nature of the ends for which work and success are the means.

Raising such issues need not lead to "bull sessions," since students' comments are based on a good deal of prior, focused discussion concerning particulars of the play itself. Rather, raising such issues serves to make the play something more than a device for filling a few empty hours, something more even than an aesthetic artifact worthy of appreciation in its own right. Such issues serve to make the play important to students' lives outside a literature classroom. In addition to entertainment and aesthetic gratification, *Death of a Salesman* offers its readers practical advice for achieving success in the socioeconomic world. Burke argues that literature induces our consent to certain sociopolitical beliefs, and Booth argues that as readers we cannot escape this persuasive element. Frank Lentricchia builds on these positions in *Criticism and Social Change,* arguing to those who would teach such works as *Death of a Salesman* that "our potentially most powerful work as university humanists must be carried out in what we do, what we are trained for. . . . [T]he point is not only to interpret texts, but in so interpreting, change our society" (7, 10). If students can see, through drama, how to change their lives for the better, we can assume that our society will be changed for the better as well. I must believe that Miller would approve of this use of his play.

APPENDIX

Chart: Analysis of Text

Agent   The characters: emphasis on Willy; on other characters' relations to and with Willy. Questions: Can Willy control, and so be responsible for, his life? Can and does he understand what is happening to him?

Scene   The environment for characters and action: 1940s Brooklyn and recent past; Lomans' backyard and its recent past; family, social, and economic conditions. Question: Is the dramatic universe ordered or chaotic?

Act   The central dramatic action: Willy's suicide as a relatively brief act at the end of the play; his death as the impending act introduced by Linda's concern over the hose; his slow, year-by-year destruction brought on by his refusal to come to grips with his failed professional life and dreams.

Agency   The means of the dramatic action: Willy's automobile, which serves as the vehicle for his livelihood and for his death; his flawed perspective on the nature and pursuit of success.

Purpose   The reason for the dramatic action: preservation of dignity (Miller's suggestion); response to exhaustion and defeat; no purpose, because no ability to act.

Dream: Analysis of Authorial Ethos

Agent   Miller as artist, as author of the successful *All My Sons* as well as the early "In Memoriam" and the 1936 unfinished play about a salesman; as a native New Yorker who likes to work with his hands; as the son of an unsuccessful businessman.

Scene Miller's family life; the United States of the late 1940s and the preceding period, including the socioeconomic history of the great depression, World War II, and the subsequent economic revival.

Act An artistic account, staged and written, of the destruction of everyman, destroyed by his inability to understand and manage himself and his place in his world.

Agency Miller's dramaturgy, including plotting, style, and development of characters.

Purpose A catharsis for Miller; a ritual of rebirth that adjusts the playwright to his society or his society to himself. (It is here that ethical analysis is most explicitly psychoanalytic and most intrusive.)

Prayer: Analysis of Effects

Agent The audience of the play; their perspective on matters central to the play's dramatic development.

Scene The audience's environment at the time of their exposure to the play; their family lives and social relations; their business knowledge, experiences, and attitudes.

Act The viewing or reading of a play that condemns certain standard American attitudes toward family, business, and society; the effects of this viewing or reading.

Agency The analytical skills of the audience; focus on how and through what means the effects are brought about.

Purpose The use of the play as equipment for living a better life; catharsis and education; focusing on the need to know oneself, on the need to make changes, admit mistakes, and move on.

Miller's Use and Modification
of the Realist Tradition

William W. Demastes

Approaching *Death of a Salesman* through the discussion of dramatic form has been, for me, a particularly useful way to place the play in a variety of contexts for a number of courses. In a seminar on Miller alone, showing the development from the naturalistic *All My Sons* to *Death of a Salesman* would be an obvious part of class discussion. An American Drama class would reveal America's obsession with the realist-naturalist form, which naturally leads to Miller's own interest in and modification of the form in *Death of a Salesman*. World Drama classes could establish comparisons between an Ibsen "problem play" and Miller's deviation from that form. And for literary surveys, comparisons between *Death of a Salesman* and novels of the period often promote interesting discussions about the nature of literary form in general.

Integral to placing any work in context is, of course, the consideration of theme. But if we are to teach more than an "issues" course, form should rejoin content in our discussions. Miller himself often emphasizes the inseparability of form and content, confirming the coequal need to highlight a play's formal aspects as well as its much-discussed thematic ones.

No single document argues this case for form-content discussion more forcefully than does Miller's 1956 essay "The Family in Modern Drama." Its use in my class has served me well in a number of ways. First, the comparison of any author's theories with his or her actual practice can reveal to students the difficulties in what we call the intentional fallacy: Does the author succeed at doing what he or she plans to do? Second, this essay provides an opportunity to work toward definitions of elusive terms—realism and expressionism, among others. This pursuit of definitions, in turn, reveals the relative and inconclusive—though still fruitful—nature of trying too hard to objectify literary studies. Of course, the age-old question "Is it tragedy?" is still a favorite that works particularly well in World Drama classes, but this realist-expressionist issue has also been a productive topic of discussion in my courses, especially those in which tragedy is not a natural issue.

In "The Family in Modern Drama," Miller observes that twentieth-century audiences already know realism by heart. Ibsen, he notes, pressed the form close to its ultimate limits: "It is written in prose; it makes believe it is taking place independently of an audience which views it through a 'fourth wall,' the grand objective being to make everything seem true to life in life's most evident and apparent sense." Despite its nearly journalistic appearance, however, realism "is a style, an invention quite as consciously created as Expressionism, Symbolism, or any of the other less familiar forms" (220).

As with other forms, its selection reveals an author's personal projection of significance onto selected events.

Key to the discussion of realism in relation to *Death of a Salesman* is Miller's observation that "by means of cutout sets, revolving stages, musical backgrounds, new and more imaginative lighting schemes, our stage is striving to break up the old living room." To this point Miller adds that "the perceiving eye knows that many of these allegedly poetic plays are Realism underneath" (221). In a given play, surface features may conform to one convention while the pervading spirit essentially aligns with the spirit of yet another.

Consider a parlor play using a set and costumes to depict a certain period, utilizing natural dialogue and presented with no attempt to manipulate simple chronology. It appears to be a realistic drama. Suppose, however, that the plot operates in a fashion forcing the characters to act "out of character" in order to demonstrate a desired "moral." This example of melodramatic form suggests that realism must involve more than presenting the illusion of material reality onstage. Television sitcoms are perfect common examples of such manipulations of realism.

If material reality were the sole, or even central, criterion, *Death of a Salesman* could quickly be dismissed as antithetical to the realist form. The reasons for questioning the play's adherence to realism, however, are significantly different from those that apply to evaluating melodrama and sitcoms. It is not inconsistent characterization but a more superficial aberration that marks the play, at first glance, as nonrealistic. For example, offstage music permeates the play, the set is a multipurpose "unrealistic" construction, and time constantly violates chronological sequence. These features are not standardly realistic techniques.

So if *Death of a Salesman* is even partly realist in its direction, what constitutes realism in the drama? Miller asks that we move beyond mere form and technique to consider content—specifically, the creation of "family relationships within the play"—then goes on to offer a good example of how form is determined by content:

> [O]ne of the prime difficulties in writing modern opera, which after all is lyric drama, is that you cannot rightly sing so many of the common thoughts of common life. A line like "Be sure to take your bath, Gloria," is difficult to musicalize, and impossible to take seriously as a sung concept. (221)

Realism is well suited to present the unencumbered intimacy of family relations, Miller argues. We don't "perform" for our family members, at least not to the degree and in kind that we perform for those outside our family circle.

It is worth noting that this observation explains America's general obsession with realism: we are obsessed with the form because we are centrally concerned with the family institution, perhaps more so than most other societies, which tend to be less private.

If realism is well suited to reveal the intimacy of the family, what is it unsuited to present? Miller argues that the private domain of realism may be contrasted to the more public applications of expressionism, which he argues "goes back to Aeschylus." Miller calls expressionism "a form of play which manifestly seeks to dramatize the conflict of either social, religious, ethical, or moral forces *per se*, and in their own naked roles." Expressionism presents the conflict of forces "rather than [the] psychologically realistic human characters" that discretely occupy those roles (224).

Defining these terms is a slippery matter. Of many critical works that attempt to do so, J. L. Styan's *Modern Drama in Theory and Practice* is the most thorough, and I often refer students to these three slender volumes for more detail. Styan admits that though realism "is the desire to reproduce on the stage a piece of life faithfully" (1: 164), "[i]t is, of course, the conception of dramatic reality which changes, and realism must finally be evaluated, not by the style of a play or a performance, but by the image of truth its audiences perceive" (1: 1). With this confession in mind, perhaps we can more easily accept Miller's definition or description as a fair perception of what constitutes realism. Because Miller does a less thorough job in describing expressionism, we might look more closely at Styan's effort in volume 3 of his *Expressionism and Epic Theatre*. One point he makes, in agreement with Miller, is that in realism "actors sit about on chairs and talk about the weather, but in expressionism they stand on them and shout about the world" (1). I find that Styan's thoughts help clarify what Miller is arguing, substantiating that Miller's seemingly unique interpretation of expressionism is not far off base and providing groundwork for any potential future discussions of the terms that may evolve as the course proceeds.

For Miller, then, when a work strives to explicate the personal actions of private individuals, expressionism fails and realism shines. So what Emile Zola would call milieu is an important contributing feature for pursuing the personal—and the "real"—since particular objects and possessions are excellent means of personalizing a type. But milieu alone is ultimately insufficient. When used alone, it is little better than a cheap trick (as in the melodrama example above). What we need to complete the personalization process is psychological depth—not the abstractions provided by expressionism but the particular avenues, choices, and consequences that realism can best articulate. As Miller notes, "The moment realistic behavior and psychology disappear from the play all the other appurtenances of Realism vanish too" (225).

We must consider language as well. Miller observes that "the language of the family is the language of the private life—prose. The language of society, the public life is verse" (225). So realism-prose stands in contrast to expressionism-poetry.

Applying these generalizations to Miller's *All My Sons* allows us to make an obvious conclusion: the play is a good example of realism at work. It is a family drama that uses all the personal appurtenances that grant its central characters individual personalities. Interestingly, many critics have argued that the play's attempt to universalize the theme of responsibility to a broader, social level is not a successful effort. For example, Patricia Schroeder notes:

> [T]he linear, Ibsenian method of *All My Sons*, which ultimately demands Keller's [the father's] confession, depends upon Keller's relationships with his wife, his sons, his business partner, and Ann; Miller's attempts to place Keller's crime in a larger social context are thus disruptive and tedious. (81–82)

Given Miller's own thoughts on form and content, he should actually agree with this assessment. The play's content unnaturally strives to step beyond its form, moving from realism to the realm of expressionism.

But Miller may have a defense, as well, against this criticism. Though the realism-family pairing may be read literally, Miller is comfortable with expanding the concept of family. All great plays, he contends, deal with a single, albeit complex, problem:

> How may a man make of the outside world a home? How and in what ways must he struggle . . . If he is to find the safety, the surroundings of love, the ease of soul, the sense of identity and honor which, evidently, all men have connected in their memories with the idea of family? ("Family" 223)

The root of all great conflict—throughout history, it seems—is family. I think it would be fair to qualify this sweeping inclusion by saying that realism is most appropriate when personal struggle, rather than the public good, is foregrounded. This qualification is especially necessary since art rarely isolates one sphere from the other.

So it is no wonder that the ancient Greeks never developed a realistic format. Their dramas were highly public affairs, to the point that family was subsumed by community, by public and even metaphysical-religious repercussions. *Antigone* and *Oedipus* could be described as family plays, but they involve the state and finally highlight the public role of the families involved. To produce a drama disconnected from public duty was unthinkable to Greek dramatists, though we do see a glimpse of realism and disconnection in the work of the latter-day playwright Euripides. Similar "antirealist" arguments may be made for Elizabethan drama and French drama of the seventeenth and eighteenth centuries.

Only with the Romantic revolution's insistence on the rights of the individual freed from a consuming dependency on social identity could realism begin to make headway. And it is no coincidence that the less public, more private form of the novel took the realistic initiative since the novel could discuss private affairs without the communal impulse of an audience group. But even the communal impulse of the stage was eventually broken by ingenious techniques such as the fourth-wall concept, which separated the audience from the stage and made the audience sneaky voyeurs. Add to those developments the ability to bring down the lights in the auditorium, which isolated individuals in the audience from their neighbors, and the stage (literally) was set for a drama of "certain private conversations" (Miller's subtitle for *Death of a Salesman*), of which Ibsen was the early master.

In fact, Ibsen himself reveals a realist-expressionist diversity. In his realist dramas *A Doll's House* and *Ghosts*, Ibsen highlights personal, family affairs that have only incidental public consequences. In *The Master Builder*, however, he uses symbolism-expressionism to a greater degree, thereby allowing social-public functions to surface more effectively.

Focusing on American drama, we can achieve the same degree of contextualizing by examining Elmer Rice's work. *The Adding Machine* demonstrates the public abilities of expressionism, while the realistic *Street Scene* is a testament to humanity's search for family. And Eugene O'Neill's plays offer many examples of expressionistic-social successes (*The Hairy Ape*, for example) and realistic-family masterpieces (*Long Day's Journey into Night* and *The Iceman Cometh*). Miller's theory, interestingly, even explains why O'Neill's "nonrealistic" family plays are less successful than his "realistic" family masterpieces.

So if Miller's theory about a natural marriage of realistic form and family content works this well in general, how does it apply to *Death of a Salesman*, a play that can only arguably be called realistic? Miller suggests an answer when he writes:

> If, for instance, the struggle in *Death of a Salesman* were simply between father and son for recognition and forgiveness it would diminish in importance. But when it extends itself out of the family circle and into society, it broaches those questions of social status, social honor and recognition, which expand its vision and lift it out of the merely particular toward the fate of the generality of men.   (223)

To what degree are Miller's expressionistic devices in *Death of a Salesman* the elements that elevate the play to a universal level? (Are they the same elements missing from *All My Sons*?) The background melody intermittently played on a flute, "small and fine, telling of grass and trees and the horizon," reminds us of Willy's father but also suggests Pan's music in Arcadia, a universal image. And Miller's calling Willy simply "the Salesman" (11) is just as expressionistically abstract (and significant) as Rice's calling his central character in *The Adding Machine* Mr. Zero. The name Loman also harkens back to the title character of the allegorical *Everyman*, which Miller calls a prototypical medieval expressionist play.

Biff's much-discussed football prowess and "big man on campus" status identify him as an abstraction of youthful promise. Bernard's arguing a case before the Supreme Court (leaving with tennis racket in hand) marks him as a symbol of success. Willy's "handy-ness" and final urge to plant a garden seem inserted to depict an element of American self-reliance, as does Biff's joy at working on a ranch out west. Similarly, Ben's Alaska proposition symbolizes the American urge to "go west"; when Ben walks into the jungle and comes out a rich man, we see the fantasy of the rugged individual come true. And Howard hardly seems real at all, the archetypal businessman whose contact with the personal, with family, extends only to a mechanized, taped recording of his family. One could argue convincingly that all these devices (and students should find even more) depict expressionistic forces at work and add a public, universal quality to the issues at hand, amid an otherwise personal, realistically rendered struggle. Such devices could easily be described as examples of "psychological characterization forfeited in the cause of the symbol" (Miller, "Family" 228).

Miller's use of language expresses a desire to move beyond the personal as well—though, as students should readily echo, with mixed success. The use of metaphor transcends the personal, informal dialogue of family discussion, striving for poetic-lyric elevation that is an attempt at moving beyond the personal realm. When Willy argues, "You can't eat the orange and throw the peel away—a man is not a piece of fruit" (82), he is admittedly on the public stage pleading with Howard, and it hardly sounds like realistic dialogue. Neither does Linda's assertion that Willy is "only a little boat looking for a harbor" (76). And though many critics have faulted Miller for such insertions, the intent seems clear: to abstract Willy's struggle to a level beyond the merely personal. Two contrasting speeches in the Requiem clearly demonstrate the realist and personal versus the poetic (expressionist) and public dichotomy that Miller has set up. When Biff observes that "there's more of [Willy] in that front stoop than in all the sales he ever made" (138), he evokes Willy the private, family man with touching, personal simplicity. By contrast, Charley's final speech ("Nobody dast blame this man. . . ." [138]) is a metaphoric speech that depicts Willy the public man. Some argue that Charley has missed the point, but if both public and private perspectives are important, as Miller claims they are, then both speeches are accurate, and both are accurately crafted to marry form to content.

Whether students do—or should—accept these points is irrelevant as long as the students are aware of the bases from which their positions derive.

One can be sure that debate will occur. After all, throughout history audiences have been uncomfortable accepting hybrid forms, and in *Salesman* Miller asks that we accept one. From a purist's position, such a request cannot be obliged, while from a more moderate position, some compromises may be granted.

This debate leads to another question: Did Miller have to be so metaphorically obtrusive? He argues that "familial emotions" and "social emotions" in fact do not "spring from different sectors of human experience but end up by appealing to different areas of receptivity" ("Family" 225). He therefore uses different levels of language to illustrate the differences between characters and roles. But how different must that language be? Here we can turn to Miller's introduction to his *Collected Plays*. Very nearly in the tradition of Walt Whitman (and other "concrete" modern poets), Miller argues that poetry is made up of concrete, specific images rather than of emotional abstractions. (Submitting to students samples of Whitman's poetry often helps clarify his point; Wallace Stevens and William Carlos Williams also make good examples.) Miller claims he found such wonder in *The Brothers Karamazov*, noting that "if one reads its most colorful, breathtaking, wonderful pages, one finds the thickest concentration of hard facts" (15). Concrete detail exacts the greatest wonder from the world (a lesson often resisted in freshman composition classes). In fact, Miller sees this poetic effect in Ibsen as well: "A situation in his plays is never stated but revealed in terms of hard actions, irrevocable deeds; and sentiment is never confused with the action it conceals" (19). This vision of a realistic, concrete poetry is one that Miller himself, perhaps, should have pursued more completely. Perhaps realism *is* capable of capturing the universal in its particulars even more effectively than the obtrusive devices he uses in the play. For example, can we not view Willy's character as particular (real) while seeing certain of those particulars as universal-archetypal? From the weary father-husband to the silently suffering wife-mother to the dopey younger brother–son hungry for attention, the detail provides "wonder" at how universal the particulars really are. It seems that we do wonder at material concretely depicted rather than merely described through metaphor or other abstractions.

So the debate may go either way. Miller may be justified in mixing realism with nonrealism and expressionism. Or, ironically, he missed the opportunity to use the tools for abstraction that were right under his nose, in the technique of realistic detail he was using all along. Furthermore, either conclusion has its aesthetic justification. The task here is to get students to articulate those premises.

Finally, we address the issue of time manipulation. It may be interesting to begin by noting that the original movie version rearranged events in simple chronological order. Is this simplification of material more realistic than Miller's own use of time? Miller states:

> There are no flashbacks in this play but only a mobile concurrency of
> past and present, and this, again, because in his desperation to justify
> his life Willy Loman has destroyed the boundaries between now and
> then.   (Introduction 26)

Admittedly, there is a standard beginning, middle, and end to Miller's play
(culminating in suicide and a requiem), but within this frame time is constantly shifting. Miller has put Willy in charge of chronology, has put us
into *The Inside of His Head*, as the play's original title declares. The result
is the ultimate in "personalizing" the play. Can this be realism? If we recall
Styan's observation that we should not rigidly judge realism "by the style
of a play or a performance, but by the image of truth its audiences perceive"
(1: 1), then we need to discuss whether or not stream of consciousness is or
can be a realist strategy. Should we accept such subjectivity as ultimately
"real"? Again, we are getting to the heart of an aesthetic debate.

If the course in question has covered the works of James Joyce or William
Faulkner, perhaps students have already addressed this issue. What Miller
presents is a distortion of the conventional, objective vision of time, but the
distortion does not fly into some surreal flight of fancy; it is still concrete.
And for Willy the order that he imposes on the stage *is* reality, *is* simple
chronological order.

No clear answer can be made to this question: conservative definitions
will lead to the conclusion that Miller is not using a realist strategy, while
more flexible approaches will see Miller as advancing realism to a new level.
Whatever the answer, do not let this debate confuse a question, perhaps
even more important, about the general success of the strategy over the
earlier-noted cinematic simplification.

The above concerns about realism and the place of *Death of a Salesman*
in that tradition have led to different discussions and conclusions in every
class I have taught. In dealing with any work of art, there are, of course,
certain matters of fact; one hopes, nevertheless, to generate opinions and
defenses of those opinions. And when the work in question is a highly
accessible play like *Death of a Salesman*, students seem forever eager to
present opinions.

The Crisis of Authenticity:
Death of a Salesman and the Tragic Muse

Stephen Barker

> In *Death of a Salesman*, Miller has formulated a
> statement about the nature of human crises in the
> twentieth century which seems, increasingly, to be
> applicable to the entire fabric of civilized experience.
> —Esther Merle Jackson

Even those who have disputed the right of *Death of a Salesman* to claim the stature of modern tragedy have been highly aware of its dialogue with that enigmatic and elevated genre. Ironically, Miller's defense of the play as modern tragedy only serves to conceal, within its humanistic fervor, many good reasons for treating the play as tragic. Other critical approaches to the play also conceal, inadvertently, tragic treatments of it. In fact, the standard generic battle over the play produces numerous puzzles and opportunities for interpretive response. To consider the play within the context of traditional notions of the tragic, notions that date back to Plato, is to invite an altered tragic vision. As mimesis of cultural crisis, *Death of a Salesman* must be treated as an exemplum of the tragic vision in the twentieth century, quintessentially defining the crisis of authenticity that is the tragic.

In this essay I consider the context, pretext, and text of *Death of a Salesman* as tragic crisis itself.

Context

Crisis

> The tragic vision, a product of crisis and of shock, is an expression of
> man only in an extreme situation, never in a normal or routine one. . . .
> a distillate of the rebellion, the godlessness which, once induced by
> crisis, purifies itself by rejecting all palliatives.   (Krieger 20)

Tragedy, tragic vision, and the Tragic Muse are normative cultural identifiers.[1] They are a collective reminder of what we were and what we imagine we want to become; from its inception in the *tragosodos*, the "goat songs" whose dithyrambic intensity galvanized early Greek audiences of tragedy, the tragic has served this self-reflexive purpose. As a result of its role as cultural identifier, the tragic idea defines itself as a function of that crisis to which Murray Krieger refers. Krieger's crisis-context, articulated in *The Tragic Vision*, for both tragedy (a literary work) and the tragic vision (its cultural context) rely on two misunderstood Greek words, *katharsis* and *mimesis*.[2] *Katharsis*, mentioned only once (vaguely) by Aristotle in the *Poetics* (1449b), means "purity" or "purgation" but is widely interpretable depending on one's view of purity or purgation. Aristotle is impossibly vague on this subject; *katharsis* becomes, as a result, a diachronic, culturally determined concept bracketed within the tragic vision. *Mimesis*, which we have come to understand as "imitation," obscuring Aristotle's practicality, should be thought of, rather, as "illusion" or "pretense" (see Kaufmann 33–41).

How different is Aristotle's definition of tragedy when it appears this way: "[A] tragedy, then, is the illusion of an action that is serious and also, as having magnitude, complete in itself" (1449b), or "[T]ragedy is essentially an illusion not of persons but of action and life" (1450a). Tragedy, in this revised view, is not the agent and result of the correspondence of planes of existence but a sign of their disintegration—not the representation of an external "reality" but the transmutation of external reification into performative illusion. As Miller points out, "[T]he Greeks could probe the very heavenly origin of their ways and return to confirm the rightness of laws, and Job could face God in anger, demanding his right, and end in submission. But for a moment everything is in suspension, nothing is accepted." All culture is threatened, and in the moment of this crisis, "this stretching and tearing apart of the cosmos," the tragic vision is born. What is "in suspension," for Miller as for the Greeks, is man's ability rightly and fully to "secure his rightful place in the world," to lay claim to "his whole due as a personality," through "the indestructible will of man to achieve his humanity" ("Tragedy," *Salesman: Text* 146). For Miller, the tragic vision provides man and humanity with the tear through which to glimpse him and itself.[3] The tragic vision thus presents "a crisis and a shock," "an expression of man only in an extreme situation." Willy, at his first entrance, is disoriented and frightened, in crisis, indeed at a critical crossroads in his life: unable to travel but defined by traveling, this man must redefine himself and thus everyone around him. Miller's response to this crisis—including its self-delusions and rebellions against constraints in which, "rejecting all palliatives," Willy gropes through his downfall—depicts the illusion of Willy's psychic crisis and suggests our own individuated one in contemporary culture. Indeed, this critical introspection occupied Miller from his conception of the play, whose original title, *The Inside of His Head*, came from Miller's original idea of a huge human head that, suspended above the stage, would literally open up; the play was to depict the "experience of disintegration" (R. Williams, *Modern Tragedy* 12) in Willy but as experienced by the viewer or reader.

Authenticity

Death of a Salesman portrays the crisis of contemporary culture; culture, in turn, is the perpetual crisis of authenticity, according to Freud's use of the term (*kultur*) in *Civilization and Its Discontents*, in which civilization's purpose "is to combine single human individuals, and after that families, then races, peoples and nations, into one great unity, the unity of mankind" (69) for reasons of safety, control, and "order." Cultural identity is the rooted goal of civilized man. Even though it must be remembered that in general (and specifically in terms of Willy, Linda, and their sons) this goal is contrary to the raw individuality and aggression of "human nature," it is still the goal of Homo sapiens.[4] This critical struggle for authenticity occurs within the context of the tragic vision:

> The tragic visionary may at the crucial moment search within and find himself "hollow at the core," because he has been seized from without by the hollowness of his moral universe, whose structure and meaning have until then sustained him. What the shock reveals to its victim— the existential absurdity of the moral life—explodes the meaning of the moral life, its immanent god and ground.   (Krieger 15)

This absurdity, which is not meaningless but, on the contrary, fraught with meaning, explodes the myth of the moral life precisely because it will not fit obediently into a synchronically operable view of "immanent god and ground." Within this context of tragic self-revelation Willy (qua salesman) strives to experience himself as somehow authentic. Throughout our tradition this quest has been an urgent concern and has formed our idea of the tragic.

A further complication of Aristotelian tragic authentication as Miller uses it in *Death of a Salesman* is its reliance on a certain jargon. An appropriate reference in the investigation of this issue is Theodor Adorno's critique of Heideggerian existentialism, *The Jargon of Authenticity*, which explores ways in which "false" rhetoric (tautology) produces an "ideological mystification" of human experience that "bars the message from the experience which is to ensoul it" (6). The aptness of this jargon of authenticity to *Death of a Salesman* is clear: Willy becomes a function of the "high spiritual language" of the capitalist ethic, with its camaraderie and alienation; his involvement with Dave Singleman and with Ben are nothing less than spiritual; what is most unauthentic is taken for the grounding of life. Biff, Happy, and Linda all buy into this jargon in their own ways. Adorno's critique of the jargon of authenticity declares that it distances one from the "aura" of the authentic to which the words point but which they do not and cannot "capture"—and which is in fact undermined by its own nature. The nomenclature of America's "religion of success" shows itself as what Adorno calls "words that are sacred without sacred content, as frozen emanations; the terms of the jargon of authenticity are products of the disintegration of the aura" (9–10). For example, Willy Loman's repeated reference to being "well-liked" and statements such as "in those days there was personality in it. . . . There was respect, and comradeship, and gratitude in it" (81) manifest this dangerous jargon. As Adorno writes,

> [T]he nimbus in which the words are being wrapped, like oranges in tissue paper, takes under its own direction the mythology of language, as if the radiant force of the words could not yet quite be trusted. . . . The jargon becomes practicable along the whole scale, reaching from sermon to advertisement. In the medium of the concept the jargon becomes surprisingly similar to the habitual practices of advertising.
> (43)

In just this way, Adorno suggests, Willy's jargon of self-authenticity, which is purportedly a language for life, becomes one for death.

One of Adorno's central ideas, linking him closely to Nietzsche's tragic mode, is the challenge to "real experience" that the dialectic with authenticity enforces: "The bourgeois form of rationality has always needed irrational supplements, in order to maintain itself as what it is, continuing injustice through justice. Such *irrationality in the midst of the rational* is the working atmosphere of authenticity" (47; emphasis mine). These remarks echo Nietzsche's on the Dionysian and Apollonian in *The Birth of Tragedy* and on cruelty in *The Will to Power*. They play a central part in Willy's sense of injustice and his fearful indignation. Tragic authentication can never be trusted, since it is always a function of authenticating jargon.

Identity

Tragic authenticity and its perpetual crisis stage themselves, as is increasingly clear, as a crisis of identity. When we ask what authentication authenticates, we (and Miller) must answer "the self." This imperative, however, is self-evidently another tautology of rhetoric, as Adorno—echoing Nietzsche—shows:

> Authenticity, in the traditional language of philosophy, would be identical with subjectivity as such. But in that way, unnoticed, subjectivity also becomes the judge of authenticity. Since it is denied any objective determination, authenticity is determined by the arbitrariness of the subject, which is authentic to itself.
> (126)

Our great hope, like Willy's, is that we will be "identical with subjectivity as such"; this "identity thinking" (Adorno 139) consumes Willy, who is naively caught in what Nietzsche calls "imaginative" lying (*Human* 54). This perpetual crisis of identity has been evolving at least since the Enlightenment and continued to do so even after Hegel's undermining of the noble tragic hero and his relation to moira, a notion necessary to Miller's claims about tragedy and the common man. Krieger's tragic vision asserts, indeed, that since Hegel's turn toward introspection (which is still bound up in the divine as pure knowledge), the conditions for the tragic have shifted and are no longer determined by Hegelian universality justly imposing itself on the tragic individual; now, Krieger says, the tragic figure stands "outside the universal," solipsistically isolated in a world where justice has passed from the universal to the individual whose rebellion is often inadvertent or unconscious—from Büchner's Woyzeck to Willy Loman. In the latter we confront a tragic "hero" who not only lacks heroism but desires to merge with and be a part of a social landscape that cannot or will not accept him.[5] The home Willy has built ("he was so wonderful with his hands" [138]) is purportedly the symbol of that resting place among the "vastness of strangers" (Miller, "Family" 233) that the solipsistic individual seeks; but Willy's hands are useless to build the home he desires, defined by Miller as "the everlastingly sought balance between order and the need of our souls for freedom" (233), which is a condition, not a place.

Willy carries his tragic homelessness around with him wherever he goes, since it is something by which he knows himself. This homelessness of self-division is what finally makes *Salesman* the tragedy of the common man. Willy is the exemplar of (American capitalist) society, attempting to achieve his humanity and his identity in the face of numerous tragic sunderings. Willy's typicality is explored provocatively by Raymond Williams in *Modern Tragedy*, in which Williams supports the view that Willy is neither a rebel nor a nonconformist but, rather, a frustrated conformist to Nietzsche's lie of culture: "Willy Loman is a man who from selling things has passed to selling himself, and has become, in effect, a commodity which like other commodities will at a certain point be discarded by the laws of the economy. He brings tragedy down on himself, not by opposing the lie, but by living it" (104). Miller corroborates Williams's view of the "laws of the economy" as they affect Willy, as though Willy's condition is quantifiable on a social ledger: *Salesman*, he writes, "was meant to be less a play than a fact; it refused admission to its author's opinions and opened itself to a revelation of process and the operations of an ethic, of social laws of action no less powerful in their effects upon individuals than any tribal law administered by gods with names" (Introduction 27).

An inevitable result of the contemporary tragic vision's anomie is its sense of the failure and falling off of culture. The cancellation of "old truths" in *Death of a Salesman* has had this effect; anomie and alienation occur in the context of the memory of a previous, better state of things, real or imagined. Miller sees all tragedy as deriving from this sense of loss, as showing "man's deprivation of a once-extant state of bliss unjustly shattered—a bliss, a state of equilibrium, which the hero (and his audience) is attempting to reconstruct or to recreate with new, latter-day life materials." It is as though we "once had an identity, a *being*, somewhere in the past, which in the present has lost its completeness, its definiteness" ("Family" 223). In Willy's effort at reconstruction, his hands are not in fact so wonderful. The tragic vision entails a fear of cultural enervation. Miller's tragic sense here has an interesting correlative in William Faulkner's. Combining the social and the personal, both Miller and Faulkner demonstrate an ambivalence concerning inner and outer realities; in this ambivalence the American dream is portrayed. The complex admixture of inner and outer states orchestrated in the great vortex of *As I Lay Dying*, with its downward spiral toward Jefferson and the replacement of Darl's narrative voice by the inarticulate Jewel (after Darl is committed to an asylum at the end) is a tremendously tragic diminution, the dying off of culture. Tragedy has fulfilled this role since before the earliest Dionysian festivals, as Nietzsche asserts: the cultural crisis portrayed by tragedy is always a fear of (cultural) death, which is the death of the self. Willy Loman tries in death to reaffirm his lost identity and his lost will, as Miller declares: "the lasting appeal of tragedy is due to our need to face the fact of death in order to strengthen ourselves for life" (Introduction 27). Tragedy, as reaffirmed by Miller, is truly a life-or-death crisis.

Pretext: The Contemporary American Tragedy

> I identify myself in Language, but only by losing myself in it like an object.   (Lacan 63)

I use the word *pretext* here in two ways: first, in its sense of falseness or deception; second, in the sense by which we are here opening a wide circle of texts before closing and in order to close in on a single text. Both senses exude a trace of *praetexere*, "to weave before," to pretend. In this sense, *pretext* carries the same burden as does *mimesis*, according to Walter Kaufmann's analysis of the latter as pretense (see appendix 1). To suggest that *Death of a Salesman* is a play about the interweavings of pretense, that the American tragic dream is one of illusion unfulfilled, would be to claim the obvious. But Miller takes the critique of American illusion a step farther: for Willy, "the [tragic] motif is the growth of illusion until it destroys the individual and leaves the children to whom he transmitted it incapable of dealing with reality" (Schumach 6). "On the play's opening night," Miller recounts in *Timebends*, "a woman who shall not be named was outraged, calling it 'a time bomb under American capitalism'; I hoped it was, or at least under the bullshit of capitalism, this pseudo life that thought to touch the clouds by standing on top of a refrigerator, waving a paid-up mortgage at the moon, victorious at last" (184).

In illusion, Miller attacks illusion; but here I want to recontextualize, using a patently Lacanian image by which to present the illusory self against which our illusions echo: "The American Dream is a largely unacknowledged screen in front of which all American writing plays itself out—the screen of the perfectibility of man. Whoever is writing in the United States is using the American Dream as an ironical pole of his story. It's a failure *in relation* to that screen" (Roudané, *Conversations* 362). Evoking the shade of Lacan's impossible dialectical self, the *je* that can never be uttered, Miller introduces the reader to the project of contemporary tragedy—without whose critical urgency, Miller says, "a genuine onslaught upon the veils that cloak the present" ("Family" 233) would be impossible.

In fact, the crisis of the American illusion is rhetorical, as Lacan suggests. The law is a rhetorical superstructure of "success," self-serving and duplicitous (a constant pretext); Willy's hamartia is a transgression against this law. Miller shows that a "failure" in business and in society has no right to live; he conceived of the play as a "race" between the meting out of this sentence of death and the opposing system of love that Biff finally learns, too late to save Willy. But even this system of love is a structure of pretexts: Willy can feel nothing beyond the veil or screen of his constitutive fictions. Harold Clurman anticipates this falsehood in a review of the play:

> Salesmanship implies a certain element of fraud: the ability to put over or sell a commodity regardless of its intrinsic usefulness. . . . To place all value in the mechanical act of selling and in self-enrichment impoverishes the human beings who are rendered secondary to the deal. To possess himself fully, a man must have an intimate connection with that with which he deals as well as with the person with whom he deals. When the connection is no more than an exchange of commodities, the man ceases to be, a man, becomes a commodity himself, a spiritual cipher.   ("Nightlife" 49–50)

That Willy's "product" is never identified becomes even more interesting in the light of Clurman's comments: Willy is the cipher of an empty signifier. His jargon of authenticity actively prevents his reifying himself. As the author of his own tragedy, Willy is prevented from taking meaningful action by the narratives that identify him. These narratives are themselves active illusions (e.g., Ben's apocryphal life stories and the epos of Dave Singleman) that put Willy into the role of Krieger's tragic visionary, the "extremist" who "despite his intermingling with the stuff of experience . . . finds himself transformed from character to parable" (20). Willy tries to learn the requisites of self-consciousness from Ben and Dave, but since they are themselves dialectical constructs within Willy's mind, and since Willy does not know this, he must fail. Willy misunderstands the ontological dilemma in which he is caught, a dilemma that has an ancient pedigree in the pretext of tragedy. Greek tragedy ends with choral closure, *Hamlet* with the perpetuation of the tragic story in Hamlet's charge to Horatio: the resolution of tragedy, structurally, is in its transformation into tragic narrative.

Willy's tragic error, his hamartia, failure to succeed, is in general that self-*méconnaissance* at the heart of the American illusion. Inherent in its rhetoric of transcendence is a crisis of transcription in which Willy is caught in his own crisis of self-vision, unable to clarify his attitude toward value and meaning, ambivalent about the nature of ethical action, and finally unable even to define the tragic; he does not see the tragedy of his own life. He searches perpetually through the "wordless darkness that underlies all verbal truth" (*Timebends* 144), not because that darkness has secrets which would finally ground him but because he fails to recognize the source of his own identity—his and his culture's constitutive tragic self-narratives. The disease of unrelatedness, whose symptoms are growing despair and a loss of meaning, is the ontological absence at the heart of ego-consciousness, ignored or transcended by the American illusion.

Text: The Civilizing Act

> WILLY. I'm not interested in stories about the past or any crap of
> that kind because the woods are burning, boys, you understand?
> There's a big blaze going on all around. (107)

Death of a Salesman seems to want us to see Willy authenticated in Biff's embrace in the play's penultimate scene; in Miller's view, Willy goes to his death exalted in this authentication: he "has bestowed power on his posterity" (Introduction 27). But even Willy can see that the insurance policy for which he has sold himself is a fiction, a text founded on illusion. The myth of authenticity in which Willy believes is an aesthetic of absence: Willy's real insurance policy is the texture of stories with which he has fought for his authentication. Willy's suicide is an embracing of a last chimerical myth. The unbridgeable gulf between Willy's desire for authenticity, for "full human character," and his blindness in achieving it replicates the great Dionysian crisis at the epicenter of the tragic vision. Willy's mounting frenzy through the course of the play, culminating in the (mock-)Zarathustran heights of that penultimate scene, reminds us of Nietzsche's admonition at the beginning of Zarathustra's self-authentication story:

> "Man is a rope, tied between beast and overman—a rope over an
> abyss. A dangerous across, a dangerous on-the-way, a dangerous look-
> ing-back, a dangerous shuddering and stopping.
> "What is great in man is that he is a bridge and not an end: what
> can be loved in man is that he is an *overture* and a *going under*."
> (*Zarathustra* 4)[6]

Willy is stretched on that same abysmal rack, never an end but always a bridge, a traveling man, on the move, wandering through a life that at numerous levels acts as a mimesis of the fundamental dilemma of tragic *méconnaissance*; he does not and cannot recognize himself. This tragedy, according to Miller, is the crisis and the reality of American life.

The play's world, like Zarathustra's, is one not of characterological reality but of civilizing texts, from Willy's first travel story of his last, abortive New England trip, to Happy's story of how he is going to show everyone that Willy had a "good dream" (139).[7] Willy speaks to Ben before Ben enters and after Ben leaves (44, 52) because what matters most to Willy is not Ben but Ben's stories. Since Willy has never "solidified" (72), never understood his own sublimation into the epos from which he fabricates himself, he has not passed this self-analysis to his sons; thus Happy is the incarnation of Willy (both are cheats, philanderers, and princes), and Biff, whose "training" has been much more complex (as we discover in the surfacing of the ultimate repression, what I call the Standish Arms Epiphany, which is not so much a repressed experience as the repressed story of an experience), "can't take hold of some kind of life" (54) and so takes hold of the dark side of the commodity exchange ritual by becoming a thief. Since Willy's stories center on his and Biff's success, the story of Bill Oliver is a vital one; when Willy is at his nadir, in Stanley's restaurant after Biff has gone through the illusion-destroying facts about his relationship with Oliver, Willy simply responds that he has been fired and that now "[t]he gist of it is that I haven't got a story left in my head" (107). Deprived of stories, Willy is "just a guy," as Happy so brutally declares (115).

The crisis of authenticity in *Death of a Salesman*, a subset of the crisis of rhetorical power, can finally be unlocked with three keys: self-naming, figures of desire, and the compensation of art for the tragic vision.

Self-Naming

In *Timebends*, Miller describes Willy as a man "who could never cease trying, like Adam, to name himself" (182). But if the self, so-called, is a palimpsest of texts written over one another, and if the original inscription, the apochryphal true identity, is chimerical, then the self is a system of dysfunctional metaphors in which, while one is always trying to "make one's mark," that mark is always a sign of absence.[8] Nonetheless, self-naming is a vital part of the tragic misrecognition in *Death of a Salesman*. Willy has had to name himself because "well, Dad left when I was such a baby and I never had a chance to talk to him and I still feel—kind of temporary about myself" (51). Unable to inscribe himself solidly, Willy has (or believes he has) named others: Biff, Happy, Howard ("I named him. I named him Howard" [97]). Willy does not see, as Charley tells him, that naming "don't mean anything" (97). If one's name is Salesman, what one sells names one; being unable to sell means having no name. When Happy denies Willy's identity in Stanley's bar, he thus speaks accurately: the now storyless Willy is not his father but "just a guy"—in some respect not Hap's father at all. Willy is simply the central figure in a convocation of characters whose need, greater than "hunger, sex, or thirst," is "to leave a thumbprint somewhere on the world," to know "that one has carefully inscribed one's name on a cake of ice on a hot July day" (Miller, Introduction 25). This urge toward self-naming accounts for Biff's otherwise incomprehensible act of stealing Bill Oliver's pen: by appropriating the signing tool, Biff tries to appropriate the ability to sign for himself. He realizes immediately that this goal is impossible and even embarrassing; he throws the pen away.

Figures of Desire

Miller gathers around the play a web of figures who exist only as subjects and objects of desire. This "chorus" of characters takes Willy as its focus and acts as a cultural medium. Seen in the light of this cultural medium, Willy's desire to be "well-liked" takes on new significance. To be well liked is a challenge to any salesman, but in the cultural medium every man is a salesman, every woman a saleswoman, acting out the desire to sell a whole and complete self to others, who will then judge the salesperson as substantial.[9] This cultural web of emblematic characters and their stories of desire for self-authentication range outward from Willy to his family to those in close proximity to it (Charley, Bernard, Howard) to those at a greater distance (Happy's boss, Stanley, people in Stanley's bar) to those who are pure narrative (Willy's father, Ben, Dave Singleman). We have seen how Hap's and Biff's stories center on a desire to be substantiated; Biff's "I know who I am" (138) is as much a rhetorical dream as is Willy's. Linda, too, has struggled for this solidification, fought Ben for Willy, won, and built a dream of security. Linda's tragedy is that she has achieved everything she set out to achieve yet can save neither the family nor Willy because she does not understand the narrative nature of her life. Like Happy's boss, the merchandise manager who cannot be satisfied with anything he has, the concentric circles of characters emanating from Willy, the play's central well of desire, reenact the crucial act of narratized desire.

Most interesting in this respect are the play's absent storytellers of desire, the chorus of chimerical figures who frame Willy's self-search. These characters—Dave Singleman, Willy's father, Ben—ground the central narratives of the play and establish the perimeters of its tragic vision of rhetorical power. Each of these figures acts as a custodian of self-ratification. Dave Singleman is the model upon whom Willy bases his standards of success; we must work our way back through Dave Singleman to reach Willy's two deeper father figures. In fact, Dave Singleman is a palimpsestic story written over that of the "real" father:

> Oh, yeah, my father lived many years in Alaska. He was an adventurous man. We've got quite a streak of self-reliance in our family. I thought

> .I'd go out with my older brother and try to locate him, and maybe
> settle in the North with the old man. And I was almost decided to go,
> when I met a salesman in the Parker House. His name was Dave
> Singleman.   (81)

The famous story of the gentleman-salesman shows two things: Singleman's
legend and Willy's failure to emulate his idol.[10] Willy's vital long speech to
Howard concludes, "[T]hey don't know me any more" (81). As for the father
as figure of desire, Willy evokes his ghost through Ben, precisely because
he feels "kind of temporary" about himself. Willy invokes Ben to tell Biff
and Hap the story of the father in an apotheosis of desire:

> WILLY.   . . . Please tell about Dad. I want my boys to hear. I want
>   them to know the kind of stock they spring from. All I remember
>   is a man with a big beard, and I was in Mamma's lap, sitting
>   around a fire, and some kind of high music.
> BEN.   His flute. He played his flute.
> WILLY.   Sure, the flute, that's right!
> *New music is heard, a high, rollicking tune.*
> BEN.   Father was a very great and a very wild-hearted man. We would
>   start in Boston, and he'd toss the whole family into the wagon,
>   and then he'd drive the team right across the country; through
>   Ohio, and Indiana, Michigan, Illinois, and all the Western states.
>   And we'd stop in the towns and sell the flutes that he'd made on
>   the way. Great inventor, Father. With one gadget he made more
>   in a week than a man like you could make in a lifetime.
> WILLY.   That's just the way I'm bringing them up, Ben—rugged, well
>   liked, all-around.   (48–49)

The original inventor, the great man whose every idea was a gold mine and
who was at the same time an Odyssean wanderer: this man is not Willy's
father but a wonderfully and impossibly romanticized narrative of the Ur-
father, the narrative behind Willy's self-crisis. Because he does not understand his own narratives, Willy cannot dissociate himself from the impossible
romanticism the story of the father establishes. Like Miller's flute music,
which implicates the reader-audience in the dream of the father, that paternal
epos operates as a pervasive index of desire.

By the same token, the teller of that story (Ben) is himself a kind of father-
narrator whose stories have a more direct impact on Willy's tragic dilemma
than Willy's actual father does. Ben, not the father, receives Willy's accolade
as "the only man I ever met who knew all the answers" (45). Ben knows all
the answers because he has a story (of success) for all occasions: his story
anticipates all Willy's inadequacies and desires for himself. Ben's triumph
is not just that he went into the jungle and came out rich but that in the

jungle Ben became solid, substantial. Ben has reified himself and solidified his story (he always tells the same one) in a way that Willy never could. Willy never understands, though Linda does, that Ben's threat is precisely this solidification: Ben and his story represent the breakup of the family, success at the price of humanness. Ben, like Faulkner's magical bear of the same name, is pure story divorced from life, and indeed when Willy is able to tell his own story in the same solid way, he is at the threshold of death. It is Ben who counsels Willy to kill himself for Biff's "inheritance." This insane advice, which completely ignores both Biff and Willy and manifests itself as a heap of platitudes ("it does take a great kind of a man to crack the jungle" [133]) is the aberrant vision of Willy's desire—and its tragic formulation. The "diamonds in the jungle" Ben seems to offer Willy are the chimerical authentication Willy cannot achieve.

Tragic Compensation

Death of a Salesman concludes not with Willy's death, of course, but with its Mass for the Dead, the Requiem, a ritual of final narrative authentication; it is Willy's memorialization. One by one, the four mourners name Willy: first Charley ("Nobody dast blame this man"); then Biff ("the man didn't know who he was"); then Happy ("he had a good dream"); and finally Linda, the remnant of the tragic chorus, who shows us the blindness to which we are all consigned in Willy's end (138–39). Linda is accurate in her elegiac statement that, in her having "made the last payment on the house today . . . there'll be nobody home" (139). Just as Willy is buried, as his house is now buried in the great tombstones of apartment buildings surrounding it, down among which no seed will grow, his tragic narrative is formalized and rigid. The family's catharsis is one of narrative ossification. As Krieger points out, "[T]he cathartic principle is ultimately a purely formalistic one, even as tragedy, despite its foreboding rumblings, can retain a force for affirmation through its formal powers alone" (4). Krieger, like Miller, invokes the Nietzschean compensation offered by tragic narrative's response to the tragic vision, which would be unbearable without that compensation. This balance is neither moralistic nor romantic but aesthetic, concerned not so much with the "lesson" of the play as with the aesthetic power of self-ratification.

In response to Willy's blindness, his inability to read his own stories accurately—indeed, his lies about himself and those around him—we must see in Miller's Requiem (as a culmination of the play's tragic vision) a portrayal of the Nietzschean tragic world, one that is "false, cruel, contradictory, destructive, without meaning. . . . *We have need of lies* in order to conquer this reality, this 'truth,' that is, in order to *live*—That lies are necessary in order to live is itself part of the terrifying and questionable character of existence" (*Will* 853). Willy Loman becomes the fabricator of a tragic truth-narrative out of which he enables those he leaves behind. Willy's stories and the framework Miller provides for them are a Nietzschean compensation for the tragic vision. Miller says that "the very impulse to write springs from an inner chaos crying for order, for meaning, and that meaning must be discovered in the process of writing or the world lies dead" (Introduction 28). In Miller's invocation of the tragic vision, "art is a function of the civilizing act quite as much as the building of the water supply" ("Family" 223). While art, for Nietzsche, is our redemption from negation and nihilism, Miller shows that tragic art is itself redemption from the negation into which tragic insight seems to force us. Willy only glimpses the abjectness of his own illusions: the anagnorisis of *Death of a Salesman* lies in its reader or viewer, for whom tragedy is the tonic and the antidote for anomie and nihilism.

The tragic in *Death of a Salesman* acknowledges the affirmation of life, which is not, finally, Aristotelian catharsis or Hegelian synthesis but what Nietzsche calls "a joyful participation *in tragedy*, as an artistic ritual, which denies and transcends the tragic" (*Birth* 7). In this vision of the tragic, unlike Aristotle's or Hegel's, "understanding" does not occur; Willy sacrifices himself for nothing. This principle is endemic to the contemporary tragic mode, which can be seen, as Krieger says, "using self-destructive crises to force itself to confront the absurdities of earthly reality—those which have always been there lurking beneath for the visionary who would dare give up all to read them." Krieger goes on to say:

> [W]e must admit that, at least in our time, driven as it is by crises and 'arrests' and blind as it is to the healing power and saving grace of tragedy, the tragic has come, however unfortunately, to loom as a necessary vision and . . . as one that can be neither reduced nor absorbed. (21)

In this way, the unrelenting tragedy of Linda at the end of the play, asking "Why did you do it?" and sobbing as she repeats "We're free" (139), demonstrates the blindness to the healing power of tragedy by which those left behind are driven. In Linda's blindness, a final coda to that of Charley, Biff, and Happy, the intensity of Miller's tragic vision reaches its peak. In the drama, for Miller, lies "the ultimate possibility of raising the truth-consciousness of mankind to a level of such intensity as to transform those who observe it" ("Family" 232). Through Miller's art in *Death of a Salesman* we confront neither the dangers of the success ethic in American business nor the lost self but the critical and tragic notion of the unfindable self in a condition of anomie, struggling through a narrative structure of differentiation and distance. Contrary to Linda's final assertion, Willy—like the rest of us, who feel it less intensely—is not, nor has he ever been, free; he is in a perpetual crisis of authentication predetermined by a rhetorical ground. This ground constitutes itself as the tragic father and the tragic muse he has never known, that chimerical author(ity) figure who is always on the road.

NOTES

[1]The Muses, as daughters of Zeus and the Titaness Mnemosyne ("memory"), served a normative cultural role: they were conceived of as a coupling of the heavenly and earthly functions of the fine arts, aspiring to superhuman synthesis and calling on our own human past for their power and effect. The word *muse*, linked to the Latin *mens* (mind, discernment, thought—but also purpose) and our own *mind*, denotes in Greek "memory" or "a reminder," since early poets had no books from which to read and so had to rely on their memories; gradually, the Muses came to be reminders to poets of the rules by which to write properly, of what to write about, and of why those subjects are "worthy." Interestingly and appropriately, in the light of Nietzsche's thought (which I discuss later), while "inspiring" the poet with subjects to be presented in, for example, the Tragic Dionysia, the Muses are associated with Apollo, traditionally their leader.

The so-called Tragic Muse, Melpomene, whose name means "singing," is an appropriate emblematic figure behind *Death of a Salesman*, preoccupied as it is with music and musical form.

[2]For Krieger, the tragic vision is nothing less than a view of reality, which inevitably alters with cultural views of reality:

> The tragic vision is born *inside* tragedy, as part of it: as a possession of the tragic hero, the vision was a reflection in the realm of thematics of the fully fashioned aesthetic totality which was tragedy. But fearful and even demoniac in its revelations, the vision needed the ultimate soothing power of the aesthetic form which contained it—the tragedy itself—in order to preserve for the world a sanity which the vision itself denied. (3)

The working out of the tragic in a literary form returns a sanity to a maddened world—regulates it (remember Nietzsche's declaration that we have art so that we will not go mad); this passage from Krieger is vital to an understanding of the form of *Salesman*.

[3]Anyone irritated by the previous passage on grounds of gender bias should recall that although many of the issues in *Death of a Salesman* are specifically gendered (i.e., pertain to the role of father, mother, son, or a socially conditioned gender-model orientation), many are not; I do not attempt to address the politics here. Note that Miller did not write *Death of a Saleswoman* or *Death of a Salesperson*; concerns specific to men are a central part of the play's thematic weight and of its tragic impetus.

[4]*Civilization and Its Discontents* is full of insightful references to this phenomenon, without which the tragic vision is significantly less understandable. Freud's case is that we deny our nature by "naturally" forming ourselves into societies:

> Man's natural aggressive instinct, the hostility of each against all and of all against each, opposes the programme of civilization. This aggressive instinct

is the derivative and the main representative of the death instinct which we have found alongside of Eros and which shares world-dominion with it. And now, I think, the meaning of the evolution of civilization is no longer obscure to us. It must present the struggle between Eros and Death, between the instinct of life and the instinct of destruction, as it works itself out in the human species. This struggle is what all life essentially consists of, and the evolution of civilization may therefore be simply described as the struggle for life of the human species.   (69)

Each sentence of this passage bears directly on Willy's and Linda's, as well as Biff's, condition, allowing us to achieve a more deeply tragic perspective on it.

[5] Some recent studies of social discontent as endemic to Western culture, and particularly as seen in themes of alienation and anomie, bear interestingly on this condition, again as grounds on which the tragic vision is to be built. From Marx to Nietzsche, and then into twentieth-century social and political theory, this issue is central to an understanding of recent social structure. Emile Durkheim, Georg Lukács, and others explore this terrain. A useful source of information on the polar opposition of alienation and anomie, a lack of identity and the lawlessness it breeds, is Gary Thom's *The Human Nature of Discontent: Alienation, Anomie, Ambivalence*, which could serve as the basis of a provocative theoretical investigation of the social structure in *Death of a Salesman* and the condition of all its characters.

[6] Willy Loman is Nietzsche's "last man," the low man in an enervated Western culture, the man of little will (willie) whose rhetoric always consists of meaningless dreams of guilt and *ressentiment* and who is unconsciously dominated by a rhetoric of oppression, as opposed to the overman, who, as master of willful rhetoric, does not succumb to the systems of signs he produces but rises above them.

Yet lest we too cleverly try to interpret Willy's name, Miller tells the story, in *Timebends*, of its "discovery": sitting in a showing of Fritz Lang's *Testament of Dr. Mabuse*, Miller was struck by the character of the director of the Sûreté, a "terror-stricken man calling into the void for help that will never come" (178–79). That character's name is Lohmann.

[7] Belief in stories is identical to and concealed in belief in "essences." Willy and Hap will not be disillusioned: Brooklyn is rural, Dave Singleman is a god, Biff is a star, Willy is well liked. Indeed, Willy sees himself as déclassé nobility, the essential man, the pioneer, the father, the holder of power, uncorrupted and clean (the language Willy uses to refuse Charley's proffered job shows this self-image clearly [97]).

[8] See Derrida's discussion of this phenomenon in "Signature Event Context": "a written sign is proffered in the absence of the addressee . . ." (315). Further:

Every sign, linguistic or non-linguistic, spoken or written (in the usual sense of this opposition), as a small or large entity, can be *cited*, put between quotation marks; thereby it can break with every given context, and engender infinitely new contexts in an absolutely nonsaturable fashion. This does not suppose that the mark is valid outside the context, but on the contrary that there are only contexts without any center of absolute anchoring.   (320)

[9] See Sartre's investigation of the gaze of the other, of the *en-soi* and the *pour-soi* in *Being and Nothingness* (73–84). Willy's desire to be well liked is also a simplified version of Hegel's *schöne Seele*, the "beautiful soul" that is possible only in the synthesis of self and other, the resolution of the conflict of master and slave. In a psychoanalytic context, Anthony Wilden comments on the beautiful soul as being "a consciousness which judges others but which cannot take action on itself in terms of judgement" (289). This is precisely Willy's dilemma: he cannot learn to judge himself or others properly, nor can he take appropriate action in response to self or other.

[10] Dave Singleman carries the name of the raw individualist, the singular man who is divorced from society and makes his own way, who is self-reliant, the successful manipulator of the system who can be aloof from life and still be well liked. Singleman is the embodiment of Lukács's view that tragedy is "the full depth of solitude," the struggle between existence and annihilation (56).

APPENDIX I

A measure of the way in which *Death of a Salesman* fits into the Western tragic tradition is the application of Greek terminology to the play. Some of the terms by which, through which, and parallel to which the tragic vision has evolved, and which provide a fruitful context for consideration of writing that claims tragic status, have given me a useful teaching tool to show *Death of a Salesman*'s relation to the tragedy of antiquity. The ways in which the terms apply to *Salesman* are indicated, but by no means exhaustively.

adikia: disruption of the right order (sexual transgression, Willy's lying to Biff about it, general deceit, being poor); see *dike*

arete: virtue (Willy's hypocritical or fictional sense of virtue, adaptable to his rhetorical sense of the world)

dike: right order (being well liked, making one's mark, being a success, going to Alaska—in particular, taking a risk for big gain; living for one's family; knowing the etiquette of the home office, as Howard does)

hamartia: error (Willy's not taking the job offered by Howard, Willy's treatment of Charley, not understanding the narrative of the social fabric, losing his temper at Biff, suicide)

mimesis: "illusion" or "pretense," as Walter Kaufmann suggests in *Tragedy and Philosophy* (33–41), rather than "imitation" or "representation" (the style and form of the play)

moira: fate (Willy's misunderstanding of his relationships with Biff and himself, Willy's inevitable sinking into self-destruction as a ratifier of his already-destroyed self)

APPENDIX II

A unifying trait in the diverse theories of the tragic since Plato is that they formulate and portray a cultural crisis that must be resolved, synthesized, accommodated, eradicated, transcended, acknowledged, suffered—according to the vicissitudes of the *épistémè du jour*. The tragic is a dramatic mechanism for crisis accommodation and authenticity portrayal. Tragedy affirms some particular view of the issues by which a particular culture sees and defines itself. Following are sketches of the history of tragic tradition that I find useful in teaching *Death of a Salesman*.

Plato

Dispersed throughout the *Republic*, Plato's elusive tragic idea relates to the nature of a proper education. It is a subset of his concerns about poetry and the state, which must be so tightly controlled in the *paideia*, the body of knowledge which any properly educated aristocrat must command. The tragic notion in Plato is to be found in sections 376–403 of the Cornford translation (see Kaufmann 9–29). Because in Plato all poetry, including the tragic, must have a didactic and heuristic ground supporting the conservative and moralistic conception of the *aristos* that Plato is at such pains to support, it must be "a model of virtuous thoughts" (Plato 75) or must not be tolerated. Plato would exclude Sophocles's *Antigone* and *Electra*, Euripides's *Medea*, *Hippolytus*, *Electra*, and *Trojan Women* from the canon: these works do not authenticate the vision of humankind that Plato wishes to foster. For the same reasons, he must have had trouble with Aeschylus's *Oresteia*. Understanding human beings as rational creatures in danger of irrationality, Plato turned away from the Dionysian origins of the tragic vision, altering it to fit another paradigm or social goal. He would not have known what to make of Willy Loman and his chimerical *paideia*.

Aristotle

Asking students to reread parts of the *Poetics* (particularly 1449a.7–1455a.19) in the context of tragic authentication leads to the interesting realization that Aristotle's project is much more like Plato's than one might have thought. It is also important to remember that Aristotle is almost incomprehensibly vague in his definition of the tragic: he does not explain any of the key terms on which he models that theory; of course, this is a reason for his lasting influence on changing ideas of tragedy.

For Aristotle the tragic is a catharsis of fear and pity that the audience of tragedy feels in the presence of a good person's sufferings; through the character's anagnorisis we see our own shortcomings and their possible transcendence. We identify with such characters as they cross the threshold of realizing that they are indeed human. For Aristotle this threshold of recognition and discovery requires unity in and concentration by the audience of tragedic drama. Catharsis is a quieting, a distancing of personal and cosmic discomfort at the level of the viewer. In Aristotle's stress on "action" (which we might now call theme) and plot over character (e.g., Miller's references to the Salesman rather than to Willy by name), he counters Plato's view of tragic poetry—as depicting the good person doing good—by introducing the central concept of hamartia, the tragic error or misjudgment by which the heroic individual must be made to gain insight into the nature of the Logos. It is ironic that Aristotle, rather than Plato, is held to initiate the concentration on the tragic hero in Western literature and drama; he would have been displeased at this perception. Aristotle was concerned with the integration of the whole, with the organic unity of humankind with all other things in a condition of ordered, analytical structure.

To Aristotle tragedy concerns itself with *eleos* (pity or mercy) and *phobos* (fear), but we may only speculate on how he intended them to interrelate, if indeed he did, and how they fit into a cathartic context. The *Poetics* is simply too allusive and unclear. What is clear in Aristotle's thought is that the point of tragedy, toward which all the formal elements of the drama work, is to arouse and purge certain emotions. According to Aristotle, Sophocles's *Oedipus Tyrannus* represents the highest instance of this function, since it shows the purest and most powerful form of this cultural normalization and the assertive emplacement of the order of the Logos (Aristotle does not mention that *Oedipus Tyrannus* won only second prize in the Summer Dionysia; apparently the audience was not behaving in proper Aristotelian fashion).

Both Plato's and Aristotle's notions of the tragic, severely limiting in terms of what can properly be called tragedy, are moralistic and didactic. They see the role of tragedy as offering a lesson to society in general on what constitutes its best interests. That is, both Plato and Aristotle take a generalist view of the cultural authentication that tragedy as a public spectacle offers.

Medieval and Renaissance Tragedy

The idea of tragedy becomes even more programmatic in its medieval (Catholic-Christian) form—as demonstrated, for example, in Boccaccio and Chaucer, who deal with the inevitable fall of illustrious men. In medieval tragedy, the trappings of the world are undermined and the lesson of humility and obedience taught. Tragedy becomes an authentication of the Christian cosmos and of humankind's place in it.

When we teach Renaissance tragedy, we tend to make the most of its developments over medieval models, with its creation of the exuberant "modern" notion of *humanitas*, the power and energy of individual man, but Renaissance tragedies from Thomas Kyd through William Shakespeare and Ben Jonson also work as moral exempla, urging attendance to the lessons of the consequences of evil (with two great exceptions: Christopher Marlowe's *Dr. Faustus* and Shakespeare's *King Lear*). This complex and familiar tragic drama is an exuberant exercise in the authentication of a new sense of the self as confined by Providence but holding immense powers of observation and action, uneasy in its role as subservient to externals but still obeying (as in *Hamlet*).

Hegel

With Hegel's idea of the tragic, explored in *The Philosophy of Fine Art* (particularly 1: 272–313; 2: 213–15; 4: 295–303, 308–26, 330–42) though never developed into a concerted theory, several new elements of tragedy as cultural authentication appear. Hegel's view of tragedy entails a new urgency concerning the human condition: the sundering of the social from the particular in human experience, inherent in Renaissance *humanitas*, reaches critical proportions in Hegel's dialectical philosophy. A person cannot act on one plane at a time, cannot be an individual and a collective being simultaneously, and so is tragic. Tragedy in Hegel destroys the individual but reconciles the dialectical position from which that destruction takes place. Individuals destroy themselves though the rigid one-sidedness of their characters, or they must identify themselves with a course of action to which they are fundamentally opposed. For Hegel tragedy, then, is the collision of opposing positions that are reconciled by the tragedy itself, by the portrayal of that collision and reconciliation. The most significant action in the tragic mode is the presentation of the tragic reconciliation itself. Ancient tragedies—the best of which is, for Hegel, not *Oedipus* but *Antigone*— portray the collision of ethical positions; modern tragedies should portray humanity as inwardly torn, self-centered, ripped apart by the forces driving the tragic vision (one can readily see the seeds of Miller's notion of Willy's self-sundering in the Hegelian tragic view). Tragedy now is a reconciliation into unity of the moral and ethical substance of Aristotle's hamartia in the hero. Hegel calls this principle the "too-assertive particularity" of the tragic figure, who is made heroic by this particularity. It is ironic that Hegel's view is the basis of modern existential tragedy, in which the particular has become the alienated and disenfranchised, for to Hegel the aim of tragedy, like all art, is the revelation of the eternal and divine in sensible form. Tragedy again teaches its lesson of order and structure and of the need for self-authentication in terms of this order. The Hegelian universe remains serenely and implacably calm in the face of human tragic furor.

Nietzsche

Nietzsche develops a radically different sense of the tragic, starting in *The Birth of Tragedy* and continuing through his later works, out of Hegel's dialectical sense and Schopenhauer's response to it. Schopenhauer's development of the tragic vision undermines and destroys Hegel's. For Schopenhauer, humanity is tragic because it is born human: our condition itself is tragic. The tragic is the acknowledgment of the "unspeakable pain, the wretchedness and misery of mankind, the triumph of wickedness, the scornful mastery of chance, and the irretrievable fall of the just and the innocent" (1: 253). Since to Schopenhauer the world, and the human life that is its measure, can never give satisfaction and therefore is not worthy of our affection, the tragic anagnorisis leads to resignation in the face of futility.

Nietzsche categorically rejects this idea, reversing Schopenhauerian resignation and stasis. For Nietzsche the tragic vision is one in which we experience tragedy in the living of life; by affirming the dichotomy of joy and suffering that defines life, we achieve tragic insight. In section 7 of *The Birth of Tragedy*, Nietzsche declares that we must look boldly right into the "terrible destructiveness" of nature, where we will see neither Hegelian synthesis nor Schopenhauerian stasis but a dramatic glimpse of the gulf between "the real truth of nature and the lie of culture that poses as if it were the only reality" (*Birth* 8).

Nietzsche reverses not only Hegel and Schopenhauer but all of tragic tradition back to Plato, as indeed is his goal. By exposing the "lie of culture" on which tragic visions have been posited, Nietzsche declares a new sense of life itself. As he develops it throughout his writing, Nietzsche shows us a tragic world with no orderly structure but opposing forces, a world of chaos, without laws, reason, or purpose. These forces are superadded by humankind, that "clever beast who invented knowing" ("On Truth" 79). To be tragic is to glimpse the truth of human nature, which is the chaos of its joy and suffering. The world of laws and systems, of love or success or business acumen or religion, that orderly and purposeful world we posit around us, is an illusion (a mimesis) that we have erected to keep the "real world" out; that real world goes on in its chaos without us, without acknowledgment of our "views, values, and our desires" (Nehamas 43). While we see the world revealed in its fearfulness, however, we see nature itself; this shock of recognition, which the tragic shows us, has nothing to do with nobility or transgression, with sin or hamartia or hubris, but reveals the universal joy and suffering in the interplay of forces defining life. Our culture rejects the real world in favor of a predictable one over which we pretend to have some control.

Nietzsche declares that Aristotle's notion of *katharsis* is simply not borne out by human experience: in the presence of fear-inducing action, we are not relieved of our fears but maintain and deepen them. "Aristotle's great misunderstanding," Nietzsche says, "is believing the tragic affects to be two *depressive* effects, terror and pity. If he were right, tragedy would be an art dangerous to life: one would have to warn against it as notorious and a public danger" (*Will* 851). For Nietzsche tragedy is a tonic, reminding us of our chaotic existence. It is, in other words, a cultural (individual and collective) self-authentication frightfully complicated by our lack of a self, as we generally define it, to authenticate. Nietzsche's affirmation of the tragic in the new context he creates for it is the tragic watershed for my interpretation of *Death of a Salesman*.

The Sociosymbolic Work of Family in *Death of a Salesman*

Linda Kintz

Postmodern theory has involved itself in complex questions about the relation between live bodies and the signs "propped" on them, about connections
between dramatic and performance texts, and about the devices and techniques that construct what we think of as reality. These abstract theoretical
questions can be made much more concrete in a study of Arthur Miller's
Death of a Salesman, which can also, very powerfully, bring together aesthetics and history through a grammar of space by showing the relation between
urban social space in the twentieth century and the different ways in which
people live themselves as human subjects.[1]

A look at the staging of social space reveals how the family, in its various
historically specific forms, works as the mediating link between individuals
and society, in terms of both symbolic imagery and political arrangements.
Analyzing social space also helps make visible the way in which families
perform what might be called sociosymbolic work, work that shows up both
in social conditions and in cultural formations and helps prepare individual
subjects either fit into society or attempt to change it. In teaching drama,
we should focus on this sociosymbolic work of family and urban space so
that students can historicize and deconstruct the concept of character in
different historical periods and so avoid collapsing all dramatic characters into
people just like them. It is also important to show how ideas of subjectivity,
character, and the individual are historically relative and depend on larger
questions of social organization. Students may gain insight into the implications of what it might mean, in historical and cultural terms, for a character
to appear "just like them."

The organization of urban space, seemingly invisible because it surrounds
us like air, is of special significance in *Death of a Salesman*. As Jean-Pierre
Vernant argues about urban space in the classical Greek city-state, "The
first urban planners were in fact political theorists: the organization of urban
space was but one aspect of a general effort to order and rationalize the
human world" (76). Though periodically (almost cyclically) dismissed and
resurrected, Aristotle's *Poetics* remains the foundational text in dramatic
criticism that sets out the formal requirements for the aesthetics of a rationalized social space—that is, the division of social space in ways that conform
to the requirements of the concept of reason dominant at the time. The
requirements for occupation of the public social space of the polis in the
Greek city-state also set the requirements for those who could do philosophy,
science, rhetoric, politics, tragedy. The divisions between occupants of the

public and private spaces matched divisions in epistemology, in beliefs about who was capable of thinking and who was not. The characteristics of the protagonists in Aristotelian dramatic plot link this politically rational space to aesthetic criteria.

The *Poetics* provides one of the most powerful analyses of the relation between the requirements for "good" drama and the requirements for participation in the public life of the polis. Participation in the polis proves to be the same thing as legitimate subjectivity. Aristotle's discussions of the protagonist bring together art and politics, art and the state, in a kind of political poetics.[2] The continuing impact of the *Poetics* has inspired feminist, Brechtian, and postmodern resistances to the Aristotelian plot (the mimesis of an action) and its dependence on a linear development of action, on an unproblematized notion of cause and effect, a hierarchical valorization of characters, and interpretations that depend on concepts of fate and universality.

Despite the historical differences between the Greek polis and urban America in 1949, when *Death of a Salesman* was first produced, certain Aristotelian requirements for protagonists, requirements that are linked to a rationalized social space, are repeated in Miller's play and reveal a structural similarity that needs to be identified. Such a comparison, however, should be accompanied by a caution to respect the historical differences that distance the two periods. Though Miller claims, in "Tragedy and the Common Man," that *Death of a Salesman* investigates the possibility of tragedy as a form suited for the common man, taking his cue from the Aristotelian notion of tragedy as suited only for the uncommon man, one may argue that his attempt to reclaim the common man's tragic stature overlooked the ways in which race, gender, and class help construct that common man's identity through the sociosymbolic work of the family and the interaction between unconscious and cultural meanings. Miller's look at Willy Loman bypasses more radical questions about race, gender, and class issues that, differentially, are necessary to make his position as protagonist possible. Simply inserting a different kind of protagonist in an Aristotelian structure obscures more than it reveals.

Willy Loman's pathos has much to do with historical ambiguities in the position of white middle-class men after World War II and their possibilities of being protagonists in American social life. In particular, Willy Loman's circumstances are connected to a reaction to racial diversity in the cities after World War II and pressures on middle-class women to return home and make more jobs available for returning soldiers.[3]

In teaching Miller's play, one should examine the stage setting in careful detail because of its rich allegorical structure, which sets up a kind of grammar of space that formally comments on the race, class, and gender issues that are not always overt in the content of the play. Many readings of *Death of a Salesman* concentrate on the futile choices presented to Willy Loman as he takes seriously the overt message of an unforgiving competitive capitalism that promises him a certain valued position as a salesman when, in fact, in that particular political economy, value can be defined only as infinite increase, upward mobility in class and wealth. Built into that message is the inherent contradiction between an admonition to be number one, which Willy takes seriously, and the inevitability that there will be far more losers than winners, a message he hears only too late. The very concept of firstness demands a guarantee that there will be many who are not first.

Similarly, Miller shows how the free-enterprise notion of value leaves no place for the confused moral qualities that Willy tries to use in his attempts to make sense of the American dream.[4] This is a dream based not on quality but on quantity: the increase of wealth taking over all questions of value, even the value of human life. As in the publicity images of advertising, anything can be bought and sold. Willy will ultimately, literally, turn himself into a commodity, acting out what Marx called alienation and Lukács called the reification of human beings under capitalism—that is, the process by which human beings come to be treated as things. Willy sells himself as thing, or commodity, selling his life for an insurance payment, logically enacting the result of a value system based on quantitative increase or profit—that is, the American dream.

If we focus on the spatiality of the stage setting, it will also help show how Willy's failure puts him, first, in a kind of limbo, and afterward on a downward trajectory, unlike the upwardly mobile track of most white middle-class citizens after the war, those who benefited from the expansion of the economy. Willy's downward movement is apparent in his inability to move with much of the white middle class to the suburbs, a move that accelerated after the war as the cities were increasingly abandoned by whites to people of color and the poor.[5] Before tracing some of those factors further, one should spend a good deal of time sketching out the detailed setting, which provides a semiotic field that encompasses these contradictions and tensions in the play as a whole. Rarely does an opening scene work so powerfully to suggest a historical context that is allegorized, whether or not in the way Miller intended. (Another American play that uses this kind of spatial allegory in a powerful way is Susan Glaspell's *Trifles*, which might be taught before *Death of a Salesman*. Glaspell's play, too, comments on the opposition between rationalized spaces—that is, between public and private spheres, between the city and the country—and between aesthetic and political forces in twentieth-century American drama.) I work here with Miller's dramatic, or written, text rather than with a particular performance text.

Initially suggesting an opposition between country and city, rural and urban, jungle and city, First World and colonies—an opposition that will structure much of the play's commentary on Willy and capitalism—Act I opens with a flute melody, "small and fine, telling of grass and trees and the horizon." The flute later proves to be connected not only to this dream-backyard space but to one of Willy's missing origins: his father, the flute salesman. The curtain opens on the salesman's house and "towering, angular shapes behind it, surrounding it on all sides." A blue light falls on the house, while the apartments that tower over it are suffused in an "angry glow of orange." The apartment houses have the appearance of a "solid vault," lending the image connotations of finance.[6] This heaviness sets up a striking contrast to the "fragile-seeming home," which has a dreamlike air, "a dream rising out of reality." In the middle of this dreamlike structure of home is a kitchen, abstractly represented. The frame of the house is "wholly or, in some places, partially transparent," with a view of the apartment buildings under and over the roof-line of the house. And downstage of the house is a backyard, a carved-out space that functions as the site of those scenes disrupting linear time, scenes that take place as memory, fantasy, or dreams (11–12).

The plot of soil, the yard overwhelmed by threatening, solid, angry apartment buildings, comes to mark the site of Willy's attempts to make a stable place for himself in reaction to what is soon revealed to be his downward movement in a class-structured world. The backyard—the real earth, or real estate—is juxtaposed with the movement inherent in his job as a traveling salesman, but this movement isn't upward. It is a constant movement back and forth in his car, the symbol of mobility in industrial capitalist society, a mobility that helped break up an extended family structure in the interests of a more mobile nuclear one. Willy spends more time in the car (that proves to be junk) than he does at home (full of things that break down), in a kind of limbo out on the highway. In his backyard, he attempts to "ground" himself, to offset this futile motion by valorizing, even romanticizing, a connection to earth through his fantasies of Alaska, of Africa. Here, too, Biff relives his memories of Texas and spins his unrealistic dreams of living on a farm or ranch. The mobility of the highway limbo also suggests a sense of unsettled identity which desperately looks toward that plot of ground and that home, though the stability of both has perhaps always been illusory, their increasingly obvious ephemerality necessitating the time Willy spends in dreams. Miller's stage directions suggest that the fragile home is dreamlike, its dream rising out of a reality, but it is, ironically, a reality that makes the fulfillment of the dream impossible.

Finally, the stage directions provide a description of Linda Loman; again, the information here is rich for what it says about the possibilities that will arise for Willy as protagonist. Besides this house, this yard, this kitchen that await Willy, Linda waits and worries about him:

> Most often jovial, she has developed an iron repression of her exceptions to [his] behavior—she more than loves him, she admires him,

as though his mercurial nature, his temper, his massive dreams and little cruelties, served her only as sharp reminders of the turbulent longings within him, longings which she shares but lacks the temperament to utter and follow to their end.   (12)

It is not only the backyard plot of soil that the settings posit as increasingly impossible and lost; it is a nostalgic view of the plot of the universalized masculine protagonist of the *Poetics*. That plot, which depends on the sociosymbolic work of an idealized family, requires the woman to wait at home, to console and civilize both husband and children, roles that provide a structural, narrative guarantee of masculine agency even in very different historical periods. For example, in Sophocles's *Women of Trachis*, the character Deianeira functions as a civilizing influence to tame the excesses of men like Heracles, whose heroic behavior outside the city walls threatens the political world of cooperation among male citizens inside the Greek city-state. Her function is, like Antigone's, to serve as a medium for coherence in the service of the public contract among males. The purpose of Antigone's act, often read as feminist (a reading that is hard to sustain), is to ensure that civilization continues; civilization is defined here as a contract between men. Women are relegated to the space of the hearth to serve as masculine civilization's glue.[7]

In *Death of a Salesman*, Linda, too, is the civilizing element, the glue of the household, her function in part to focus the audience's gaze, as well as the gaze of the sons, on Willy.[8] Linda Loman, of course, has the most memorable line of the play: "Attention must be paid." But to what? To whom? To Willy. She is the mirror that makes possible his image of himself. In a scene juxtaposed with one in which Willy is in the hotel room with The Woman, Linda darns her old stockings and tells him that he's "the handsomest man" (39). And though she seems at times to function as the site of what is most concrete and real, her relations with her family are also built on lies. Willy's dilemma throughout the play is one of loss: a lost frontier, a lost fortune, lost sons, a lost image. Yet Linda, from the play's beginning, already occupies a site of loss. The domestic space of the house, ostensibly a female space, is there not in fact for her but as a space in which she must wait for Willy; part of the pathos of the play arises out of his inability ultimately to claim what is, by right, his.

The kitchen that is set out in the opening scene as a place that waits for him to occupy it, with Linda listening for his arrival, suggests another historical factor in Willy's dilemma.[9] Max Horkheimer, a Frankfurt school theorist, argues that late-nineteenth- and twentieth-century industrial capitalism produced what he calls a society without fathers. With the development of state bureaucracies and social welfare policies, the power within individual families passed from fathers to the state. Social workers, psychotherapists, health workers, and judges came to exercise the authority once held by fathers within families. The American social critic Christopher Lasch also argues that during this development of the Western bureaucratic state "[e]nlightened opinion . . . identified itself with the medicalization of society: the substitution of medical and psychiatric authority for the authority of parents, priests and lawgivers, now condemned as representatives of discredited authoritarian modes of discipline" (qtd. in Barrett and McIntosh 117). Echoing Lasch's view, Jacques Donzelot, who draws on Michel Foucault's analysis of the intersection of state social services with the rise of the social sciences, warns of an "unhealthy alliance between women and the plethora of agencies that disguise state intervention in the family as 'expertise' . . ." (117).

What begins to emerge in Miller's staging is what Michelle Barrett and other feminists have criticized in the work of Horkheimer, Lasch, and Donzelot: a nostalgia for a time when fathers were fathers and women were mothers, a masculine resistance to the predations of an impersonal bureacracy and competitive capitalism. Their view does not address gender and race but, instead, produces important descriptions of the serious effects of industrial capitalism on men. Miller's play, like the work of Horkheimer, Lasch, and Donzelot, laments the loss of dignity for someone like Willy, the falseness of the values of capitalism, but this powerful and painful play about Willy's degradation is undercut by a romantic nostalgia for lost masculine authority.

This nostalgia is also linked historically to a longing for a certain kind of neighborhood without "angry" teeming apartment houses, a neighborhood where people like Willy can live around others "like" themselves. The most effective way to teach this play is in juxtaposition with Lorraine Hansberry's *A Raisin in the Sun*, which makes these connections explicit. Hansberry's characters, drawing on the strengths and tensions of an extended family organization rather than on those of a nuclear one, live in one of these apartments, or tenements, that tower over the fragile, threatened white nuclear family in all its disarray. Both the Lomans and the Youngers have been left behind in the urban space.

In showing how Willy's dream is inseparable from a historical ordering of race and gender as organized through an idealized model of the nuclear family, Mimi Abramovitz's concept of a "family ethic" is helpful and direct. Abramovitz argues that, historically, North American middle-class culture developed this idealized, normative model of the nuclear family—that is, a heterosexual couple, living in a space separated from extended family members, with several children; an autonomous "normal" family unit. To this day, American cultural values, land-use planning, and urban zoning, as well as financial systems based on the single-family home and mortgage deductions, continue to structure and organize American social space in the interests of such a family, even though few families—either in 1949, when this play was first produced, or now—fit this mythical Donna Reed pattern.[10]

Abramovitz argues as well that the social services Horkheimer sees as threatening the authority of fathers are based on the idealized model that places women in the home, subordinate to men. It is in fact the privileging of that model, she argues, that destabilizes family life and oppresses women.

Because the family ethic idealizes marriage and motherhood while devaluing women at home and at work, "permit[ting] societal institutions to view non-nuclear families as deviant and unworthy" (9), it supports conditions that benefit those who live in traditional family structures "while penalizing alternative family forms where poor women and women of color tend to predominate" (2). It is, ironically, not feminism, drugs, permissiveness, or loss of male authority that destabilizes families, she argues. It is this normative family ethic that attempts to "save" one kind of family rather than to broaden the definition of family.[11] In Willy's case, the very conditions that underlie the mythical family of that ethic, those of a developing competitive economy, are precisely the conditions that make his participation in his own family impossible. He is gone all the time, and both he and Linda are, as Abramovitz argues is true of the family ethic, "frozen into rigid gender roles" (2).

In the late forties the race and class dimensions of this ethic became more and more evident. Veterans returning from World War II were assured of Federal Housing Administration loans that required no down payment and small monthly mortgages, women who had gone to work during the war were pressured to return home, and an industrial system that had been geared toward defense production was shifted to production for consumption, rather than directly for defense. The central areas of most American cities were increasingly abandoned by young white workers and their families as they moved to the suburbs, and minorities were left behind in the inner cities. Housing starts became a major indicator of economic growth, highway construction was expanded, and the automobile industry grew. The suburban home became the primary site of consumption, the primary target of advertising, the bedrock of the American economy, helping stabilize the workforce with long-term mortgages. As Delores Hayden writes, "Housing Americans was . . . a big, big business, and American banking, real estate, and transportation interests were intimately involved" (38).

The development of the family ethic, the normative white nuclear family and its connection to housing patterns in the United States, provided spatial evidence of the distribution of wealth, prestige, and opportunity in postwar American communities. That spatial evidence was a strange new area, neither city nor country but the suburbs, the privileged site of the emergence of the isolated, single-family home as the ideal living situation for the ideal family. As Abramovitz argues, the privileging of that site meant that other kinds of families were rejected as nonideal, in particular the extended family structure of immigrant and African-American families in the city, as well as utopian models of communal arrangements, many of which were tried in

American cities in the nineteenth century. Hayden has analyzed this shift in the American dream from the ideal city to the American dream house as the spatial representation of hopes for individual freedom, expression, and privacy, with serious consequences for politics as well as for the environment.

Middle-class white women were increasingly located in a highly contradictory space. As the move out of the inner cities to the suburbs physically separated the middle class from the lower classes, and whites from people of color, allowing the white middle class to surround themselves with others "like" themselves, white women's place after the war again became the home, their job to develop and increase cultural capital rather than earn wages, to provide the "haven in a heartless world" (Lasch) that was a haven defined in opposition to the harsh, competitive public space of men, the world Willy faced. Along with consoling the breadwinner for the wounds inflicted in that world, middle-class women were charged with increasing the family's status through the care, education, and training of their children. Linda Loman, in Willy's transitional, threatened, delicate, and finally empty house, its mortgage finally paid off, waits in the threatened privacy of the single-family house left behind in the city. The futility of this lifelong job of Willy's is made concrete: to buy a "home" that then proves to have no family in it, he has devoted and lost a life.

Women of color, in contrast to middle-class women, were already in the public sphere in the cities, more likely struggling for privacy in the face of a growing corporate state whose agencies were charged with enforcement of social policies based on that mythical white nuclear-family model. A comparative study of *Salesman* and *A Raisin in the Sun* can also foreground the different ways in which white women and women of color relate to their families, challenging the supposedly universal definition of family. The conflict in Hansberry's play has to do with the attempt of an African American extended family to buy a house in the suburbs, an attempt that brings into stark clarity who the ideal occupants of these houses should be and throws into relief the model of the family that is the ideological foundation of an economy and a culture.

White middle-class women, at a disadvantage within the family because of their gender (a disadvantage that shows up in Miller's nostalgic use of Linda Loman to provide consolation and audience to her sons and to Willy), also came to assume an identity that superseded their identification with women of other classes. The move to the suburbs reinforced that class difference, as the lack of race and class consciousness in the early years of the feminist movement showed.

Situating *Death of a Salesman* within a historical discussion of the importance to the American economy and its dream of the single-family home can also help make more concrete a postmodern discussion of Jacques Lacan's notion of the symbolic, showing the power of symbolic systems and sign systems to construct the ways historical subjects come to live themselves and, in fact, the culturally specific ways in which they think of themselves as human subjects. The mythical nuclear family that underlies the concrete relations of industrial capitalism shows up in symbolic form as the Freudian triangular family of Oedipus—father, mother, and son—a model that can be used to describe how subjects come to live themselves as desiring subjects in a particular form of society, that is, industrial capitalism. Lacanian and Freudian theories provide useful descriptions of the European and American middle class in the nineteenth and twentieth centuries; they do not, however, provide theoretical descriptions of a universal form of subjectivity. Miller's play simultaneously critiques the restriction and damage perpetrated by the rigid gender roles of this oedipal model of family with the white male as head and longs for the imagined stability of a time in a mythical American past when men could unproblematically own their plot of ground and plant it, wives were always available, and men really were the head of the family.

When teaching this play, one should foreground the historical and cultural constructedness of both character and subjectivity so that young men do not have to participate defensively in discussions as if they were merely the enemy. White masculine identity, like that of white women and people of color, is a part of this social construction, and in many ways its strictures are complex and oppressive for young men. Neither Willy Loman nor most of our white male students benefit unambiguously from the nuclear-family myth, though it is far more immediately apparent that women and students of color do not. The histories of these students, at least in the public universities, are highly contradictory and varied.

Once the historical and structural importance of the work of families is set out to show that Willy's struggle cannot be universalized as the struggle of the "individual" but, rather, must be seen as the struggle of a white man falling out of the middle class in late 1940s urban America, there is much to be gained by focusing on that very myth of individuality that works to reinforce the family ethic. Miller's determined dissection of the promises and contradictions of the myth of the individual are important.

Willy's internalizing of the jumbled myths that surround success point to a particular opposition: the relation between style and substance, a relation that initially presupposes substance but at every turn finds style and appearance to be poised over emptiness. For example, Willy buys a particular refrigerator because it had the best ads; the refrigerator breaks down. The images of the flashy Chevrolet lose their gleam next to a stack of repair bills. The paid-up mortgage has, of course, bought an empty house. Biff's success in sports has no substance to rest on; his cheating, his faking, has destroyed it, though that fakery is a logical response to what he has been taught. Willy himself, in the image of father and husband that he cultivates, proves to be a fake. On the night out with Willy, Biff and Happy tell stories that are lies, and the reason behind their party is a lie. The notion of fatherhood for Willy has always been a lie, his own father having abandoned his family.

The importance of style, of appearance, of personality, of being liked, of image over substance, links Willy's position to another historical feature of American culture, the predominance of advertising, of images that establish standards and values that, paradoxically, make it impossible to establish standards and values. In particular, advertising, as students can attest, provides multiple images of possible selves. In a culture that praises the power of the individual, individuals are bombarded with mass-produced possibilities for being like everybody else, since advertising plays on promises of uniqueness to sell identical products. Buy Euphoria perfume to set yourself off from all the rest, who, by the way, are also watching this commercial, with its promise of uniqueness for them, too. Willy's desire to be number one falls into this space of the production of desires whose satisfaction is impossible; there will always be something else one can buy to make oneself more desirable. The impossibility of satisfaction is necessary to make the infinite increase of profit possible.

The art critic John Berger argues that in late capitalist society publicity comes to function as the model by which we assess value, not just the value of objects but of art, of people, of ourselves.[12] Publicity is about the future buyer of an object: it offers the buyer "an image of himself made glamorous by the product or opportunity [the ad] is trying to sell. The image then makes him envious of himself as he might be" (132). Value here rests on the envy of others, the happiness of being envied by others. There is no center, simply a constant need to increase that envy. Willy is thus both the buyer and the seller of the image of himself. He has bought an empty notion of success, which is, in fact, a model based on publicity: its very definition places style over substance. This is a model of success that is, like celebrity, intrinsically grounded in the appearance of success, of personality, of being liked.

But Charley has given him the key to "reading," or deciphering, publicity and appearance, though Willy missed its implications. In talking about J. P. Morgan, Charley deconstructs the notion of being liked and locates the "real" within the image: "Why must everybody like you? Who liked J. P. Morgan? Was he impressive? In a Turkish bath he'd look like a butcher. *But with his pockets on he was very well liked*" (97; emphasis added). Money, as Charley knows but Willy does not, is the site where value is established. As Berger argues, "[T]hose who lack the power to spend money become literally faceless. Those who have the power become lovable" (143). In the logic by which he tries to become number one, Willy has become faceless, or, as Biff says, "He never knew who he was" (138). Willy has tried to establish an identity based on the model of an advertising image for a competitive system he did not understand: "What's—what's the secret?" (92). Willy

Loman is a failed publicity image, a failed style whose substance is its ability to pass itself off as real.

What Willy's confused, sad fakery reveals is the contradiction Berger isolates in a publicity culture. Such a culture has "moved towards democracy and stopped halfway there. . . . The pursuit of individual happiness has been acknowledged as a universal right. Yet the existing social conditions make the individual feel powerless" (148). That powerlessness, which Willy feels, is reinforced by his working conditions. In an alienation so profound that fewer and fewer people vote, the choice of what to buy replaces significant political choice.

The publicity culture has, of course, made the systems that construct the "real" even more indecipherable since 1949. The Reagan years were years characterized by the most sophisticated orchestration of publicity and image in American history. Peggy Noonan, whose speeches were instrumental in this dizzying play of publicity, style, and images, compared Ronald Reagan with Willy Loman: "They say he was like Willy Loman, going through life on a smile and a shoeshine and telling his sons you've got to be liked. Well, he was Willy without the angst, and he was Ben too . . ." (183).

But perhaps Reagan needed Willy's angst. Willy's painful but futile attempt to be the image is marked by a paradoxically innocent guilt about his own role within his family. There is, in his confusion about images of success, a construction of innocence; guilt or responsibility can only sneak around those images in the form of unease, of angst, of a worry that something is not right, though one cannot say quite what or "read" those images in order to gain some control over them. Perhaps Willy's innocence is a metaphor for a certain notion of America, for "what the publicity image achieves as it masks and compensates for all that is undemocratic within society" (Berger 149). The deep violence done to subjective experience, the impossible paradox of mass-produced individualism that mythologizes the family, leaves Willy's identity poised over an anguished emptiness—the emptiness of death and of Linda's final words in the play, "We're free . . ." (139).

NOTES

[1] One of the best texts to use in defining the connections between subjectivity and cultural formations is Silverman's *The Subject of Semiotics*, in which she draws on Freud, Lacan, and Foucault while developing her own original and highly accessible feminist theory. (In particular, see chapter 4.)

[2] Unless students in such a drama class have some background, it helps to begin by teaching the *Poetics* in depth, with discussions of the historical circumstances of the Greek city-state, to provide a context for later discussions of dramatic form. Of particular help is the work of Zeitlin, Winkler, duBois, and Else.

[3] The documentary film *The Life and Times of Rosie the Riveter* traces the pressures on women to leave jobs, particularly jobs that were formerly held by men, such as

work in shipyards. The film also follows shifts in medical and psychological advice given to middle-class women about the importance of their presence in the home; during the war, when women's labor outside the home was needed, psychologists minimized the influence of that presence on young children's development.

[4]"Moral" qualities themselves need to be historicized, as Friedrich Nietzsche argues in *The Genealogy of Morals*. What certain Western groups think of as moral has a history in the rise of the middle class. Their notion of morality operates in the interests of that class, as George Bernard Shaw argues in *Major Barbara*. Charity, for example, may have more to do with middle-class needs than it does with the needs of the poor. This reasoning does not imply that "moral" behavior, or ethics, is pointless. Rather, it suggests that as we develop new ways of thinking about morality, we need to ask whose interests our morals serve.

[5]Now this move has been partially reversed, and the poor are being forced out of certain urban areas, often onto the streets, as the affluent reclaim and gentrify these areas.

[6]Miller's play is filled with contradictions. Here the vaultlike appearance of these apartments suggests the weight of investment and the monumentality of Wall Street buildings, which could be analyzed interestingly in this kind of grammar of space. Yet it is the apartments that look like vaults, sites of investment rather than of investors.

[7]Froma Zeitlin refers to *The Women of Trachis* as a "schematic model of gender relations," a cultural artifact that, among other things, sets out an epistemology which continues to structure gender even now (77).

[8]Teresa de Lauretis's influential work on plot and the relation of the protagonist, who occupies the active plot space, to the inscription of gender into texts is helpful in coming to grips with Linda's function here in relation to Willy, the occupant of that space. See in particular chapter 5, "Desire in Narrative."

[9]Glaspell's *Trifles* is also set in a kitchen. In and out of this space move male characters who are representatives of the law and language. The women alternately acknowledge their own secondary status when the men are present and work out subtle forms of resistance and resistant ways of speaking and "reading" when the men are not onstage.

[10]According to the 1987 census, only seven percent of American households fit the pattern of a mother who stays at home, a working father, and children.

[11]Marsha Ritzdorf has traced the history of land use and zoning in the United States in relation to the privileging of the nuclear family:

> Research into the exclusionary uses of municipal zoning ordinances has focused on the exclusion of minority and low- and moderate-income residents from American communities by limitations upon or of alternatives to large lot single-family housing, yet the family definitions affect an even wider variety of people. A sample of affected groups would include foster children, communal living arrangements, students, elderly, single parents and their children, handicapped, mentally retarded, developmentally disabled, ex-convicts, ex-mental patients, juvenile offenders, and rehabilitating drug and alcohol users. (15)

Mina Davis Caulfield argues that colonization by the First World has used the nuclear-family model to break up kinship groups in which women often had more power than they have had since the introduction of manufacturing. Western systems of education introduced a certain model of family into other cultures and favored boys over girls, as did Christianity's holy family and masculine concept of God. Labor in manufacturing, rather than subsistence or agricultural labor, favored men's contribution over that of women. Caulfield argues, however, that "family" cannot be seen only as a site of oppression. Extended families continue to provide sites of resistance, both in the Third World and in the United States, in the inner city and other poor areas such as Appalachia.

[12] Berger's explanation of the mechanisms of the publicity image in *Ways of Seeing*, chapter 7, is very accessible, both for background and for use by students.

Beyond the Male Locker Room:
Death of a Salesman
from a Feminist Perspective

Jan Balakian

If Biff and Happy placed an ad in the classified section it would read:
WANTED: WIFE
Must be able to cook, clean, pay bills, keep peace, be supportive,
soft-spoken. Above all praise me in whatever I do.
> —Student paper, Kean College of New Jersey

The Male Gaze

Contrary to the common feminist argument that *Death of a Salesman* paves
the way for the displacement of women in contemporary plays, I think it
cries out for a renewed image of the American woman. Feminists who claim
that the play does not attempt to redefine women but instead contributes
to the perpetuation of female stereotypes forget that Miller is accurately
depicting a postwar American culture that subordinated women. He thus
depicts America through the male gaze. We see everything from Willy's
perspective and never from a female point of view. His mind becomes a
vehicle through which Miller unveils the flaws of a postwar American society
that has "come to serve the machine," that values "production for profit and
production for use" (*Theater Essays* 61) at the expense of creating a world
in which one can live humanly.

My working-class students at Kean College readily identify with the play's
critique of capitalist values. "I've worked in a factory, and I know what Willy
is feeling! I know what it's like to be a cog in a wheel," an older student
exclaims. A younger student replies, "I'm a clerk at the Marriott in Jersey
and I'm always being bossed around by the guys making the profit." A third
student, a woman, responds, "I drive a school bus every morning, and I
know what it's like to be on the road all the time." Another female student
corners me in the corridor after class to tell me, "This is the story of my
family." Students' initial responses to the play and their urges to identify
with it are thus remarkably similar; their perceptions of Linda, however,
vary radically.

A Hybrid Form

Before approaching the play from a feminist perspective, I clarify the connection between Miller's dramaturgy and the play's social character. While the
play uses expressionism to probe the psychology of character, it dramatizes

social forces in a symbolic fashion, breaks the illusion of the fourth wall, and is therefore also in the poetic tradition of Aeschylus and of medieval morality dramas like *Everyman*. To put it a bit differently, this hybrid of realism and expressionism results from the fact that *Salesman* is both a family drama and a social drama. Miller realizes that realism cannot bridge the gap between the private and the social and that expressionism has its limitations because it forgoes psychological realism. Indeed, the form of the play is not unlike the stream of consciousness or T. S. Eliot's effort to show the world as it appears to a troubled mind in *The Waste Land*. In *Salesman*, characters walk through walls, and when they do so, they walk through years. This form enabled Miller to dramatize the way in which our society shapes and breaks the psyche. The only problem, I remind my students, is that we see only the male psyche.

The Male Locker Room

When we explore the play as Miller's requiem for an America with all the wrong dreams, it becomes clear that this flawed America is a male world, a locker room where women are voiceless, marginalized, or perplexed; they are either wives who mediate between fathers and sons or objects of male sexual exploitation. I ask my students, "What connection do you find between, on the one hand, the fact that the dislocations of Willy's private life are those of a society chasing material success and, on the other, the pervasive sexism in the play? How do you measure success? Do the guys in the class equate the number of women they date with their success? How many women here have been sexually harassed? What would Gloria Steinem say about the women in this play? Is Murphy Brown better off than Linda Loman?" We discuss Susan Faludi's *Backlash*, which challenges the belief, prevalent in some quarters, that feminism is women's worst enemy, that the very changes that have strengthened women have actually made life worse for them. Are women really enslaved by their own liberation? Have women grabbed at the gold ring of independence only to miss the one ring that really matters? Have they gained control of their fertility only to destroy it? Have they pursued their own professional dreams and lost out on the greatest female adventure? (See Faludi x.) Does Linda Loman's happiness really rest on Willy? Furthermore, I ask, "Is the Loman family the American family that conservative groups wave as a banner, or does it exemplify the family as an icon for an American ideal that is shattered beyond repair?" These questions ignite student debate.

I then link Miller's use of expressionism with the objectification of women in the play. As Willy is confiding in Linda about his insecurities and she is telling him how handsome he is, we flash back to the laughter of The Woman, which continues through Linda's lines. While Linda tells him that few men are idolized by their children the way he is, we hear music and dimly see The Woman dressing (37). Nameless, she is merely an expressionistic, objectified symbol, without identity, much like Willy's sexual relationship with her. Her laughter, her appearance in a black slip, and the music suggest that she is temptress and femme fatale (Stanton 81). Indeed, The Woman, like Miss Forsythe and Letta, the call girls in the restaurant, has no power and almost no characterization. As Gayle Austin says, the women in the restaurant are objects that can be traded, but because they are not wives, they are not totally under men's control. They can tempt sons to desert their father or cause fathers to alienate sons. Indeed, women are dangerous property (63). Moreover, when Letta says that she is to begin jury duty on the next day and Biff says that he has been in front of a jury (113–14), the scene suggests that women are judges and determiners of truth and value yet are subjugated by a patriarchal world (Stanton 73).

In the present, Willy tells Linda that she is "a pal." He says, "On the road . . . I want to grab you sometimes and just kiss the life outa you." The Woman's laughter is loud now. She has come from behind the scrim and is standing, putting on her hat, looking into a "mirror" and laughing. In the present, Willy tells Linda, "There's so much I want to make for—" and in his memory, The Woman replies, "You didn't make me, Willy. I picked you" (38). Here, rather than being object, The Woman is subject, choosing Willy rather than having been chosen. In a world where Willy feels valueless, he is flattered to have been chosen. But if The Woman fleetingly attains subject status, Linda, as betrayed wife, remains an object in this fused conversation. In the flashback, Willy slaps The Woman's bottom and gives her Linda's stockings; her laughter blends in with Linda's. As The Woman disappears into the dark, the area at the kitchen table brightens, and Linda is sitting where she was at the kitchen table, but now she is mending a pair of her stockings, the emblem of Willy's betrayal (39).

Although the Loman home seems feminized from the start—it is a "small, fragile-seeming home" that is surrounded by "a solid vault of apartment houses"—the "air of the dream" that "clings to the place" is a male dream of success (11). Willy breaks down because the values that have shaped him break: "It's who you know and the smile on your face!" "It's contacts" (86). "Be liked and you will never want" (33). He believes that appearances matter, and when they do not result in success, he is baffled: "In the greatest country in the world a young man with such—personal attractiveness, gets lost" (16). The silver athletic trophy is an important icon for the world of athleticism in the play, a world in which we never see women participate. For Willy, making the grade, being well liked, playing ball, having dates, doing whatever it takes to get ahead (Happy's lying, Biff's stealing), playing tennis "with fine people" (91), walking into the jungle and coming out rich (48), knowing what one wants and going out to get it all derive from a masculine American ethos that has instilled these values in him. His language is full of clichés: "The world is an oyster, but you don't crack it open on a mattress!"(41). "Knocked 'em cold in Providence, slaughtered 'em in Boston" (33). "We've got quite a little streak of self-reliance in our family" (81). Ben "started with the clothes on his back and ended up with diamond mines" (41). Wielding his valise and umbrella, telling Biff never to fight fair with strangers, assuring Willy that "[o]pportunity is tremendous in Alaska" (45), Willy's brother Ben personifies the male world of capitalism, imperialism, and the American myth of success.

The dominance of Ben's male point of view becomes most consequential when Willy is debating his own suicide. Ben is no longer conjured from Willy's past but becomes a force in the present, appearing after Willy is fired so that Willy can discuss his suicidal "proposition" with him. Ben initially dissuades Willy, but when Willy asks, "Does it take more guts to stand here the rest of my life ringing up a zero?" Ben tells him, ". . . twenty thousand—that *is* something one can feel with the hand." He encourages Willy to believe that there can be materialistic values even after death: "Oh, Ben . . . I see it like a diamond, shining in the dark, hard and rough, that I can pick up and touch in my hand. Not like—like an appointment!" (126). Death will allow him to make the errand into the wilderness that he never made with Ben and to retrieve the pioneering spirit of his father. Ben confirms these notions when he reappears to validate Willy's plan: "It's dark there, but full of diamonds. . . . A perfect proposition all around" (135). What would this conversation be like if Willy were talking to a sister or if he listened to Linda, who at this moment is calling him inside? When Linda says, "I think this is the only way, Willy," meaning that Biff should leave, Willy confuses it with the suicide plan: "Sure, it's the best thing" (134). Ben agrees. They all agree, but on different terms. When Linda calls, Willy's reply—"Coming!"—answers Ben rather than her. She has offered acceptance based on love. Responding to Linda's call, he tries to quiet her. "Sounds, faces, voices" swarm in on him, and then we hear the flute music (135–36). As Kay Stanton notes, Willy tries to silence the female voice one last time. Ironically, while Ben represents the American myth, he ultimately affirms that Willy cannot attain it in America but that the promised land is a dark place called death where Willy can exchange himself for cash. Death becomes both frontier and stock exchange in Willy's imagination; even it is defined by the male ethos of Wall Street.

In this 1949 play businessmen are the measure of success. Emblems of a patriarchal world fill the stage: football equipment, the boys' bedroom, the salesman. Although the flute recalls the pastoral world of Willy's father, the ruggedly self-sufficient craftsman, it also suggests a lyric, feminine quality that Willy has denied in himself. Clearly, Miller exposes the problems of postwar America when men were men.

When we enter the boys' room, moreover, we step into a locker room, where Biff and Happy, now in their thirties, discuss the women they have had. As Happy says, "About five hundred women would like to know what was said in this room." Biff reminds him of Betsy on Bushwick Avenue: "I got you in there." Happy replies, "Yeah, that was my first time—I think. Boy, there was a pig! . . . You taught me everything I know about women." In addition, when Biff explains that he is lost, that he does not know what he is "supposed to want," that the business world repulses and alienates him, he suggests this remedy: "Maybe I oughta get married" (20–23). Although women are exploited in the play, they also provide stability for lost men, and all the Loman men are lost.

The Transaction of Women

Before continuing to point out examples of the way men in the play view women, I tell students about an influential text in feminist theory, Gayle Rubin's "The Traffic in Women: Notes on the 'Political Economy' of Sex." As Austin points out, Rubin uses the theories of Marx, Lévi-Strauss, and Freud to develop a theory of how women are exchanged among men, mainly through marriage, to maintain the "sex-gender system" of a society (59). Rubin states:

> If it is women who are being transacted, then it is the men who give and take them who are linked, the woman being a conduit of a relationship rather than a partner to it. . . . If women are for men to dispose of, they are in no position to give themselves away. . . . Women are given in marriage, taken in battle, exchanged for favors, sent as tribute, traded, bought, and sold. Far from being confined to the "primitive" world, these practices seem only to become more pronounced and commercialized in more "civilized" societies. (157)

In class, one of my female students pointed out that Linda married at such a young age that she literally moved from her father's house to Willy's. We discuss the custom in weddings whereby fathers, rather than mothers, give away their daughters. Happy and Willy clearly verify this view of women as commodities. Further, in *Salesman*, not only do men betray women, but sons and fathers betray each other, using women as the means of betrayal. In the restaurant scene near the end of the play, Happy coldly leaves Willy babbling in the men's room, tells the woman he has picked up that Willy is not his father, and leaves the restaurant with her. Happy's betrayal of Willy is juxtaposed with the flashback of Willy's affair with The Woman in the Boston hotel. The Woman is laughing in her black slip as Willy buttons his shirt (116). Willy tells the teenage Biff, "[S]he's just a buyer. . . . She's nothing to me, Biff. I was lonely" (120). In a play about broken faith, women are commodities that alleviate men's pain and alienation; they are also the scapegoats for men's betrayals of one another.

The Marginalized Mother

Linda, along with Willy's mother, further exemplifies the marginalization of women in the play. Ben does not even know when their mother died. As Stanton points out, both Willy and Ben trivialize the role of mother. Ben calls her a "[f]ine specimen of a lady" and "the old girl" (46). Willy's only memory of her is of being "in Mamma's lap, sitting around a fire" as his father—"a man with a big beard"—played the flute. She is mediator between father and son without making her own music. What is her story? When Willy asks Ben to tell his sons about their father because "I want my boys to . . . know the kind of stock they spring from," it becomes clear that Willy sees only a patriarchal lineage (48).

We know a bit more about Linda, especially about what she is lacking:

> Most often jovial, she has developed an iron repression of her exceptions to Willy's behavior—she more than loves him, she admires him, as though his mercurial nature, his temper, his massive dreams and little cruelties, served her only as sharp reminders of the turbulent longings within him, longings which she shares but lacks the temperament to utter and follow to their end. (12)

Linda is there to support Willy, to participate vicariously in his dreams without being a subject in her own right, without having a vision that is distinct from his false one. As she tells Biff, "[I]f you don't have any feeling for him, then you can't have any feeling for me" (55). In her inability to actualize her longings, she lacks the stature of Miller's idea of a tragic figure, one who risks everything to gain a righteous place in the world, because she has no sense of self. Even Miller concedes this fact:

> My women characters are of necessity auxiliaries to the action, which is carried by male characters, but they both receive benefits of male mistakes and protect his mistakes in crazy ways. They are forced to do that. So, the females are victims as well.
>
> (Roudané, *Conversations* 370).

Willy is always interrupting Linda, silencing her, rendering her voiceless, against Biff's protest. I remind students that this voicelessness is a historical phenomenon, that not until 1920—after the National Woman's Party members began picketing the Capitol, chaining themselves to the White House gates, enduring imprisonment and forced feedings—did women (half the population) finally get the vote (Faludi 456). Willy calls Linda "kid," and Biff knows that Willy "always wiped the floor" with her, "[n]ever had an ounce of respect" for her (55). It is not clear, however, whether Linda knows about Willy's affair. Students tend to think that she knows about The Woman.

Nevertheless, Linda is highly sensitive to Willy's predicament, and she confronts her sons with it:

> I don't say he's a great man. Willy Loman never made a lot of money. His name was never in the paper. He's not the finest character that ever lived. But he's a human being, and a terrible thing is happening to him. So attention must be paid. He's not to be allowed to fall into his grave like an old dog. (56)

She understands that Willy is exhausted from the complexity of social factors that have dehumanized him. "He works for a company thirty-six years this March, opens up unheard-of territories to their trademark, and now in his old age they take his salary away" (56). Clearly, she is a tough and perceptive woman, but she asserts herself for Willy rather than for herself. Miller, however, does not entirely acknowledge that perception of Linda:

> Critics generally see my female characters as far more passive than they are. When I directed *Salesman* in China, I had Linda in action. She's not just sitting around. She knows from the beginning of the play that Willy is trying to kill himself. . . . My women characters are very complex. They have been played somewhat sentimentally, but that isn't the way they were intended. . . .
>
> (Roudané, *Conversations* 370)

For whom is she in action? Does she ever actualize her own needs? Can she distinguish her needs from Willy's? When Happy and Biff arrive home without Willy, Linda is outraged: "Did you have to go to women tonight? You and your lousy rotten whores!" (124). She refuses to pick up the flowers that have fallen because she refuses to be her sons' "maid." When Happy turns his back on Linda's order, refusing to acquiesce to female dominance, Biff gets on his knees and picks up the flowers. I ask my students, "Who takes charge when men betray each other?" "Women!" they answer.

Student Debate about Linda

I always take a vote in class about Linda as a character. How many students think she is a strong character? How many think she is weak? We are all a bit torn. I pull out the 1949 *New York Times* review by Brooks Atkinson of the original production and read to them: "Mildred Dunnock gives the performance of her career as the wife and mother—plain of speech but indomitable in spirit" (27:2). I ask, "Do you, with your 1990s perspective, view Linda as 'indomitable'?"

My students debate fiercely. One female student thinks women in the play are either Madonnas or whores: "Women are not portrayed as complex personalities! Without her family, Linda would have no purpose; her identity *is* her family. And then there's the other extreme—The Woman as whore. Women are either sexual or maternal in this play."

"Could you argue that without Linda there would be no family?" I ask.

A male student insists, "She's a really strong woman; she's not an Edith Bunker! Willy even tells her, 'You're my foundation and support.' If she were weak, it would be total chaos, because Willy is so far gone." Another male student exclaims, "She's totally dependent on Willy, and she feeds his illusion. It's like codependency with an alcoholic. There is nothing she can do to save him. But on important issues she runs the show. She's in charge of everything." A woman retorts, "She tries to help Willy, but there's a limit to what she can do. After all, this is the forties! Women had no power then!" A male student responds with a feminist viewpoint: "Happy says he wants somebody with character like his mother, but for him that means somebody who will cook and clean and mend. Remember, Biff says, 'They broke the mold when they made her. She's a saint for putting up with Willy.'"

They are all correct. Not only does Linda lack her own sense of identity, but she also supports Willy's illusions. As Miller says:

> Linda sustains the illusion because that's the only way Willy can be sustained. At the same time any cure or change is impossible in Willy. Ironically, she is helping to guarantee that Willy will never escape from his illusion. She has to support it; she has no alternative, given his nature and hers.   (Roudané, *Conversations* 370)

In an effort to protect Willy, Linda creates excuses about his breakdown: "Maybe it was the steering again. . . . Maybe it's your glasses. . . . you'll just have to take a rest. . . . Your mind is overactive, and the mind is what counts, dear. . . . Take an aspirin. . . . It'll soothe you" (13–14). In the end, all she can say is "He only needed a little salary. He was even finished with the dentist" (137). In contrast to my point of view on this remark, one of my students pointed out that Linda means that Willy did not need a huge salary, just a "little" salary, that Willy set his goals too high. I pointed her to Charley's reply—"No man only needs a little salary"—which implies that the human soul needs to be fed in other ways. For Linda, being "free and clear" for the first time in thirty-five years should have been reason for Willy to live. While she wants to protect her husband—"[T]ell Howard you've simply got to work in New York" (14)—she ultimately cannot prevent his suicide. When Willy is planning his suicide, they talk past each other rather than to each other. Still, the question remains, Can anyone prevent Willy's suicide? Linda cannot, but neither can Charley or Biff.

Moreover, what else could a wife in the forties tell a husband who was in Willy's predicament? I present Stanton's argument that Linda cannot understand why Willy's dreams of inflated masculinity are more important than family love, compassion, and respect (94). Linda is at once nurturer and confidante as she takes off Willy's shoes. She tells him, "You've got too much on the ball to worry about," to which Willy responds, "You're my foundation and my support" (18). In fact, she is the foundation and support of the Loman home. Her role in Willy's life embodies that of the ideal wife in postwar America, infinitely supportive of her husband. But even this kind of wife is not enough for Willy (Stanton 74). Still, in her support she demonstrates strength. Dismissing Biff's concern about his father's strange behavior, she says, "Oh, my dear, you should do a lot of things, but there's nothing to do, so go to sleep." Mending the lining of Willy's jacket, she demands to know why Biff and Willy are so hateful of each other (53–54). While she cleans and repairs, the sons rebuild through theft. In short, she cleans up the male mess on all levels. And just as Willy leaves the repair of household appliances to Linda, the boys leave the repair of their broken-down father to her. The Loman men are not able to keep account of themselves; only Linda understands what has value, what things cost, and how much must be paid to maintain and repair home life (Stanton 76). When Willy fabricates the number of sales he has made, she checks him. For her, family matters are financial ones. She tells Willy not to forget to ask for a little advance to cover the insurance premium, reminding him, "It's the grace period now" (72). In fact, Miller originally toyed with the title *A Period of Grace* for *Salesman* because of Willy's preoccupation with overdue insurance payments and his fear of being swallowed up by the system (Bigsby, *Critical Introduction* 2: 185). Linda is quick to point out that weathering a twenty-five-year mortgage is an accomplishment, and she thwarts Willy's grand aspirations to go west with Ben to make a fortune. In discussion, I raise the importance of the Lomans' social class; being middle-class in an urban Brooklyn setting has everything to do with the way this family ticks.

At the end of the Requiem we are left with a choice between Happy and Linda, as Willy had a choice between Ben and Linda. For Linda, having made the last payment on the house should sustain Willy's soul; Happy also has a limited perception of Willy's situation. He chooses to "show . . . that Willy Loman did not die in vain. He had a good dream. It's the only dream you can have—to come out number-one man. He fought it out here, and this is where I'm gonna win it for him" (138–39). But Charley, speaking as a choral voice earlier in the Requiem, has a more complex understanding. Even in the end, the play privileges the male voice as the conveyer of truth:

> Nobody dast blame this man. . . . [F]or a salesman, there is no rock bottom to the life. He don't put a bolt to a nut, he don't tell you the law or give you medicine. He's a man way out there in the blue, riding on a smile and a shoeshine. . . . A salesman is got to dream, boy. It comes with the territory. (138)

Although Charley has thrived in the American system, he has scruples and compassion; indeed, he represents a humanized, perhaps a feminized capitalism. He aches for Willy, offers him a job and money, tells him to take care of himself and pay his insurance. With the same kind of understanding, Biff has to light out for the West, a bit like Huck Finn, because he cannot bear to be eaten by the business world as Willy was. He realizes that Willy "didn't know who he was" (138). Charley and Biff articulate the facts that Willy could never acknowledge.

The Marginalization of Willy: The Empty Funeral

I also look at the Requiem in another way. Not only has the male myth caused Willy to perceive himself as an outcast in life, but Miller depicts him as such in death. In the Requiem the sacred ritual of the funeral is broken because only Willy's family, Charley, and Bernard attend. *Salesman*, then, is finally about the absence of ritual, of community, and therefore of a religious world that has no place in Miller's entirely secular dramatic world. Willy must plant his garden in the end because he feels entirely deracinated by industrial America. Ultimately, there is no audience for Willy, just as there is no voice for the women in the play. He is as marginalized as they are.

Death of a Salesman does not condone the locker-room treatment of women any more than it approves of a dehumanizing capitalism, any more than *A Streetcar Named Desire* approves of Stanley Kowalski's brash chauvinism or David Mamet's *Glengarry Glen Ross* approves of sleazy real-estate salesmen. Instead, the play asks us to question whether the dichotomized image of woman as either mother or whore is a desirable cultural value. Indeed, I believe Miller helped create the need for women's voices in the plays of such writers as Ntozake Shange, Adrienne Kennedy, Pam Gems, Marsha Norman, Caryl Churchill, and Wendy Wasserstein, plays that grapple with the complex interplay of gender, race, and class, raising women to the forefront of the American scene.

Why Willy Is Confused: The Effects Of a Paradigm Shift in *Death of a Salesman*

Paula Marantz Cohen

The conventional "social" reading of *Death of a Salesman* conceives of Willy Loman as the alienated man, conditioned to seek success within a system that transforms him into "a commodity which like other commodities will at a certain point be economically discarded" (Williams, "Realism" 75). When I used to take this approach to the play with my students, however, they angrily opposed me. Most of them were headed for careers in business, and they agreed with Happy that Willy "had a good dream" (139). At first, I saw their reaction as part of the problem: they were benighted victims of the system they defended. But in time I found myself questioning my own tendency to discard their views. Largely as a result of their resistance, I grew uncomfortable with my assumptions about the play and revised my interpretation.

My present approach is to locate *Death of a Salesman* in respect to an important transition in Western society: the transition from industrialism to postindustrialism. This approach has the advantage of focusing on the development not of capitalism but of technology (Bell), a focus that renders certain conventional ideological arguments less relevant. The transition to which I refer has been described as a move from labor and machine power to intellectual and technical power and from a linear, closed model for work and family interaction to an ecological, open network of relations in which boundaries and hierarchies break down. Although the theorists who have identified this paradigm shift are often referred to as social forecasters, their work tends to involve an extrapolation on conspicuous events and trends.[1] Miller's play, predating these social analyses by several decades, seems truly to forecast (albeit in ways that are especially telling in hindsight) the shape of the future that lay ahead—a future that has become our present. I suggest to students that part of Miller's greatness as a playwright lay in his intuitive grasp of the direction of his society's evolution.

As background for my teaching of the play, I assign students readings in Gregory Bateson's *Steps to an Ecology of Mind*, Bell's *The Coming of Post-industrial Society*, and Marshall McLuhan and Quentin Fiore's *War and Peace in the Global Village*. We discuss the fact that these theorists, different as they are, are all essentially concerned with describing an evolution in communication as it affects the functioning of Western society. This evolution takes two forms. On the one hand, it involves the development of advanced communication technology and a related shift in the content of business from industrially manufactured products to high-tech services—from things to words, as it were. On the other hand, it involves a shift in the nature of communication itself. In an industrial social context, communication was defined according to a one-way, sender-to-receiver model. An organization framed a message that it wanted to relay to its public and transmitted this message through available channels. In the postindustrial paradigm in which we presently find ourselves, communication is defined according to a two-way, symmetrical model (Grunig). An organization's public thereby ceases to be a passive, undifferentiated receptacle for its messages and becomes a collection of individuals or groups, each with particular interests and needs. According to this model, the public (the receiver) is not only taken into account through the development of public opinion and marketing studies but becomes a sender as well; consumer advocacy, investigative journalism, and government regulation serve as lobbying tools by which that public can pressure an organization to amend its policy. In short, where feedback is substantive and ongoing, the labels *sender* and *receiver* cease to be meaning-ful. What Miller's play records is a case of communication that has begun to be inadequate to a changing social context. Willy Loman is trapped by a communication model that does not allow him to recognize, much less incorporate, feedback.

In attempting to locate Willy in the history of business communication, I first ask the class to identify the aspect of his job that is most obviously outmoded. We discuss how, in the early phases of an industrial society, salemanship consists of reaching existing markets. Willy, as Linda tells her sons, opened up unheard-of territories to his company's trademark (56), just as Willy's hero, the old salesman Dave Singleman, traveled around the country by train, bringing products to customers in thirty-one states (81). This early form of salesmanship shares in the pioneering and extractive imagery of preindustrial enterprises. Willy's brother, Ben, who presumably made his fortune through either timber in Alaska or diamonds in Africa, is another role model. He exists in Willy's imagination as the pioneer entrepreneur, carrying on the legacy of their peddler father. But the increasing difficulty Willy experiences in getting to his destination and in making sales once he gets there dramatizes the end of the myth of the businessman as pioneer. Willy's father traveled by covered wagon; the old salesman Singleman by train; Willy, by automobile. By the end of the play the car, too, has been symbolically superseded. Not only has Willy been fired from his road job, but he has also, literally, ended his driving career by killing himself—doing so, it must be added, in his car.[2] Daniel Bell calls transportation "the first infra-structure in society . . . for the movement of people and goods" (xv). In Willy's exhaustion and failure, Miller symbolically represents, if not the obsolescence of that infrastructure, at least its decline in the context of an evolving economy.

Willy's bone-wearying journeys to New England are only part of what defines him as a salesman, however. His belief that success is a function of personal style is not a pioneering mentality; it serves to locate him in mid-twentieth-century America. Following World War II, people had more money to spend, productivity increased, and competition began to emerge among products. The result was a "massive growth in the apparatus of persuasion and exhortation that is associated with the sale of goods" (Galbraith 3). This was the period when the sales departments of corporations began to encompass advertising and marketing functions and when the professional PR man became a fixture at the local bar, ready to buy a reporter a drink in the hope of "placing" a story for a client (Raucher). Willy's cult of personality and his fixation on the Loman name are in keeping with the promotional spirit of this period. He is his own product. When he is "up," he boasts of being "well liked," the quality that is supposed to send him "right through" to the buyers and give him an edge over the competition; when he is "down," he complains of being fat, laughed at, and hence unable to sell as much as the next guy. As a consumer, he responds to product packaging and promotion in the same fickle, superficial way. He buys the refrigerator with the biggest ad but then, when it breaks down, derides it for its lack of reputation: "Whoever heard of a Hastings refrigerator?" (73).

His consumerism is never informed by a knowledge of the product, and his salesmanship is never informed by a knowledge of the consumer. It does not occur to him that a "receiver" might want more or different kinds of information than that which he is conditioned to provide. In teaching the play, I often ask students to critique the scene in which Willy is fired based on their own experience hunting for jobs or dealing with employers. (Almost all my students work.[3]) In trying to convince his young boss to give him an office job, Willy chooses a strategy, my students say, that is all wrong. He focuses not on what he can offer but on what he wants. Even when he invokes his history with the company and recounts a personal anecdote that directly touches on his employer's life, he never turns it into a matter for dialogue. He says not "Did your father ever tell you . . . ?" but "Your father came to me the day you were born and asked me what I thought of the name of Howard, may he rest in peace" (80). Delivered this way, the statement allows no room for a response. It is packaged sentiment and seems drawn out of that very salesman's kit that can no longer sell the buyers in New England. Willy ends up selling himself out of a job because his plea brings home to his employer, if only subliminally, the ineffectiveness of the old-style salesmanship with its reliance on one-way communication.

In discussing this scene, I ask the class to analyze the reciprocal relation that can be said to exist between an informed sales force and an informed consumer public. Although consumer rights to information and product regulation were spurred by activists like Ralph Nader, consumerism can also be understood as the result of an evolution in sales strategy—a mode of response taught to the public by business in its effort to improve or revitalize itself. After all, when the consumer has become saturated with one-way messages, whether they are the glib claims made on behalf of a product or the programmed lines that the salesman uses to sell himself, they lose their power to seem real and to move. That Willy can no longer make sales (even when he succeeds in reaching his destination) and that he cannot sell Howard on the value of giving him an office job demonstrate that the mode of salesmanship which served him in the past is, like himself, used up—that something new is required.

Significantly, it is Howard who introduces the single symbol of the new in the play. He is fiddling with his new toy—a tape recorder—when Willy broaches the possibility of an office job. Here is a device that is mechanical without being productive in any obvious sense. It doesn't make anything except noise and, when not mobilized for communication purposes, it seems a childish indulgence. Yet the machine is meaningful in a historical context. It symbolizes the beginning of a new wave of communication devices for business use. Although Howard appears unaware of any practical use for his machine, Miller provides us with a clue to such use in the figure of Bernard, the play's representative of the future. Bernard is in the field of communication: he is a litigator, and his profession is destined to play a powerful role in the coming information society and to be among the first that use the tape recorder to full advantage.

After the class has discussed Willy's problems at communicating in a business context, I ask students to relate them to the communication problems within the Loman family. How, I want to know, are the public and private spheres connected? What we discover is that they are not—or, rather, that there is only distortion and confusion as messages struggle across the boundary that separates home from work. As background for this discussion, I generally draw on the history of the nuclear family (Shorter) and discuss the Victorian notion of the family as a retreat and refuge from the industrialized workplace. We discuss how aspects of this family ideal were retained in the stereotypical American nuclear family of the 1940s and 1950s (a model of family life familiar to my students through TV reruns). Willy's family is—or tries to be—a closed system, organized according to stereotypical role assignments that enforce that closure. Yet ironically, the family, designed as a retreat from the pressures of the world outside, duplicates the one-way communication patterns of that outer world. Willy appears never to hear his wife and his sons, and they, with the possible exception of Biff, seem neither to receive nor to expect a response to their messages. By the same token, Willy fails to see how lessons he has taught at home may take shape in other contexts. In the flashback scenes, Willy thus praises Biff for his initiative in stealing a football and in taking lumber from a nearby site to rebuild the front stoop; later, when an adult Biff confesses to his father that he stole Bill Oliver's pen, Willy will not hear the confession. We see that Biff has become a thief because of the messages he received at home and that the home, which should be a source of comfort and forgiveness, is precisely the place where his confession cannot be heard.

By highlighting the one-way, uncontextualized nature of the communication within the family, Miller shows us how completely the family has failed to fulfill its presumed function as a site of moral guidance and emotional intimacy. As a class, our most extensive analysis of this failure centers on the scene in the hotel room after Biff discovers that Willy has a woman with him:

> WILLY.   She's nothing to me, Biff. I was lonely, I was terribly lonely.
> BIFF.   You—you gave her Mama's stockings! *His tears break through and he rises to go.*
> WILLY, *grabbing for Biff.*   I gave you an order!
> BIFF.   Don't touch me, you—liar!
> WILLY.   Apologize for that!
> BIFF.   You fake! You phony little fake! . . .   (120–21)

After reading this scene for the first time, many of my students will argue that Biff's reaction is thoroughly justified. It reflects his moral outrage at his father's infidelity. But such a conclusion never holds up in class discussion. Biff calls Willy a fake, but on what basis? Biff has blithely succumbed already to Willy's cavalier attitude toward related values, such as stealing and lying. To give the scene its shock value, Miller seems to be invoking the clichéd sanctity of the mother and the dramatic titillation attached to sexual promiscuity. If this shock were the whole function of Biff's discovery, it would be no revelation but a reinforcement of the kind of one-way messages that permeate Willy's world. Ultimately, the students come to see how the scene draws on a stereotyped response from Biff—and, arguably, from themselves—to expose the inadequacy of this response. Biff lashes out at his father, accusing him of being a fake, but this is the accusation of a boy who, while he now rejects the messages that he received from his father, has nothing with which to replace them. He can no longer believe in the paternal image that his father sold him all his life, but neither can he find meaning in what lies behind or escapes the image. Biff is thus just as unwilling to accept his father in a new role as a vulnerable individual, desperately in need of friendship ("I was terribly lonely"), as he is to accept his father in his old role as an authority figure ("I gave you an order!").

Of course, any discussion of the family scenes must acknowledge that these scenes contain moments of constructive, affirmative action. Students are receptive to the positive values attached to Willy's carpentry and his love of nature, but they are distressed by the compartmentalized and regressive way in which these activities exist for him. If I talk about a nostalgic, elegiac aspect to the play, about its invocation of a rugged individualism associated with cowboys and first settlers, my students are impatient. They want to connect Willy's abilities to something contemporary and useful. They want him to succeed in business just as much as he wants to succeed, but they want him to do so by exploiting his gifts rather than repressing them. "Can't he put his skills to work for him on the job?" they ask, as if the problem were simply a matter of writing a more effective résumé. I have had the challenge of facing a class that has no sympathy for Biff's final decision to go off, presumably back to the farm for twenty-eight dollars a week, and is more supportive of Happy in his insistence that Willy "had a good dream."

In dealing with such reactions, I often encourage the class to list what they consider to be the positive images in the play: Willy's family moving together across the West; Willy and his sons building the stoop together; Biff, on the farm, engaging in a collective exertion in the service of nature; Biff and Happy dreaming of a business featuring the Loman brothers, a business based literally on teamwork. Although these images are presented as either nostalgic or impractical in the context of the play, we conclude that they all reflect a sense of reciprocity between nature and human beings that need not be relegated to the past or to fantasy. Social networking and ecological awareness are hallmarks of the postindustrial society. Such a perspective leads us to a consideration of McLuhan and Fiore's argument that advanced communications technology can create a "global village"—can replicate and extend the unity, once present in a more primitive society, that was lost with the advent of industrialization. Some of my students even try to reclaim Dave Singleman to a new communications paradigm: "And old Dave, he'd go up to his room, y'understand, put on his green velvet slippers—I'll never forget—and pick up his phone and call the buyers, and without ever leaving his room, at the age of eighty-four, he made his living" (81). They argue that the image of the man on the phone, plugged into a social network, is prophetic and stands in direct opposition to the figure of Ben, the true representative of the past, who made his fortune plundering the earth's resources and whose guiding dictum is distrust rather than reciprocity: "Never fight fair with a stranger, boy" (49). Ben also believes that one can profitably trade only in material things, and so he scorns Willy's line of work: "Lay your hand on it. Where is it?" (86).

In a new information age, as Bell points out, knowledge replaces capital. Because it cannot be owned in the same way as capital, knowledge requires a far more interactive and mutually supportive business philosophy. If Willy could only have connected with those around him as he did with nature and materials in his free time, he would have emerged in 1949 as the new man rather than the worn-out, tired one whom "they don't know . . . any more" (81). But he could not do so. The communication model of his age and his self-definition, itself the product of that model, were against it. As Charley sums him up, "He's a man way out there in the blue, riding on a smile and a shoeshine" (138)—a man dissociated from any context whatsoever. Like his vision of his son, frozen forever in his glory on the football field, Willy does not acknowledge a receiver, much less listen for a response.

Thus, while the play can be said to contain the components destined to make up a new paradigm for social interaction, it does not integrate them. The majority of the play's messages are truncated or confused. They do not make the desired connection across boundaries: between work and home, father and son, personal interests and personal goals. We cannot see how relations would be adjusted were the boundaries between home and work opened up, were sex roles and hierarchical organization questioned, were new technology used to foster individual talent and social networking. Biff tries to shout across the personal and institutional boundaries that define his world, but he is not heard. But then, his own efforts to communicate may well be part of the problem. Biff fails to be heard not only because the others are deaf to him but also because his language, for all its earnestness, resembles the language of the other characters. This recognition helps us further account for Biff's insensitivity to his father in the hotel room. Like his father, Biff is limited by a communication model that does not allow for feedback. And, indeed, the same can be said of the character's creator, Arthur Miller. Eric Bentley seems to have been aware of this limitation when he referred to the play's language as "bad poetry" ("What Is Theory?" 82), and Harold Bloom also acknowledges the problem when he suggests that the play manages to be great while suffering from "indifferent or even poor writing" (*Critical Views* 1).

We look at Linda's final soliloquy ("Forgive me, dear. I can't cry" [139]) and her earlier tirade at her sons ("I don't say he's a great man" [56]), both speeches meant to evoke our sympathy and to be taken uncritically. They are initially powerful, but on rereading they lose some of that power and seem overly generalized and flat. Such an evaluation of the play's language leads inevitably to a conscious appraisal of the play as a historical artifact. It is a work that both diagnoses its time and is of its time. It shows as well as tells us the dilemma of a historical transition, when language has begun to fall short of changing social structures but has not yet broken free of the old maxims that once served it well. In assessing the play's power, we conclude that Miller's gift as a dramatist lies not in an ability to write resonant dialogue but in an ability to heighten the language of his age so as to bring into relief its inadequacy. I suggest that the tape recorder is a metaphor for the play's relation to its historical moment. It is a device that cannot register feedback, yet, as it functions in the play, it seems to parody that inability—to announce its own limitation. No communication technology could become an important tool for change until society had recognized its value and adapted the technology to a context in which it could effect change. The play appears to record a stalled moment between past and present without providing a solution for starting the motor again. But it becomes a catalyst for change when it is shown to an audience ripe to take it in. In concluding my teaching of the play, I generally discuss details of the play's first staging and reception: how its opening in 1949 produced a sensation, catapulting Miller to fame while making it impossible for him to write anything afterward to equal that early triumph. My students are always impressed by the story that Miller tells in his autobiography, *Timebends*, about how the retail magnate Bernard Gimbel, watching an early production of the play, strode to the front of the theater to announce that henceforth no employee in his company would be fired for age (191). The story is worth discussing because it is one of the most powerful, albeit one of the crudest, examples of how a play, when presented at the right moment, can produce immediate and dramatic feedback.

It is harder to discern feedback in its more long-term, less dramatic manifestations. But that is what we look for when we try to measure the distance between the picture of life represented in *Death of a Salesman* and the life we see transpiring around us today. This assessment is what I try to make my goal in teaching the play. *Death of a Salesman* is about the communicational difficulties attached to a historical moment of which it is itself a part. Miller stands in a position that allows him to see the limitations of his characters and, to some extent, beyond them. But he is also subject to the contradictions and what to contemporary readers must seem the limitations inherent in the communication model available to him. For this reason, perhaps, his play appears both more flawed and more interesting the farther away we get from it.

NOTES

[1] See Daniel Bell's discussion of social forecasting and its relation to the present in the introduction to *The Coming of Post-industrial Society*.

[2] Lois Gordon, discussing the car-road symbolism in the play, observes that for

Willy "the road, which had idealistic as well as realistic meaning for his father, has become merely a journey devoid of significance" (102). Yet for Gordon this symbolism reflects Willy's individual obsolescence rather than that of the more general system of which he is a part.

[3]At Drexel University, almost all students participate in a cooperative education program: they alternate three terms of coursework with three terms on a job. Students in my classes, therefore, tend to have had a recent experience in the business world and can give firsthand accounts of office politics.

Family and History in *Death of a Salesman*

James Hurt

When I teach *Death of a Salesman,* I generally begin by asking the students to join me in constructing on the blackboard a family tree for the Lomans. The exercise is a quick way for us to enter the lives of the Lomans and to start excavating the story behind the discourse of the actual text, that skittering alternation of memory and present action that Miller, in *Timebends,* says was suggested in part by the structure of the Brooklyn Bridge (144). We address that discursive structure later in the course, but I focus first on the lives of the Lomans and then on the America in which those lives are played out. Our family tree eventually looks something like the chart in figure 1.[1]

Once we put this simple chart on the board, I ask the students to think, first, about this family as a system; second, about history, about the dating and chronology of the events in the family history and how they illuminate the play; and, third, about the relation between the two, about the family and the United States as parallel systems and what such a conception includes and leaves out.

The Loman family history, as it is presented in the play, includes three generations. The unnamed eldest Loman was an itinerant flute maker with a wife and two sons, Ben and Willy. Ben remembers him as "a very great and a very wild-hearted man" who would take his family on long wagon trips through the Midwest and far West selling flutes and another unspecified

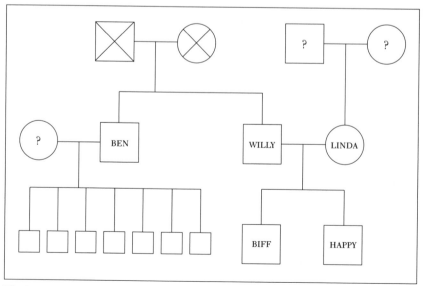

Fig. 1

"gadget" of his own invention (49). On one of these trips, the father abandoned his family in South Dakota and went to Alaska to seek his fortune in the gold fields. At the time Willy was "three years and eleven months" old. Ben also deserted the family, apparently soon after his father's decampment. Willy remembers him "walking way down some open road." Ben was going, he says, in search of his father in Alaska but instead ended up in Africa: "When I was seventeen," he says, "I walked into the jungle, and when I was twenty-one I walked out. . . . And by God I was rich" (47–48).

In Willy's narrative a period of about fifteen years is very shadowy. Most crucially, we are told nothing of his childhood from the age of "three years and eleven months," when his father and brother abandoned the family, to the age of "eighteen, nineteen," when he was "already on the road" as a salesman (80). He was presumably reared by his mother, but she is never referred to except when Willy tells Ben, during a remembered visit about twenty years before the present action, that she "died a long time ago." Ben remarks that she was a "[f]ine specimen of a lady, Mother" (46) but apparently has not had contact with her since his departure for Africa. Ben's activities through these years are also quite obscure; he married and had seven sons, lived in Africa but had business interests in Alaska, and has died in Africa two weeks or so before the present action (45–48). (None of these "facts" is certain; they are presented through Willy's mind and may include considerable fantasizing. See June Schlueter's essay in this volume.) As for the footloose flute-making father, he drops out of the record completely. "Heard anything from Father, have you?" Ben asks Willy at one point, but there is no reply (46).

The narrative, such as it is, picks up when Willy is "eighteen, nineteen." He has apparently worked in various jobs for a few years and then briefly considered following his brother to Alaska but instead went to work when he was twenty-seven for the vaguely portrayed firm at which he currently works. He is now sixty-three and has worked with the firm for thirty-six years.

Willy married Linda sometime before he was twenty-nine. Biff was born when his father was that age, and Happy when his father was thirty-one. (Biff is currently thirty-four, Happy thirty-two.) We are told nothing of Linda's background and family of origin, of her parents or siblings. The crucial year in the family history, in some ways, is the one in which Willy turned forty-six. This is the year of the Ebbets Field game, the high point of Biff's life as a football hero, followed rapidly by his discovery of his father with The Woman in Boston, his failure to complete credits for graduation, and the beginning of his long slide into failure. At the time of the present action, all four members of the family are showing signs of severe distress. Willy can no longer drive a car and carry out his duties as a salesman and has made some halfhearted attempts at suicide. Linda is desperately worried about Willy. Biff has become a compulsive thief and feels deep shame about his failure to live up to his father's expectations. His brother, Happy, is stuck in a routine job and seems to be sexually compulsive, employing seduction of his superiors' fiancées as a covert means of aggression. He also still feels rejected and ignored by his parents, whom he tries to please with repeated promises to get married.

The first point that might be made about this family history, even in this sketchy form, is how distinctly odd it is. Surely Willy, as the son of an itinerant freelance flute maker, is the exception rather than the rule among lower-middle-class Brooklyn salesman. Surely, too, he is exceptional in having a fabulously wealthy African diamond tycoon for a brother (if we are to find any substantial truth in his memories-fantasies). Such details make us question not only the accuracy of Willy's memories but also the presumed realism of the play. Here, as elsewhere in the play (in the semiallegorical names such as Loman, Singleman, even Biff and Happy, for instance), we may feel that a schematic allegory has been only partially displaced into a credible, realistic story.[2]

When we look at the Loman history with a sort of clinical literalism, even more surprising is its tissue of gaps, absences, and suppressions. The most obvious of these omissions is the lack of any information about Willy's mother. Although Willy did not see his father after the age of four and so was apparently raised by his mother, he broods obsessively about his father and never mentions his mother except to say, tersely, "She died a long time ago." (The flute music Miller stipulates for the play, written for the original production by Alex North, makes the memory of the father even more insistent.) This reticence about the mother extends to other female family members. Linda's family is never mentioned, in stark contrast to the fairly detailed account of Willy's family, and Ben's wife, mother of the seven sons, is mentioned only as the writer of a letter announcing Ben's death (45). A playwright does not take an oath to tell the whole truth, of course, and Miller is under no obligation to provide a full account of his characters' family history. But if we are to take the family seriously as a system, such absences must be noted as significant.

In addition to its oddness and its sketchiness, the Loman genogram is notable for its repetitiveness. Certain motifs crop up several times in the successive generations. The most obvious is the occurrence of two sons and no daughters in both Willy's family of origin and his own family. Biff and Happy are parallel in some ways to Ben and Willy. In both pairs, the elder son has left home on an adventurous quest while the younger son has stayed home, close to the mother. Ben is a "success," Biff a "failure," but we may suspect that Biff's kleptomania is a repetition, on a humbler scale, of his uncle's activities in the African diamond mines. Questing is also abandonment, as it is passed down from the flute maker to his oldest son and then to his grandson Biff. And if the elder sons' motif of quest is passed down from Ben to Biff, the younger sons' motif of family intimacy distorted to illicit sexuality is passed down from Willy to Happy; The Woman is the direct predecessor to Happy's conquests (which are multiple, if we take his word for it). Even the motif of working with one's hands traces out significant continuities. Willy's father was a skilled craftsman and instrument maker, Willy is "so wonderful with his hands" (138), and Biff is comfortable only with manual labor: "Men built like we are should be working out in the open" (23). Such details may be seen in terms of a "green world myth," but perhaps they should be seen first in terms of family dynamics.

Traditional readings of *Death of a Salesman* tend to be couched in heavily judgmental and moralistic terms. Willy is scrutinized for his "tragic flaw," seen as either his sexual transgression or his commitment to a flawed value system of salesmanship. Linda is judged either as a good wife, Willy's "foundation and support" (18), or as an unconscious accomplice in Willy's grandiose self-deceptions. Biff's kleptomania and grandiosity are redeemed by the self-understanding expressed in the Requiem, while Happy's shallow and compulsive competitiveness, both in bed and in business, remains unredeemed by any gained insight.

Such judgments, natural enough, are limiting. Family-systems theory may provide some welcome relief from such moralizing and perhaps correspond more closely to Miller's text and audience reaction to it in the theater. Family-systems theory, developed over the last thirty years mostly in clinical situations, takes entire families, nuclear and even extended ones, as its subject and sees individual behavior within the context of a complex web of interactions with the family system; such behavior is motivated, often misguidedly, by a desire to preserve that system.[3] In such a view, the individual Lomans' acts are not "good" or "bad" behavior but merely well-intended, if sometimes misguided, attempts to preserve the family and survive within it. Willy Loman, from this point of view, must be regarded as the central character; the notion that Biff is central, since he is the one who achieves tragic insight, must be rejected. The Loman family system is a network of adjustments to Willy's various needs. Willy, in the language of the self-help movement of the 1980s, is an adult child, doubly abandoned in childhood, by father and older brother, and left with little sense of what a "normal" family might be. His longing confession to Ben, "Dad left when I was such a baby and I never had a chance to talk to him and I still feel— kind of temporary about myself" (51), might be the self-description of many children of alcoholic, abandoning, or otherwise dysfunctional parents. Willy's decision not to follow his father and brother to Alaska but instead to stay at home and pursue salesmanship (as idealized in the figure of the surrogate father Dave Singleman) is not a simple surrender to a flawed value system but in some ways a laudable attempt to break the pattern of paternal abandonment. A fuller discussion of Willy's life history might lead the class into other adult-child behaviors: his exaggerated sense of responsibility (as opposed to his father's and brother's irresponsibility), his difficulties with intimacy (his "in-and-out" strategy of sentimentalizing and belittling Linda), and the uncertain boundaries of his self (his tendency to live through Biff).

The family-systems framework may also free us from polarized interpretations of Linda as "good wife" or "bad wife" (whether those terms are defined along 1940s or 1990s lines). Linda is a classic enabler, whose own life is absorbed by the project of caring for a dysfunctional partner. Those who point out that Linda helps maintain Willy's delusions through her constant support ("But you're doing wonderful, dear. You're making seventy to a hundred dollars a week" [37]) are surely correct. But moral condemnation is inappropriate here. Both Linda and Willy are trapped in a confined system, within which they function as well as they can. The same is true of Biff and Happy, who have become in their turn adult children, inheritors of their parents' dysfunction. "I'm like a boy," Biff says in self-condemnation (23), and Happy is equally stuck in childhood roles, trying to please his parents ("I'm getting married, Pop, don't forget it. . . . You'll see, Mom" [133–34]).

For all their seeming individual isolation and loneliness, the Lomans are an enmeshed family. None of the four members is able to balance individual needs with group needs or able to go away and come back freely and without guilt. All are frozen in rigid roles: the provider, the enabler, the family hero, and the clown (to use the language of family-systems theory). And the key to the system, what allows it to sustain itself, is secrecy. Willy and Biff's shared guilty knowledge of The Woman is perhaps the least significant, if the most conscious, of the secrets in the Loman family. Biff hides his criminal record in Kansas City behind a western fantasy, Willy hides his business failure behind an idealized fantasy of salesmanship, Linda hides her doubts about Willy's effectiveness and her denial of her own needs behind a screen of wifely supportiveness, and Happy conceals his self-doubts about being only "one of two assistants to the assistant" (131) behind the bluster of business success and sexual conquest. Such a reading of the play seems to correspond closely to Miller's own conception.

Significantly, the climax of the play comes not with an Ibsenesque revelation of the "big secret"—The Woman—but with a general exposure of family deceptions. "We never told the truth for ten minutes in this house!" cries Biff (131), and there follows an awkward but telling explosion of family secrets: Happy's failure, Biff's criminality, Willy's real status as a "hard-working drummer who landed in the ash can like all the rest of them." After Willy loses his temper at Biff, his ultimate reaction is illogical but psychologically convincing: "Isn't that—isn't that remarkable? Biff, he likes me!" (132–33). Love, as opposed to obsession, can come only with truth telling, the dismantling of the toxic family system. Unfortunately, the dismantling is incomplete: Willy commits suicide so that Biff will have the insurance money, Happy reaffirms his belief in "the only dream you can have—to come out number-one man" (139), and Linda ends the play painfully "free and clear" of the person who gave her life its derived meaning. It is hard to see how the play could conclude differently without sentimentality. But the illumination at the climax is of all the Lomans' complicity in a family system that is everybody's fault and nobody's fault.

Such a representation of an American family in 1949 performed some important cultural work. The Lomans' defenses and rationalizations are culturally determined: the romanticizing of the salesman, the myth of the good wife, the dream of the West. By locating these cultural values within the context of a dysfunctional family system, Miller performs a significant critique of those values. But the play also places the Lomans explicitly within American history. To see how it does so, we must return to the family tree and fill in some dates.

June Schlueter's meticulous chronology of the play (in her essay in this book) is the best resource here. The crucial dates are 1886, when Willy was born; 1890, when his father abandoned the family; 1913, when Willy started working for Wagner and Co.; 1915 and 1917, the birth years of Biff and Happy; 1932, when Biff played the championship game at Ebbets Field and, later that year, discovered Willy with The Woman in a Boston hotel room; and 1949, the time of the present action.

This chronology may throw some light on the allegorically colored oddness of the Loman family. We can squeeze out four generations here that seem to suggest four stages in the history of American individualism. The wandering flute-maker father seems to represent a pioneer generation of westering, and he lights out for the territory at about the time the frontier closed, in the early 1890s. Ben walked into the African jungle and walked out again, rich, four years later, apparently in the late 1890s, at the height of America's imperialist and colonialist ventures. Willy's dream of salesmanship, as idealized in the figure of Dave Singleman in about 1915, is not so much a rejection of this individualist heritage—the opposite of going to Alaska—as a transformation of it, a dream of the lone wolf ("a man way out there in the blue, riding on a smile and a shoeshine" [138]) combined, paradoxically, with affectual ties (being "well liked"). Biff and Happy act out in the 1940s the contradictory and ambivalent strains in the individualist tradition, acquisitiveness becoming compulsive theft and personal charm becoming compulsive womanizing.

Perhaps even more striking, once this chronology is foregrounded, are the gaps and suppressions in the play's representation of the period in American history it covers. Drawing on story material from 1886 to 1949, the play makes no reference to World War I (although it coincided with the start of Willy's family and career) or the depression (although surely it would have played a part in the decline of Willy's fortunes after his peak year, 1928).

World War II is referred to only twice, both times elliptically: Biff recalls leaving home "before the war" (22), and the waiter Stanley says, "I only wish during the war they'd a took me in the Army. I coulda been dead by now" (99). Biff and Happy were of prime draft age in 1941—twenty-six and twenty-four—so one wonders how they escaped service in the war.

To note that the major historical events of the time are absent from *Death of a Salesman* is not to condemn it; Miller is under no more obligation to give a full history of Willy Loman's America than he is to flesh out the Loman family tree exhaustively. But noting what Miller left out as well as what he put in helps us see the kind of play *Death of a Salesman* is. History impinges on the Loman family not so much in the form of actual events—wars and depressions—as in the form of an abstract moral conflict, represented in the powerful stage image of the salesman's old-fashioned cottage, lit by a soft blue light, surrounded and dwarfed by a "solid vault" of apartment houses, lit by "an angry glow of orange" (11). The conflict between a past of vital human relationships and a present of dehumanized greed is spelled out by Willy to Howard in a speech that, however undercut by Willy's own delusions, expresses a central theme in the play:

> In those days there was personality in it, Howard. There was respect, and comradeship, and gratitude in it. Today, it's all cut and dried, and there's no chance for bringing friendship to bear—or personality. You see what I mean? They don't know me any more.   (81)

History in *Death of a Salesman* is largely a privatized network of personal relationships rather than an interplay between the individual and public events. Willy's problem is defined, by himself and perhaps by Miller, as the callousness of his young boss Howard ("That snotnose" [97]) rather than as the lack of a reasonable pension policy and other job benefits or as the result of forces like economic recession or inflation. History in *Death of a Salesman* has some of the qualities of the Loman family, as a narrow, closed, and intensely moralistic system.

Constructing a family tree for the Lomans can provide a concrete focus for analyzing the family as well as for placing it within the framework of history. There is, of course, no guarantee that the interpretation of the family tree will follow along the lines of my suggestions here; other, richer lines of interpretation may come up and doubtless will. Also, work of this sort will not lead to a full interpretation of *Death of a Salesman*. It is, rather, a form of excavation, of uncovering the story materials and the relationships implied by the finished dramatic text. But it is a good way of focusing attention on some important issues in the play: the family and history. The exercise is good spadework for a class beginning to interpret not only the materials of the play but the play itself.

NOTES

[1] For the Loman family tree, I have used a simplified version of the "genogram" developed in Monica McGoldrick and Randy Gerson's *Genograms in Family Assessment*. Males are represented by squares, females by circles. A cross drawn through the symbol indicates that the family member is dead. McGoldrick and Gerson provide other symbols to indicate various kinds of relationships (e.g., close, alienated), which might be useful in class.

[2] In his autobiography, *Timebends*, Miller says that the name Loman was an unconscious reference to a scene in Fritz Lang's film *The Testament of Dr. Mabuse* in which a terrified man repeatedly whispers into a phone, "Lohmann? Lohmann? Lohmann?" The "heavy-handed symbolism" of "Low-man" was never intended, he says. "What the name really meant to me was a terror-stricken man calling into the void for help that will never come" (179). *Timebends* includes many passages that illuminate *Death of a Salesman*, especially Miller's account of a salesman-uncle named Manny Newman, who was one of several models for Willy Loman (121–31).

[3] See Deborah Anna Luepnitz's *The Family Interpreted: Feminist Theory in Clinical Practice* for both a survey of schools of family-systems therapy and a searching critique of them. Tony Manocchio and William Petitt, in *Families under Stress: A Psychological Interpretation*, devote an interesting chapter to the Loman family from a clinical point of view, but they use the play largely as a source of examples of such topics as work roles, expectations, differentness, and secrets.

Re-membering Willy's Past:
Introducing Postmodern Concerns
through *Death of a Salesman*

June Schlueter

Death of a Salesman has become so familiar a play to high school and college students that finding new ways to approach this watershed of American drama is a continuing challenge. As years of critical commentary have shown, the play lends itself readily to a generic approach, cued by Miller's own essay "Tragedy and the Common Man," or to a social, softly Marxist approach (how responsible is capitalist society for Willy's failure?). In a postmodern literary climate, however, the challenge is to extend critical commentary to see whether this forty-year-old canonical play can be recontextualized.

In particular, my interest in approaching *Death of a Salesman* from a postmodern perspective resides in the recurring monologue that Willy conducts with himself. By focusing on Willy's several memory scenes, I have been able to encourage students to destabilize the orthodoxies of the play and have also introduced them, in accessible terms, to the concerns of postmodernism. Those concerns entail a questioning of historicity—can we, asks Linda Hutcheon in *A Poetics of Postmodernism*, "ever *know* [the] past other than through its textualized remains?" (20)—and a challenging of essentialist assumptions about identity.

I begin by assigning students the task not only of reading the play but also of reconstructing the personal history of Willy Loman. Because Miller is generous with temporal references, both fictional and historical, students who pay close attention to the text can assemble a calendar that records events from 1873 (when Ben was born) through the present (1949, "the New York and Boston of today" [*Salesman* 10]). Moreover, they seem to enjoy doing so and, in class, are eager to compare their chronologies. Typically, they list 1890 as the year when Willy, nearly four years old, watched his father head for Alaska and his seventeen-year-old brother Ben, attempting to follow, head for Africa. They identify 1913 as the year that Willy, age twenty-seven, began working for Wagner & Co. and the year that Howard Wagner was born. Biff, who was nine when his parents bought the house in Brooklyn, left home in 1939, before the war. The students record several pieces of information about the present: Biff is thirty-four and Willy sixty-three; Ben, age seventy-six, reportedly died a few weeks earlier; and Linda, on the day of Willy's funeral, makes the final payment on their twenty-five-year home mortgage. Those who are most thoughtful will succeed in dating Willy's reveries as well: it was 1932 when Biff played football at Ebbets Field, flunked his math exam, and discovered Willy and The Woman in a Boston hotel room, 1928 when Ben reappears.

We spend the first class reviewing the chronology; students explain to one another how they arrived at particular datings. (One can date Ben's appearance to 1928, for example, by connecting Linda's comment to Ben within Willy's third reverie—"Why, old man Wagner told him just the other day that if he keeps it up he'll be a member of the firm . . ." [85]—with the scene between Willy and Howard in which Willy speaks of promises made in 1928 [82].) At this point, students see Willy as a character with a carefully constructed, recoverable past. Miller's attention to temporal detail permits them the security that accompanies the chronologically intact realistic play.

But *Death of a Salesman*, despite the dismissive tendencies of critics, is not a realistic play. Its partially transparent set of imaginary wall-lines, its shifts between the present world and the past, and its reliance on a dramatized interior monologue challenge, in both form and spirit, the conventions of realism. I speak with students about expository techniques characteristic of the realistic mode, encouraging the realization that much of the recuperation of the past that takes place in Miller's play relies on the memory scenes. How reliable, I then ask, is Willy as "narrator"? Though basic to the study of narrative, such a question invites a recontextualized reading of the play and a distinctly postmodern query: To what extent has Willy assumed authorial control of his own history, consciously or unconsciously rewriting and restaging it to suit his emotional needs?

To answer the question, we turn to the present space of the play. Here students catalog the action and dialogue of characters outside Willy's reveries. Happy, they note, who has otherwise hardly been generous with his family, recently sent Willy to Florida for a rest. Charley is quick to investigate when he hears noises next door and unusually tolerant of Willy's unjust abuse. By Jenny's account, Charley gets upset whenever Willy turns up at the office, and when she hears a voice from the elevator (Willy, recalling the Ebbets Field game), she solicits the assistance of Bernard because she "can't deal with him any more" (90). Both sons worry when they hear their father talking to himself or see him going for walks in his nightclothes, and all the characters are aware of Willy's repeated road accidents, which the insurance company claims were not accidents at all. Even the faithful Linda, who moderates Biff's assessment—"You called him crazy," she says—by characterizing her husband's condition as exhaustion, makes a desperate plea that "attention . . . be paid," for "a terrible thing is happening to him" (56).

If other characters' comments suggest that Willy is suffering mental fatigue, so does Willy's own behavior; take, for instance, two incidents occurring on the fatal Tuesday. In the first, Willy asks, then begs, Howard Wagner for a transfer to the home office. Following the unproductive interview, Willy recoils in astonishment at his own irrational behavior: "Pull myself together! What the hell did I say to him? My God, I was yelling at him! How could I!" (82). When Willy accidentally switches on the wire-recording machine, the voice of Harold's five-year-old son reciting state capitals becomes a cruel, cacophonous assault on the frightened man and a prelude to his firing. Later that day, at the Forty-eighth Street restaurant, The Woman's voice, calling for Willy to open the hotel room door in response to the knocking, mentally punctuates his dialogue with the present-day Biff, who is trying to tell his father of his failure not in math, as he did seventeen years earlier, but in his encounter with Bill Oliver. Unable to suffer either moment of truth, Willy dashes off to the washroom, where, as Biff later describes it, his sons leave him "babbling in a toilet" (124).

Even when Willy is not on the extremities of experience, however, students see that his language and behavior establish certain tendencies of mind. In the opening scene, the salesman, having just scuttled a trip to New England because he was unable to keep the car on the road, speaks of opening the windshield, confusing the Studebaker he drives in 1949 with the 1928 Chevy he once owned. Students witness the chronic strain between Willy and his elder son ("Why are you so hateful to each other?" [54]) and listen as the father speaks with disdain of Biff's indolence ("Biff is a lazy bum!" [16]), then, moments later, boasts of Biff's industry ("There's one thing about Biff—he's not lazy" [16]). They hear Willy confess that he's "tired to the death" yet refuse to consider a New York transfer: "I'm the New England man. I'm vital in New England" (13–14). And they hear Linda tell her sons that their father concealed a suicide hose behind the basement fuse box. Contradictions characterize the sixty-three-year-old Willy, who habitually collapses present and past, love and loathing, confidence and despair.

Balancing the security afforded them by the earlier discussion of chronology with the present results of character scrutiny, students are ready to look more closely at Willy's reveries. Both 1928 and 1932 were, I suggest, critical years. In 1928, Willy passed up an opportunity to work for his brother in Alaska, ensuring the subsequent financial scrimping that has characterized his declining years in sales. Four years later, his son, about to graduate from high school and enter the University of Virginia on an athletic scholarship, presented Willy with his greatest moment of pride (Biff is a football hero in a championship game) and his greatest moment of shame (Biff discovers Willy and The Woman in a Boston hotel).

When students examine the four memory trips, they learn much about Willy's insecurities and habits of mind. In the first reverie, the sixty-three-year-old, imagining himself and his family in their Brooklyn backyard seventeen years earlier, glows with paternal pride at his handsome, athletic sons. Willy's red 1928 Chevy, which had made frequent trips to New England, had eighty-two thousand miles on the odometer, but it was still in pristine condition, for Biff, under his father's supervision, had regularly simonized the car. In this idyllic domestic setting, Willy rewards his sons with a Gene Tunney punching bag, speaks of hanging a hammock between the elms, gives fatherly advice about girls and school, fantasizes about starting his own business, boasts of meeting the mayor of Providence, and warms to the thought of walking through a hotel lobby in Boston with his boys carrying his bags. In this first reverie, Willy and his sons anticipate Saturday's Ebbets Field game, in which Biff promises to break out and score a touchdown for his dad.

When Bernard intrudes to remind Biff to study for the Regents exam the following week, Willy dismisses him with "Don't be a pest, Bernard!" (33), then schools his boys on the relation between success and personality. Painting a portrait of the traveling salesman for his sons, Willy boasts of his successes: "Knocked 'em cold in Providence, slaughtered 'em in Boston" (33). The Willy of the first part of this reverie is full of himself and his boys; all is well—his sons are well liked and, like himself, will succeed on a smile.

Only when husband and wife discuss Willy's commissions and the bills does Willy admit his habit of inflation. Beginning with the boast of having done "five hundred gross in Providence and seven hundred gross in Boston" (35), Willy, coached by Linda, adjusts his commission from $212 to $70. The recital of debts brings expressions of concern from Willy about the quality of the washing machine, the roof, and the car, a doubt that settles, finally, on his own inability: "Linda, people don't seem to take to me. . . . They seem to laugh at me. . . . I don't know the reason for it, but they just pass me by. I'm not noticed" (36). This portion of the reverie establishes Linda as Willy's lifelong supporter. Candid and self-reflective, if not perspicacious, Willy catalogs his failings, only to be told by Linda, "[Y]ou're the handsomest man in the world" and then, in a pronouncement that legitimizes the earlier memory, "Few men are idolized by their children the way you are" (37).

Also crowded into this first reverie, prompted by Linda's comment about their sons and by Willy's confession of loneliness and fear, is The Woman, who is filled as well with words of support: "I picked you. . . . I think you're a wonderful man. . . . you're so sweet. And such a kidder" (38–39). Though Willy's first memory sequence is of an encounter with The Woman before Biff discovers them, Willy's guilt over the affair is already apparent: Linda's mending of stockings incenses him, for he presents The Woman with a gift of stockings each time they meet. Yet, given the need for a woman's approval (students may notice that, from the age of four, Willy was brought up, alone, by his mother), we understand why Willy, during his absences from home, has an affair.

The reverie ends with Bernard's reappearance, haunting Willy with the truth about his irresponsible elder son, who cheats, steals, is "rough with the girls" ("All the mothers are afraid of him!"), and drives without a license. "If he doesn't buckle down," Bernard warns, "he'll flunk math!" Despite the claim that this portrait of the youthful Biff makes on Willy's memory, the man defends and denies: "There's nothing the matter with him! You want him to be a worm like Bernard? He's got spirit, personality. . . ."

Alone, "wilting and staring," Willy justifies his paternal role: "I never in my life told him anything but decent things" (40–41).

Willy's first reverie, which covers three events in 1932, reveals the extent to which he is devoted to an ideal: success in business, friendship, and love comes from being well liked. He himself "can park [his] car in any street in New England, and the cops protect it like their own" (31). Willy's sons, "built like Adonises" (33) and eager to please, are sure candidates for success. But the reverie reveals as well a man assailed by the missiles of truth that threaten to shatter the veneer. As uninvited recollections enter Willy's memory, the salesman, tellingly, attempts to edit them out of the drama of his mind.

Prompted to notice Willy's revisionary impulse, students begin to question the accuracy of Willy's recuperation of the past. Was Linda really so tolerant of his low commissions, so hyperbolically supportive of her husband? Was she responsible for the buttressing of self-confidence that reactivates yet paralyzes the salesman, invidiously assuring his return to the road job and preventing his making a change? Or did Willy rewrite the extent of Linda's support to transfer blame for his self-delusion to his wife? Did Linda observe that his sons idolized him, or did Willy create a fictionalized Linda to confirm that he was loved? A look at the rhetoric of the present reveals that Willy, not Linda, is given to hyperbole. Though Linda's words are filled with affection and support, she is not in the habit of idealizing a man whose failings are all too evident. We agree that Linda's language in Willy's memory trips sounds more like a refashioning of Willy's rhetoric than an expression of her own.

Having encouraged an interrogative mode, I direct students to Willy's third reverie, which slips from Ben's 1928 visit into the Ebbets Field game that the first memory trip anticipated. I point out that Ben, who is, after all, momentarily in a time space he cannot legitimately inhabit, keeps trying to leave—and finally does. As the memory shifts to 1932, Willy is adamant in his support for Biff: "Without a penny to his name, three great universities are begging for him, and from there the sky's the limit, because it's not what you do, Ben. It's who you know and the smile on your face!" (86). Preparing to depart for the game, the family and Bernard are excited. When Charley, possibly filling in for Ben, playfully mocks Biff's achievement, Willy turns into the angry armed bodyguard, indignantly protecting not only his son's honor but the set of creaky values that have shaped the Lomans' lives.

In Willy's second memory trip, chronologically the earliest, Ben stops by on his way to Alaska, promising to reappear on his return trip. Cued by his conversation with Charley, who responded to the commotion in the Loman household attending Willy's first mental excursion, the reverie first moves uncontrollably between the past and the present, as Willy tries to juggle Charley's comments with those of his remembered brother. Indeed, both Charley and Ben speak of job opportunities, which Willy refuses. Eventually, the mental trip settles into a sustained drama in which the brothers, who have not seen one another in thirty-eight years, catch up on family affairs. Willy introduces his brother to Linda and the boys: "This is your Uncle Ben," he announces proudly, "a great man!" (48). Willy tells Ben that their mother died long ago, and Ben describes their father:

> Father was a very great and a very wild-hearted man. We would start in Boston, and he'd toss the whole family into the wagon, and then he'd drive the team right across the country. . . . And we'd stop in the towns and sell the flutes that he'd made on the way. . . . Great inventor, Father. (49)

Ben confirms the values that Willy promotes in his sons ("rugged, well liked, all-around" [49]): "William, you're being first-rate with your boys. Outstanding, manly chaps!" (52). Elated, Willy ends the reverie: "That's just the spirit I want to imbue them with! To walk into a jungle! I was right! I was right! I was right!" (52).

Knowing Willy's needs and tendencies, students are primed to question this first of two memory sessions with Ben. They think it curious that Ben's description of the father who deserted the family confirms Willy's idealized perceptions of his father and—even more curious—celebrates him as a salesman and a pioneer. They also notice that the comparison concluding Ben's description—"With one gadget he made more in a week than a man like you could make in a lifetime" [49]—is much like Willy's self-characterizations, promoting, then deprecating his own worth. As when we looked at Linda, we question whether Ben actually made such pronouncements or whether the sixty-three-year-old Willy only imagines he did. Nagged by the doubts about Biff that surfaced in his first reverie, Willy needs Ben's reassurance. Moreover, he needs to understand why he himself feels and behaves as he does. When Ben arrives, Willy, shaking his hand, exclaims, "Ben! I've been waiting for you so long!" (47). When Ben motions to leave, Willy pleads with him to stay:

> Can't you stay a few days? You're just what I need, Ben, because I— I have a fine position here, but I—well, Dad left when I was such a baby and I never had a chance to talk to him and I still feel—kind of temporary about myself. (51)

Given Willy's psychological needs, we may reasonably speculate that Ben's comments are Willy's personal wish fulfillment, a private psychoanalysis in which the misremembered Ben provides the explanations and the answers Willy desires.

Ben's reappearance en route to Africa after his "short business trip" to Alaska meets with Willy's confession that "nothing's working out. I don't know what to do" (84). Yet when he met with Howard, he spoke of 1928 as a lucrative year ("I averaged a hundred and seventy dollars a week in commissions"), claiming that Frank Wagner had come to him, "or rather, I was in the office here—it was right over this desk—and he put his hand on my shoulder." In imaginary conversation with Frank moments later, Willy again recalled the event: "Frank, Frank, don't you remember what you told me that time? How you put your hand on my shoulder, and Frank . . ." (82). Although he does not complete the narration, Linda offers an account to Ben within the reverie. Again, we wonder how much of Linda's part has been rewritten by Willy, who himself may have stubbornly refused Ben's offer of a job in the Alaskan timberland even as he refuses other, more recent offers. The remembered "promise," which may have been nothing more than an encouraging boss's careless remark, provides Willy with the occasion to defend his job as salesman: "I am building something with this firm, Ben, and if a man is building something he must be on the right track, mustn't he?" (85).

Students need take only a small step now to ask whether Ben actually appeared in 1928—or whether Willy invented the story. A look at the dialogue of the present reveals that Willy's third reverie is not the first occasion on which he has recalled the visit and the job offer. As the voice of Ben intrudes on Willy's conversation with Charley, Willy tells Charley, "For a second there you reminded me of my brother Ben." Charley clearly knows about brother Ben, for he replies, "You never heard from him again, heh? Since that time?" (45). Willy also talks with Happy about Ben's visit:

> WILLY.   . . . Why didn't I go to Alaska with my brother Ben that time! Ben! That man was a genius, that man was success incarnate! What a mistake! He begged me to go.
> HAPPY.   Well, there's no use in—
> WILLY.   You guys! There was a man started with the clothes on his back and ended up with diamond mines!
> HAPPY.   Boy, someday I'd like to know how he did it.   (41)

Has Happy met the family hero, as Willy's conversation implies, or has he merely become accustomed to the story of a missed opportunity that might never have been an opportunity at all? (Students will remember that Ben hardly begged Willy to go to Alaska.)

Increasingly comfortable with the questions, students may even ask whether Ben existed at all. He does not, for one thing, ever appear in the present. A few weeks earlier, the Lomans presumably received a letter announcing Ben's death. But might Linda have contrived the announcement, in a gesture not unlike that of Edward Albee's George, who, in *Who's Afraid of Virginia Woolf?*, kills off the couple's imaginary son in a car crash? Might Linda, aware of Willy's suicidal intent, have tried to deflate the dream that has proved sustaining but toxic to her husband? Might she have felt that the invented death of the hero brother, who never existed in the first place, was a necessary step in reclaiming her husband from the obsessions that threaten his life? Only once in the present does Linda speak of Willy's brother in verifying terms, and that is when Willy cannot recall what he has done with the diamond watch fob from Ben. She reminds him that he pawned it twelve or thirteen years earlier to pay for Biff's radio correspondence course. Yet this event, too, might be part of the fiction that her compassion has allowed. If the watch fob is the only material evidence of Ben's existence, why must its absence be explained?

The possibility that Ben is part of the mental arsenal Willy has built up in his own defense becomes particularly provocative in the play's final moments. Here Ben, a prominent presence in Willy's final mental excursion, can only be a fictive construct. For Willy's conversation with his brother about the insurance money is not a recuperative moment but a present fantasy. Though Ben is dead, Willy engages him in a dialogue on the subject of suicide, responding to Ben's endorsement of the plan by going ahead with the deed. Seeing the force of Willy's imagination, students ask whether Willy's reconstructions of the past are, in fact, no more verifiable historically than this last encounter with Ben. Were they, in short, not memories at all but constructs, designed, consciously or unconsciously, to re-present one man's meaningless life as meaningful? (At this point I like to point out that Miller calls the memory trips "imaginings" [12].)

That question asked, I then invite students to consider the imagining set in the Boston hotel room. Reserved for a position near the end of the second act, that memory trip, which culminates in Biff's impassioned accusation— "You fake! You phony little fake! You fake!" (121)—is the mental companion of the restaurant scene, in which son disillusions father; not only did Biff fail to get a loan from Oliver, but he stole his former boss's pen. When, in the recollection, Biff appears in Boston pounding on Willy's hotel room door, the salesman, concealing The Woman in the bathroom, reluctantly admits him. The father-son talk that ensues appeals to the paternal ego students have seen in the simonizing and Ebbets Field sequences; Willy is ready to intervene on Biff's behalf to salvage the failed math course. Willy's recollection of The Woman's entrance seems painfully candid and precise, as though Willy, even after seventeen years, cannot rewrite this scene.

Not only does the recollection seem uncharacteristically free of Willy's habitual attempts to reshape the past, but, as students discover, it is verifiable. Here present and past interact as Willy recalls Bernard's news that Biff has flunked math and gone off to Boston. A confirming prelude, Bernard's visit must have been related to Willy by Linda, who received the news. Moreover, this event, unlike the others, is confirmed in the present. Bernard asks Willy what happened in Boston, what caused Biff to burn his University of Virginia sneakers, to have a fistfight with his friend, and to cry. "I've often thought of how strange it was that I knew he'd given up his life," Bernard remarks (94).

Yet despite the indelibility of the Boston affair, Willy has not been successful in "reading" the event. Speaking "*confidentially, desperately,*" he tells Bernard, "There's something I don't understand about it. His life ended after that Ebbets Field game. From the age of seventeen nothing good ever happened to him" (92). Unable to reshape the memory of the Boston affair or to acknowledge its devastating effects, Willy instead blames Biff for his testy behavior and, in their final argument, repeatedly accuses his son of being spiteful. Nonetheless, with its confirmations in the present, this memory is psychologically and historically intact. Students understand that the questions they asked of the other reveries yield different but productive answers here.

I also count on this final memory trip to dispel any tendencies that students might have to dismiss Willy as a psychotic. I refer them to Miller's objection to the Stanley Kramer film:

> Fredric March was directed to play Willy as a psycho, all but completely out of control, with next to no grip on reality. . . . [A]s a psychotic, he was predictable in the extreme; more than that, the misconception melted the tension between a man and his society. . . . If he was nuts, he could hardly stand as a comment on anything.
>
> (*Timebends* 315)

I refer them as well to Molly Kazan's advice, also related in *Timebends*: she felt that Miller could strip the play of "all the scenes in the past" because they were "unnecessary in the strictest sense." The playwright defended those scenes as offering a coloration and a tonality that were necessary to the characterization of Willy and to the justification of the action of the play (334). I want students to understand that a psychotic Willy would be a reductive reading, and I want them to understand that our approach to *Death of a Salesman* has moved through the psychological to the epistemological. I point out that Willy's self-assessment ("I still feel—kind of temporary about myself" [51]), with its pun on time, contains Willy's unintended validation of our approach, which explores his memories as an inquiry into the nature and the authorization of experience and the self.

The complexities of Willy's memory trips model the epistemological questions involved in any one person's relation to the past. Whether Willy's motivation at any moment is to repudiate or to reclaim, it is clear that the impulse of his recollections is transformative. Willy's (or anyone else's) relation to the past involves a series of rereadings and misreadings; the boundaries between the discourses of history and fiction are neither manifest nor firm.

With some discussion of this insistently postmodern premise, students understand that meaning rests not in the events but, as Hutcheon puts it, *"in the systems* which make those past 'events' into present historical 'facts.' " "This is not," Hutcheon continues, in a comment germane to the Miller play, "a 'dishonest refuge from truth' but an acknowledgement of the meaning-making function of human constructs" (89).

With its structural interplay between past and present, the former represented and re-presented through the consciousness of a man with particular interpretive strategies, *Death of a Salesman* can prove an effective introduction to the concerns of postmodern literary criticism. In constructing the chronology, students see the determining nature of history; in deconstructing Willy's memories, they face questions about the historicity of knowledge, the nature of identity, the epistemological status of fictional discourse. At any stage of their literary experience, but particularly when they are freshmen, an awareness of how authors of texts—themselves included—construct meaning should serve them well.

APPENDIX I

The Chronology of *Death of a Salesman*

1873   Ben born.

1886   Willy born.

1890   Father leaves for Alaska (Ben is 17, Willy 4); Ben follows but ends up in Africa.

1894   Ben is rich.

1913   Willy (age 27) starts working for Wagner & Co.; Howard Wagner is born.

1915   Biff is born (Willy is 29).

1917   Happy is born (Willy is 31).

1924   Willy and Linda buy house in Brooklyn (Willy is 38).

1928   Ben, in his sixties [sic], stops by on his way to Alaska, meets Linda and the boys; reappears on his way back to Africa, offering Willy a job in Alaska. Willy claims to be averaging $170 per week; Frank Wagner reportedly speaks of making Willy a member of the firm.

1932   *January:* Biff plays on the All-Scholastic Championship Team of the City of New York at Ebbets Field, takes Regents exams.
June: Biff fails math, discovers Willy with The Woman in a Boston hotel room.

1932–39 Biff tries various jobs, takes radio correspondence course (1936 or 1937).

1939   Biff leaves home.

1949   Ben dies (age 76); Willy kills self (age 63); 25-year mortgage on Loman house is paid. Biff is 34, Happy 32, Howard Wagner 36.

APPENDIX II

Notes on Reconstructing the Chronology

1. Miller sets the play in "the New York and Boston of today" (10). Since *Death of a Salesman* was published in 1949, I have taken that year as the present. I considered 1948, when Miller began writing the play, finding that the dates could be adjusted by one year without violating internal consistency or historical coincidence. But, with Bernard Dukore, I settled on 1949 because Biff's year of birth would then be 1915, the same as Miller's, and his high school graduation date, like Miller's, would be 1932. (In *All My Sons* [1947], Miller made Chris Keller the same age as himself.)

The time of year is probably May. Early in the play, Willy speaks of spring flowers: "This time of year it was lilac and wisteria. And then the peonies would come out, and the daffodils" (17). Although Willy's horticultural knowledge is imperfect (daffodils are the first to bloom), he establishes the time of year as May, when lilacs and wisteria are in flower in Brooklyn. Linda confirms the likelihood that the month is May when she speaks to Biff about having written to him in February about Willy's smashing up the car (164) but having been unable to write since then because "[f]or over three months [he] had no address" (54).

2. Miller obliquely but certainly establishes 1928 as the year Ben appears. In the present world, he has Willy place the conversation with Frank Wagner concerning Willy's partnership in the firm in 1928, "the year Al Smith was nominated" (82). In Willy's reverie, Linda recalls that conversation to Ben as having taken place "just the other day": "why, old man Wagner told him just the other day that if he keeps it up he'll be a member of the firm, didn't he, Willy?" (85). The year 1928 is also the year of Willy's Chevy, which, when it appears in the simonizing scene in 1932, has accumulated eighty-two thousand miles (20). Production has proved that although the text locates Ben's visit in 1928, there is no need to preserve the distinction between these reveries and the 1932 reveries. In the 1985 Volker Schlondorff television production starring Dustin Hoffman, for example, Biff and Happy wear the same clothes when they simonize the car as they do when they meet Uncle Ben.

3. The reveries involving the Ebbets Field game, the math exam, and Biff's trip to Boston return Willy to 1932, the year of Biff's planned high school graduation. In Willy's first reverie, Biff is simonizing the car a few days before the Saturday Ebbets Field game, the week before the Regents exam (32). A 1931 *New York Times* article reveals that the high school Regents exams were administered each year in January and June, making either, initially, a plausible dating ("City Pupils"). It is unlikely, however, that Miller, who elsewhere respects historical accuracy, would have placed the championship football game in June, when Ebbets Field would have been occupied by the Brooklyn Dodgers. The *New York Times* index, disappointingly spotty in the 1930s, does not include the All-Scholastic Championship Team of the City of New York. Scanning back issues of the *Brooklyn Daily Eagle*, however, I found that such a team was acknowledged at an awards luncheon in January 1932, as it had been for six years. The article refers to Abraham and Straus's sponsorship of the luncheon, noting that it had become "an integral part of the scholastic football season." Moreover, Frank Glick, personnel director, commented, "I've seen a lot of football, and I've never seen schoolboys play it any better than they do at Ebbets

Field or Boys High Field or any of the local fields" (Parrot). While it is clear from Glick's comment that high school teams played at Ebbets Field during the football season, neither the *New York Times* nor the *Brooklyn Daily Eagle* speaks of a championship game played between the selection of the team members (c. 20 December, according to the *Brooklyn Daily Eagle*) and the awards banquet (c. 9 January). It would appear, then, that Miller elaborated on the selection of these twenty-two high school players (eleven on the first team, eleven on the second) by creating a fictional championship game. Because the team was, historically, selected in late December and honored in early January, as the culmination of the fall football season, it is reasonable to assume that Biff's game took place a week before the January, not the June, Regents exams.

Two textual references also help locate the season. Willy refers to Christmas, suggesting that the holiday is still fresh in his mind: "I didn't tell you, but Christmas time I happened to be calling on F. H. Stewarts . . ." (37). As Willy and his family head for the game, Charley jokingly asks, "Baseball in this weather?" (89), a comment that implies this event is just prior not to the June Regents exam (during baseball season) but to the January exam.

The failed math course and Biff's trip to Boston take place at the end of term, in June. (Bernard, recalling the event, is explicit about the date: "Willy, I remember, it was June, and our grades came out. And, he'd flunked math" [93].) Biff, unqualified to graduate because he has failed not the Regents exam but the math course ("Birnbaum flunked him! They won't graduate him!" [110]), begs his father to talk to his math teacher "before they close the school" (118). Bernard's story of Biff's burning his sneakers on his return from Boston ("What happened in Boston, Willy?" [94]) and Willy's plaintive comment to Bernard ("His life ended after that Ebbets Field game. From the age of seventeen nothing good ever happened to him" [92]) suggest the impact of this sequence of events: Ebbets Field, the Regents exam, Biff's final grade in the math course, the Boston hotel.

Willy's comment also confirms that Biff is seventeen at the time. If he was born in 1915, as the chronology suggests, then this memory year is 1932. (It should also be noted that at the time of the reverie Biff is too young to have a driver's license: Bernard notes, "He's driving the car without a license!" [40]. In 1932, though one could obtain a junior operator's license at age sixteen, it did not permit driving in New York City; the legal driving age in Brooklyn was eighteen.)

4. Several historical references help place events. Biff, for example, left home "before the war" (22). Miller may mean before 1939, when Germany invaded Poland, or before December 1941, when Japan bombed Pearl Harbor and the United States entered the war. When Biff returns home, he has been gone for ten years (16). Since it is unlikely that Miller would have set the play later than 1949, particularly given his opening description of the setting, I conclude that Biff left in 1939. (Of course, if the present is 1948, Biff would have left in 1938, also "before the war." Any earlier date would probably not have prompted the location of the day in relation to the war.)

Other historical references include the 1928 Chevy with eighty-two thousand miles (19); a Gene Tunney punching bag (29; Tunney was world heavyweight boxing champion from September 1926 to July 1928); Howard's purchase of a mass-marketed wire recorder (76); Jack Benny's radio show (78; Benny was on radio from 1932 to 1955); Al Smith's presidential nomination (82); Red Grange (89; Harold "Red"

Grange, a University of Illinois football star, signed with the Chicago Bears in 1925 and retired after the 1934 season); and the All-Scholastic Championship Team of the City of New York (88).

5. Several fictional references also help place events. Willy, for example, who is now sixty-three (57), was "[t]hree years and eleven months" (47) when his father left home; his brother Ben was seventeen. Ben walked into the jungle at seventeen and walked out at twenty-one, having made his fortune (48, 52). Biff was nine years old when Linda and Willy bought the house in Brooklyn; the twenty-five-year mortgage on the house is about to be paid off (73). Howard Wagner is thirty-six years old (stage direction, 76); he was born the same year Willy started working for the firm, thirty-six years earlier (56). Biff, who is thirty-four (16), "spent six or seven years after high school trying to work [himself] up" (22) before leaving home; he's been tramping around for more than (almost?) ten years now (16); it's been "almost [more than?] ten years" since he worked for Oliver (26), a year since he's visited home (55). "Biff is two years older than his brother Happy" (stage direction, 19).

6. The one chronological clue that I was unable to reconcile comes in the stage direction for Uncle Ben's entrance: "He is a stolid man, in his sixties" (44). Ben, in fact, is in his fifties in 1928. I have reluctantly concluded that, although Miller is careful in constructing the chronology, he fell prey to a mathematical error here (perhaps in deference to Biff). Willy also gets his numbers wrong when he tells Howard he's "put thirty-four years into this firm" (82). Linda is more certainly accurate in observing, "He works for a company thirty-six years this March" (56). Had Willy been at Wagner & Co. for only thirty-four years, he would not have been around to "name" Howard, who is now thirty-six ("Your father came to me the day you were born and asked me what I thought of the name of Howard" [80]). Dukore, seeking a psychological rationale for these discrepancies, suggests that Willy confuses "his time with the firm with his older son's age" (14) and "imagines seeing [Ben] . . . in his sixties—Willy's age in 1949" (15).

CODA

"Oh, God I Hate This Job"

Ruby Cohn

When Arthur Miller's book Salesman *in Beijing* was published in Britain, he signed copies of it at the National Theatre. Pleased at the line of several hundred people snaking around the theater, he wondered aloud if there were any salesmen among them. No one, however, can wonder if there are any salesmen among the main roles of United States drama. Eugene O'Neill's Hickey is "[a] hardware drummer. . . . He comes here twice a year regularly on a periodical drunk" (*Iceman* 24). Like Hickey, Arthur Miller's Willy Loman is a traveling salesman, his firm's "New England man" (14). In *Glengarry Glen Ross*, based in Chicago rather than New York, David Mamet's four real estate salesmen compete for leads to customers. Histrionic to a man—and *man* should be emphasized—the several salesmen speak in distinctive idioms.

Theodore Hickman, lovably nicknamed Hickey in *The Iceman Cometh*, is O'Neill's most complex salesman but not his first. Implied in the title *Marco Millions* is O'Neill's view of Marco Polo as a prototypical businessman, who garners millions by selling at high profit. In 1923, the year after the publication of Sinclair Lewis's *Babbitt*, which satirized the American businessman, O'Neill began his turgid drama about the happy-go-lucky Italian salesman with his typically American backslapping flair. When the play was finally staged in 1928, Marco the traveling salesman went riding for a fall, and a year later all of American business suffered a disastrous fall.

The depression and another decade passed before O'Neill reconceived the figure of the traveling salesman—in Hickey, whose ambition is at once lesser and greater than that of Marco. The only million attached to Hickey's name is one of jokes, but what he sells in *The Iceman Cometh* is a stupefying confrontation with reality—a confrontation he imposes on others, so as to avoid it himself.

Setting the play in 1912, a crucial year in O'Neill's own life, the author drew upon people he actually knew for several of the characters in *The Iceman Cometh*, but the salesman or drummer Hickey seems to have sprung fully formed from his creator's imagination. Endowed with the fullest biography in the cast, Hickey is the son of a midwestern preacher, whose profession is likened to salesmanship: ". . . my old man whooping up hell fire and scaring those Hoosier suckers into shelling out their dough . . . he sold them nothing for something" (232). Hickey is aware of his heritage: "I got my knack of sales gab from him" (81). Feeling imprisoned in home and school, Hickey was attracted by salesmen who roamed far and wide: "I knew I could kid people and sell things" (233).

Even before we see Hickey onstage, we hear about his jokes, especially the one about his wife in bed with the iceman. And we hear about his generosity, buying round after round of drinks in Harry Hope's saloon. When Hickey does finally amble in under the affectionate guidance of Rocky the bartender, his first words are those of a jovial Marco-like extrovert: "Hello, Gang!" O'Neill devotes a page of scenic directions to Hickey, not only the "salesman's winning smile" and "mannerisms of speech" but also his "business-like approach" (76–77). The winning smile is part of Hickey's businesslike approach, but the mannerisms of speech are minimal—a few words of slang, a few mild oaths like "God," "hell," and "damn," and a few verbs of salesmanship: "peddling some brand of temperance bunk" (79), "sell you a goldbrick" (81), and, most significantly, "selling my line of salvation" (147).

After we have watched Hickey fraternize with his middle-aged drinking companions, whom he addresses as "[b]oys and girls" (81), we can appreciate his careerist pride: "I'm a good salesman—so damned good the firm was glad to take me back after every drunk—and what made me good was I could size up anyone" (84). Typically, O'Neill repeats the final phrase when, late in the play, Hickey reminisces: "It was like a game, *sizing people up quick*, spotting what their pet pipe dreams were, and then kidding 'em along that line. . . . Then they liked you, they trusted you, they wanted to buy something to show their gratitude" (235; emphasis added). But the denizens of Harry Hope's saloon are mistrustful of the panacea that Hickey advocates; not unlike his father before him, Hickey whoops up the hellfire of pipe dreams, in order to sell salvation through realizing the dreams. Unlike his father, however, Hickey does not seek financial gain from his parishioners; instead, he manipulates "the only friends I've got" (225) to justify his own dark deed. His pipe dream is his love for his wife. Hickey thinks he has rejected his father's "religious bunk" (232), but his guilt unmasks him as still his father's son.

During the sixteen-odd hours covered in O'Neill's play, Hickey emerges as the titular iceman who comes to sell the habitués of Harry Hope's bar the cold hardware to precipitate their pipe dreams. Although Hickey's "sales gab" exhibits few mannerisms, his speech rhythms are distinctively nervous—questions, exclamations, self-interruptions—and at odds with the' peace he promises. After Hickey is arrested by the policeman, the anarchist Hugo enunciates, "He vas selling death to me, that crazy salesman" (249). Hugo might be predicting Miller's *Death of a Salesman*.

Not that Willy Loman would deliberately sell death to anyone, but then, neither would Hickey. As O'Neill's title prepares us for the ultimate conflation of the salesman and the iceman, Miller's title hints at Willy's playlong preoccupation with death.

O'Neill was twenty-seven years older than Miller, but in 1946 the latter's *All My Sons* won the New York Drama Critics' prize over *The Iceman Cometh* (completed in 1940). Miller records dissatisfaction with the production of *Iceman*, but he seems unaware that his next play gnawed at its core. In spite of Hickey's corrosive salesmanship, pipe dreams sustain the community in Hope's saloon, but the dream of Miller's Willy Loman destroys him. As Miller wrote in the introduction to his *Collected Plays*, "The play was begun with only one firm piece of knowledge and this was that Loman was to destroy himself" (25).

In his autobiography, *Timebends*, Miller reveals that he began and abandoned a salesman play some ten years before Willy Loman, in 1949, captured the Pulitzer prize. Miller believes Willy is based at least partially on his rug-salesman uncle, whose home of boisterous sensuality he envied, as compared with his own. Authorial diversity is merely confirmed by O'Neill's sourceless Hickey and Miller's Willy, rooted in Miller's relative.

No admiring community awaits Willy's visits. We are first introduced to his house in Brooklyn and then to a weary old man who sets his sample cases down so that he can unlock the door. Before we learn Willy's profession, we hear that he is "tired to the death" (13), the definite article nuancing the cliché that first links Willy to Miller's title. Almost at once, Willy and his wife, Linda, bemoan the rigors of his calling, and Willy's self-contradiction starts. While Linda takes off his shoes to ease his aching feet, the tired traveler boasts, "I'm vital in New England" (14).

Like O'Neill's drama, *Death of a Salesman* is set in New York City, but onstage we see different corners of the city. Harry Hope's mercifully dark saloon, with adjoining rooms cheaply rentable, contrasts with "the small, fragile-seeming [Loman] home" (11). A whiskey-nurtured community contrasts with a dissolving nuclear family. Hickey the salesman is a festive visitor to his alcoholic enclave, but Willy the salesman is a troubling fixture in his small family.

Like Hickey, Willy gradually reveals his past to us, as Miller skillfully interweaves present, past, and fantasy in the play, originally titled *The Inside of His Head*. Miller has summarized this device: "There are no flashbacks in this play but only a mobile concurrency of past and present" (Introduction 26). At first the playwright shifts from the parents' bedroom to their sons' bedroom, simultaneously visible. Before the two brothers complete their conversation, however, we are inside Willy's head as he recalls the high school athletic glory of his elder son, Biff. To both his sons Willy brags more about his popularity than about his selling prowess: "I never have to wait in line to see a buyer. 'Willy Loman is here!' That's all they have to know, and I go right through" (33). Although he assures his sons, "Knocked 'em cold in Providence, slaughtered 'em in Boston" (33), he offers excuses to Linda for the paucity of his sales on the road, where each stop is "a fine city" (31).

Even in that first excursion into Willy's past, we cannot quite separate fact from fantasy, for it is unlikely that Willy's rose-colored memory would accommodate his insecurity: "I get the feeling that I'll never sell anything again, that I won't make a living for you, or a business, a business for the boys" (38). The feeling is probably an intrusion of present reality into his disjunctive recollections.

Past and present, Willy's speech resembles Hickey's in its rhythmic questions, repetitions, and interruptions, but the phrases are shorter, the vocabulary less colorful, and the expletives more juvenile. Willy's opening words are "Oh, boy, oh, boy" (12).

Younger son of a westward-trekking flute maker, Willy can scarcely recall his parents or a stable home, but his brother, Ben, assures him (in a memory scene) that their father earned good money selling the flutes he made. Ben himself represents an American entrepreneurial past, whereas Willy is a middleman, traveling between producer and consumer. At a fixed location his son Happy follows his father's calling, and Willy deflects Biff's ambition to borrow money for a ranch. Another pipe dreamer of big money, Happy persuades Biff that the two brothers can play in exhibition sports: "Baby, we could sell sporting goods!" (63). The Loman family has grown three generations of salesmen, and Willy is the least competent of the three. Even Happy admits, "he's no hot-shot selling man" (66). Although Willy never fully faces his failure, he converts suicide into a pipe dream. If Willy failed to achieve success, he can still ensure it for Biff.

Only in act 2 are we presented with Willy's retrospective entrance into salesmanship. Hickey was restless in a small town in Indiana, so traveling provided him with escape, but Willy was seduced by a sedentary vision—of eighty-four-year-old Dave Singleman in his green velvet slippers, telephoning buyers from his hotel room. Although Willy praises Dave Singleman as one who is "remembered and loved and helped by so many different people" (81), the image is one of power through success rather than affection.

Singular Singleman inspired Willy to seek institutional success (rather than Ben's adventurous enterprises), and Willy utters Miller's title in connection with the grandiose funeral of this salesman he wishes to emulate. But the play leads to the death of another salesman, since Willy's evocation of Singleman to Howard, his employer, is punctuated by the loss of his job.

No longer a salesman, Willy indulges more freely in fantasy. It is difficult to understand why Charley, "the only friend I got" (98), considers him a salesman when all evidence contradicts it. Although we never see Willy selling, we hear of his paltry profits—present and past. Willy should have worked with his hands—gardening, carpentry, masonry—but he was lured by the American dream of rags to riches, contacts to control, personality to profit. Can we imagine Hickey ascribing failure, as Willy does, to talking too much and joking too much? Emotionally attached to his family, Willy has to spend each week on the road. By the end of the play, however, he is almost euphoric, envisioning that father and son are "gonna make it, Biff and I" (135). Willy Loman drives to his death in order to obtain insurance money for Biff, but he rejects Biff's judgment of his life: "You were never anything but a hard-working drummer who landed in the ash can like all the rest of them!" (132).

When *Death of a Salesman* was diluted to a movie in the McCarthyite 1950s, it was "all the rest of them" that frightened Columbia Pictures. As Miller tells it, the studio corraled a few professors at a business school to affirm that "Willy Loman was entirely atypical, a throwback to the past when salesmen did indeed have some hard problems. But nowadays selling was a fine profession with limitless spiritual compensations as well as financial ones" (*Timebends* 315). Miller declined to accept this trumped-up testimonial, which was intended to sell a flaccid film. It would not be the last time that Miller refused to knuckle under.

In the Requiem of the play itself, Willy's only friend, Charley, pronounces an epitaph for all salesmen: "A salesman is got to dream, boy. It comes with the territory" (138). Willy's son Biff pronounces that dream wrong, but his son Happy declares it a good dream. In the decades since the first production of *Death of a Salesman*, audiences and readers have echoed Biff's verdict, while debate has shifted to the context of Willy's failure. Would Willy be a deluded dreamer in any society, or is he an inept drummer to the rhythm of capitalism? Although the 1990s bear witness to the bankruptcy of Eastern European socialism, salesmen's dreams under capitalism are scarcely reassuring. A recent magazine advertisement proclaims: "From taxi driver to millionaire: —— did it, so can you with the Top-Producer Sales System."

Would-be top producers inhabit Mamet's *Glengarry Glen Ross*, which draws upon his experience in a real estate firm, where he functioned like John Williamson, the most despicable character of his play. O'Neill and Miller are deliberately vague about what their respective salesmen sell, but

Mamet is ironic; what estate is less "real" than Florida swamplands with names resonant of romantic Scottish highlands? Yet that is the product for sale in the Chicago firm of an invisible Mitch and Murray, where salesmen are condemned to compete with one another: The top man wins a Cadillac, the second man wins a set of steak knives, the bottom two men get fired. The competition centers on the *leads*, with each man trying desperately to get the best ones.

In contrast to O'Neill's full stage and Miller's "mobile concurrency of past and present," Mamet's drama moves economically and mercilessly to its conclusion. Act 1, set in a Chinese restaurant, drives through three duologues in swift sequence; act 2 gathers all six characters in a ransacked real estate office, but the men usually converse in pairs. We meet the first salesman, Shelley "The Machine" Levene, as he pleads with the office manager, John Williamson, for leads to customers: "Our job is to *sell*. I'm the *man* to sell" (19). Boasting about his past sales, obscenely complaining about his present lack of opportunity, Levene tries to bribe Williamson for leads, but he cannot produce the necessary cash.

Abruptly, the second scene presents another two salesmen, Moss and Aaronow, also hungry for leads but angry at the competition: "Somebody wins the Cadillac this month. P.S. Two guys get fucked. . . . Someone should stand up and strike *back*" (36–37). The strike suggested by Moss is an office theft of the leads and their sale to a competing firm. Even crime includes a sale, and Moss appoints a reluctant Aaronow as the criminal-salesman: "In or out. You tell me, you're out you take the consequences" (46).

Leaving us in suspense about the burglary, Mamet opens the third scene on the fourth salesman, Richard Roma, who is a decade younger and a century more aggressive than the others. For the only time in the three salesmen plays, we watch a professional at work on a sale, and Roma's technique is a sophisticated embellishment of Hickey's "sizing people up quick." Guessing at the loneliness of a total stranger, James Lingk, Roma enfolds him in verbiage. Spoken swiftly in the theater, Roma's "knack of sales gab" is a barely comprehensible quasi-philosophic monologue, but read slowly, it reduces to amoral relativism: "I trust myself. And if security concerns me, I do that which *today* I think will make me secure" (49). Only when the two men settle down to drink gimlets does Roma murmur to Lingk, almost parenthetically, about land in Glengarry Highlands, Florida.

In act 2 the discovery of the robbery triggers foul tempers flaming in foul words. As a detective interrogates each salesman in turn (offstage), Aaronow confesses that he is too upset to work, Roma grills Williamson about the Lingk contract, and Williamson affirms that it is safe in the bank. Out of key with the visible gloom, Levene trumpets his real estate sale to an old unlikely couple. Aaronow and Roma express grudging admiration, but Moss is sour, picking a quarrel with Roma: "You're hot, so you think you're the *ruler* of this place . . . ?!" (70). Moss leaves for "Wis*con*sin" and Aaronow for the detective's inquest, while Levene regales Roma with the tale of his sale, which is also a vindication of his way of life: "I *did* it. Like in the *old* days, Ricky. Like I was taught. . . ."

When Roma responds, "Like you taught me," Levene demurs but shifts immediately to affability: ". . . well, if I *did*, then I'm *glad* I did" (73–74). Success goes to Levene's tongue, and he blends his boasts with abuse of an increasingly taciturn Williamson. Unexpectedly, Lingk appears to reclaim his contract, and Levene, on a cue from Roma, enacts an American Express executive rushing to the airport. Working as a team, the two salesmen manage to confuse Lingk about the status of his check, but Williamson inadvertently spoils the game by assuring the client that his check has been deposited.

Mamet's hell has no fury like a conman foiled, and Williamson weathers Roma's foulmouthed diatribe in silence. When Roma is summoned by the detective, Levene takes up the relay of didactic obscenities, but he unwittingly reveals that the Lingk contract was not taken to the bank—knowledge that only the thief could have. Briefly, Levene shows bravado: "So I wasn't cut out to be a thief. I was cut out to be a salesman" (101–02). But Williamson punctures that boast, too; the check of Levene's clients is worthless.

While Williamson disappears to inform the detective that Levene is the criminal, a self-absorbed Roma offers to go into partnership with him: "We are the members of a dying breed. . . . We team up, we go out together, we split everything right down the middle" (105). Before Levene can answer, he is summoned by the detective, and in his absence Roma modifies the prospective partnership: "My stuff is mine, his stuff is ours" (107). A disconsolate Aaronow, with questions unanswered, settles into his desk chair: "Oh, god I hate this job" (108). He is the only one of the four salesmen to give vent to this feeling. He is the only one of the four who has neither lied, bribed, threatened, nor committed a crime. The two facts are not unrelated.

In rage as in pride, Mamet's salesmen speak similarly. Obscenities flow so freely that they shed their literal meaning. Euphemisms, pleonasms, elisions, and interruptions energize the speech of these salesmen. The very word *talk* is often on the tongues of the four salesmen, variously synonymous with ask, boast, chat, explain, confide, bargain, deal, reveal, deceive, comfort, teach, intend, and even act. Thematically, Mamet's *Glengarry Glen Ross* indicts American cutthroat capitalism, where the salesman's second prize is, suitably, a set of steak knives but where, paradoxically, the salesmen talk a dynamic language.

Between Hickey's "knack of sales gab," with its bonhomie and good fellowship, and the Chicago quartet's "talk," with its lethally hard edge, Willy Loman is the vulnerable middleman. Distant—very distant—descendants of the mythic Yankee peddler, these theater salesmen mark progressive disenchantment with the American dream of success. O'Neill's Hickey, still proud of his sales prowess, imposes salvation on others so as to avoid his own atonement. Mamet's salesmen, wholly absorbed by their quasi-real estate, connive in the momentum of their own damnation. Miller's Willy Loman advises his beloved son Biff, "And don't undersell yourself" (67). For all his lies, clichés, and contradictions, that is exactly what Willy does during his vivid stage life, but Miller's play prices him out of the market.

CONTRIBUTORS AND SURVEY PARTICIPANTS

The following scholars and teachers contributed essays or participated in the survey of approaches to teaching Miller's *Death of a Salesman* that preceded preparation of this book. Their assistance made this volume possible.

Thomas P. Adler, *Purdue University*
Frank R. Ardolino, *University of Hawaii, Manoa*
Jan Balakian, *Kean College*
Stephen Barker, *University of California, Irvine*
Thomas L. Berger, *St. Lawrence University*
Steven R. Centola, *Millersville University*
Paula Marantz Cohen, *Drexel University*
Ruby Cohn, *University of California, Davis*
William Demastes, *Louisiana State University, Baton Rouge*
Noel Riley Fitch, *University of Southern California*
Alexander G. Gonzalez, *State University of New York, Cortland*
Susan C. Haedicke, *University of Massachusetts, Amherst*
Dabney A. Hart, *Georgia State University*
James Hurt, *University of Illinois, Urbana*
Martin J. Jacobi, *Clemson University*
Linda Kintz, *University of Oregon*
Colby H. Kullman, *University of Mississippi*
Josephine Lee, *California State University, Northridge*
Barbara Lounsberry, *University of Northern Iowa*
Julian Mason, *University of North Carolina, Charlotte*
Michael J. Meyer, *Concordia of Wisconsin, Milwaukee*
George Newton, *University of Wisconsin, Marathon County Center*
Michael Quinn, *State University of New York, Stony Brook*
June Schlueter, *Lafayette College*
Christopher Shipley, *Maryland Institute College of Art*
Susan Harris Smith, *University of Pittsburgh*
Joe D. Thomas, *Houston, Texas*

WORKS CITED

Abbott, Anthony S. *The Vital Lie: Reality and Illusion in Modern Drama*. Tuscaloosa: U of Alabama P, 1989.

Abramovitz, Mimi. *Regulating the Lives of Women: Social Welfare Policy from Colonial Times to the Present*. Boston: South End, 1988.

Adam, Julie. *Versions of Heroism in Modern American Drama*. New York: St. Martin's, 1991.

Adams, Bert N. *The American Family: A Sociological Interpretation*. Chicago: Markham, 1971.

Adams, James Truslow. "The American Dream." *The Epic of America*. Boston: Little, 1931. 415–28.

Adler, Thomas P. *Mirror on the Stage: The Pulitzer Prize as an Approach to American Drama*. West Lafayette: Purdue UP, 1987.

Adorno, Theodor W. *The Jargon of Authenticity*. Trans. Knut Tarnowski and Frederic Will. Evanston: Northwestern UP, 1973.

Altena, I., and A. M. Aylwin. *Notes on Arthur Miller's* Death of a Salesman. London: Methuen, 1976.

Anderson, Maxwell. *The Essence of Tragedy and Other Footnotes and Papers*. Washington: Anderson, 1939.

Aristotle. *The Complete Works of Aristotle: The Revised Oxford Translation*. Vol. 1. Ed. Jonathan Barnes. Princeton: Princeton UP, 1984.

———. *The Poetics*. Trans. Ingram Bywater. New York: Modern Library, 1954.

Atkinson, Brooks. "*Death of a Salesman*, a New Drama by Arthur Miller, Has Premiere at the Morosco." *New York Times* 11 Feb. 1949: 27.

August, Eugene R. " 'Modern Men'; or, Men's Studies in the 80s." *College English* 44 (1982): 583–97.

Austin, Gayle. "The Exchange of Women and Male Homosocial Desire in Arthur Miller's *Death of a Salesman* and Lillian Hellman's *Another Part of the Forest*." Schlueter, *Feminist Rereadings* 59–66.

Barrett, Michele, and Mary McIntosh. *The Anti-social Family*. London: Verso, 1982.

Bateson, Gregory. *Steps to an Ecology of Mind: Collected Essays in Anthropology, Evolution, and Epistemology*. 1972. New York: Ballantine, 1987.

Bell, Daniel. *The Coming of Post-industrial Society: A Venture in Social Forecasting*. New York: Basic, 1973.

Bentley, Eric. *The Life of the Drama*. New York: Atheneum, 1964.

———. *The Playwright as Thinker*. 1946. New York: Harcourt, 1946.

———. *What Is Theatre?* New York: Beacon, 1956.

Berger, John. *Ways of Seeing*. London: Penguin, 1977.

Berkowitz, Gerald M. *American Drama of the Twentieth Century*. London: Longman, 1992.

Berlin, Normand. *The Secret Cause: A Discussion of Tragedy.* Amherst: U of Massachusetts P, 1981.

Bhatia, Santosh K. *Arthur Miller: Social Drama as Tragedy.* New York: Humanities; New Delhi: Arnold-Heinemann, 1985.

Bigsby, C. W. E., ed. *Arthur Miller and Company.* London: Methuen, 1990.

——, ed. *The Cambridge Companion to Arthur Miller.* Cambridge: Cambridge UP, forthcoming.

——. *Confrontation and Commitment: A Study of Contemporary American Drama, 1959–1966.* Columbia: U of Missouri P, 1968.

——. *A Critical Introduction to Twentieth-Century American Drama.* 3 vols. Cambridge: Cambridge UP, 1982–85.

——. *File on Miller.* London: Methuen, 1987.

——. *Modern American Drama, 1945–1990.* Cambridge: Cambridge UP, 1992.

Bigsby, C. W. E., and Don B. Wilmeth, gen. eds. *The Cambridge History of American Theatre and Drama.* 3 vols. Cambridge: Cambridge UP, forthcoming.

Blau, Herbert. *The Audience.* Baltimore: Johns Hopkins UP, 1990.

Bloom, Harold, ed. *Arthur Miller.* New York: Chelsea, 1987.

——, ed. *Arthur Miller's* All My Sons. New York: Chelsea, 1988.

——, ed. *Arthur Miller's* Death of a Salesman. New York: Chelsea, 1988.

——, ed. *Modern Critical Views: Arthur Miller.* New York: Chelsea, 1987.

——, ed. *Willy Loman.* New York: Chelsea, 1991.

Booth, Wayne C. *The Company We Keep: An Ethics of Fiction.* Berkeley: U of California P, 1988.

——. *The Rhetoric of Fiction.* 2nd ed. Chicago: U of Chicago P, 1983.

Bouchard, Larry D. *Tragic Method and Tragic Theology: Evil in Contemporary Drama and Religious Thought.* University Park: Pennsylvania State UP, 1989.

Bowen, Murray. *Family Therapy in Clinical Practice.* New York: Aronson, 1978.

Brater, Enoch. "Miller's Realism and *Death of a Salesman.*" Martin, *New Perspectives* 115–26.

——. *The Stages of Arthur Miller.* New York: Thames, forthcoming.

——. *Why Beckett.* New York: Thames, 1989.

Brockett, Oscar G. "Poetry as Instrument." Bryant, *Rhetoric* 15–25.

Brockett, Oscar G., and Robert R. Findley. *Century of Innovation: A History of European and American Theatre and Drama since 1870.* Englewood Cliffs: Prentice, 1973.

Broussard, Louis. *American Drama: Contemporary Allegory from Eugene O'Neill to Tennessee Williams.* Norman: U of Oklahoma P, 1962.

Brustein, Robert. "Designs for Living (Rooms)." Rev. of *The Theatre Art of Boris Aronson,* by Frank Rich and Lisa Aronson. *New Republic* 1 Feb. 1988: 27–29.

——. *Who Needs Theatre: Dramatic Opinions.* New York: Atlantic, 1987.

Bryant, Donald C. "Introduction: Uses of Rhetoric in Criticism." Bryant, *Rhetoric* 1–14.

————, ed. *Rhetoric and Poetic*. Iowa City: U of Iowa P, 1970.

Burke, Kenneth. "Literature as Equipment for Living." Burke, *Philosophy* 293–304.

————. *Permanence and Change: An Anatomy of Purpose*. 1935. Berkeley: U of California P, 1984.

————. *The Philosophy of Literary Form*. 1941. Berkeley: U of California P, 1973.

————. "The Philosophy of Literary Form." Burke, *Philosophy* 1–137.

————. *A Rhetoric of Motives*. 1950. Berkeley: U of California P, 1969.

Carnegie, Andrew. *The Empire of Business*. New York: Doubleday, 1902.

Carnegie, Dale. *How to Win Friends and Influence People*. New York: Simon, 1936.

Carpenter, Charles A. "Studies of Arthur Miller's Drama: A Selective International Bibliography, 1966–1979." Martin, *New Perspectives* 205–19.

Carson, Neil. *Arthur Miller*. New York: Grove, 1982.

Caulfield, Mina Davis. "Imperialism, the Family, and Cultures of Resistance." *Socialist Review* 20 (1974): 67–85.

Cawelti, John. "Dream or Rat Race: Success in the Twentieth Century." *Apostles of the Self-Made Man*. Chicago: U of Chicago P, 1965. 201–36.

Centola, Steven R., ed. *The Achievement of Arthur Miller: New Essays*. Dallas: Northouse, 1994.

————, ed. *Arthur Miller in Conversation*. Dallas: Northouse, 1993.

"City Pupils Lead in Regents Tests." *New York Times* 23 Feb. 1931: 14.

Clurman, Harold. *The Fervent Years: The Story of the Group Theater and the Thirties*. 1945. New York: Hill, 1957.

————. *Lies Like Truth: Theater Reviews and Essays*. New York: Macmillan, 1958.

————. "Nightlife and Daylight." *Tomorrow* May 1949: 47–50.

————, ed. *The Portable Arthur Miller*. New York: Viking, 1971.

Cohn, Ruby. *Dialogue in American Drama*. Bloomington: Indiana UP, 1971.

Commager, Henry Steele. *The American Mind*. New Haven: Yale UP, 1950.

————. "Who Is Loyal to America?" *Freedom, Loyalty, Dissent*. New York: Oxford, 1954. 135–55.

Conn, Peter. *Literature in America: An Illustrated History*. Cambridge: Cambridge UP, 1989.

Conwell, Russell H. *Acres of Diamonds*. New York: Harper, 1905.

Corbett, Edward P. J. Introduction. *Rhetorical Analyses of Literary Works*. Ed. Corbett. New York: Oxford UP, 1969.

Corrigan, Robert W., ed. *Arthur Miller: A Collection of Critical Essays*. Englewood Cliffs: Prentice, 1969.

————, ed. *The Theatre in Search of a Fix*. New York: Delacorte, 1973.

Crèvecoeur, St. Jean de. "What Is an American?" *Letters from an American Farmer*. New York: Dutton, 1962. 39–68.

de Lauretis, Teresa. *Alice Doesn't: Feminism, Semiotics, Cinema*. Bloomington: Indiana UP, 1984.

Demastes, William. *Beyond Naturalism: A New Realism in American Theatre.* Westport: Greenwood, 1988.

Derrida, Jacques. "Signature Event Context." *Margins of Philosophy.* Trans. Alan Bass. Chicago: U of Chicago P, 1982. 307–30.

Donzelot, Jacques. *The Policing of Families.* Trans. Robert Hurley. New York: Pantheon, 1979.

duBois, Page. *Centaurs and Amazons: Women and the Pre-history of the Great Chain of Being.* Ann Arbor: Michigan UP, 1982.

Dukore, Bernard F. Death of a Salesman *and* The Crucible: *Text and Performance.* Atlantic Highlands: Humanities, 1989.

Eissenstat, Martha Turnquist. "Arthur Miller: A Bibliography." *Modern Drama* 5 (1962): 93–106.

Elam, Keir. *The Semiotics of Theatre and Drama.* London: Methuen, 1980.

Else, Gerald. *Aristotle's* Poetics: *The Argument.* Cambridge: Harvard UP, 1965.

Emerson, Ralph Waldo. "Self-Reliance." *Essays and Lectures.* New York: Library Classics, 1983. 259–82.

Erikson, Erik. "Reflections on the American Identity." *Childhood and Society.* New York: Norton, 1950. 285–325.

Esslin, Martin. *The Field of Drama: How the Signs of Drama Create Meaning on Stage and Screen.* London: Methuen, 1988.

Evans, Gareth L. *The Language of Modern Drama.* London: Dent, 1977.

Evans, Richard I. *Psychology and Arthur Miller.* New York: Dutton, 1969. Repub. as *Dialogue with Arthur Miller.* New York: Praeger, 1981.

Falb, Lewis W. *American Drama in Paris, 1945–1970: A Study of Its Critical Reception.* Chapel Hill: U of North Carolina P, 1973.

Faludi, Susan. *Backlash: The Undeclared War against American Women.* New York: Crown, 1991.

Ferres, John H. *Arthur Miller: A Reference Guide.* Boston: Hall, 1979.

———, ed. *Twentieth Century Interpretations of* The Crucible. Englewood Cliffs: Prentice, 1972.

Fitzgerald, F. Scott. *The Great Gatsby.* New York: Scribner's, 1925.

Foulkes, A. P. *Literature and Propaganda.* London: Methuen, 1983.

Franklin, Benjamin. "The Way to Wealth: Preface to Poor Richard." *Poor Richard's Almanack.* New York: Library Classics, 1987. 1295–1302.

Freedman, Morris. *American Drama in Social Context.* Carbondale: Southern Illinois UP, 1971.

———. *The Moral Impulse: Modern Drama from Ibsen to the Present.* Carbondale: Southern Illinois UP, 1967.

Freud, Sigmund. *Civilization and Its Discontents.* Trans. and ed. James Strachey. New York: Norton, 1961.

Gagey, Edmond M. *Revolution in American Drama.* New York: Columbia UP, 1947.

Galbraith, John Kenneth. *The New Industrial State.* Boston: Houghton, 1967.

Gassner, John. *Form and Idea in Modern Theatre.* New York: Dryden, 1956.

Gelb, Phillip. "*Death of a Salesman*: A Symposium." *Tulane Drama Review* 2 (1958): 63–69.

Giamatti, A. Bartlett. "Baseball and the American Character." *Harper's Magazine* Oct. 1986: 27 +.

Glaspell, Susan. *Trifles: Types of Drama*. Ed. Sylvan Barnet, Morton Berman, and William Burton. New York: Harper, 1993.

Goffman, Erving. *Frame Analysis*. Cambridge: Harvard UP, 1974.

Golden, Joseph. *The Death of Tinker Bell: The American Theatre in the Twentieth Century*. Syracuse: Syracuse UP, 1967.

Goldfarb, Alvin. "Arthur Miller." Kolin 309–38.

Goode, James, ed. *The Story of* The Misfits. Indianapolis: Bobbs, 1963.

Gordon, Lois. "*Death of a Salesman*: An Appreciation." Koon 98–108.

Gottfried, Martin. *A Theater Divided: The Postwar American Stage*. Boston: Little, 1968.

Gould, Jean. *Modern American Playwrights*. New York: Dodd, 1966.

Greenfield, Thomas Allen. *Work and the Work Ethic in American Drama, 1920–1970*. Columbia: U of Missouri P, 1982.

Grunig, James E. "Organizations, Environments, and Models of Public Relations." *Public Relations Research and Education* 1 (1984): 6–29.

Hadomi, Leah. "Fantasy and Reality: Dramatic Rhythm in *Death of a Salesman*." *Modern Drama* 31.2 (1988): 157–74.

Hansberry, Lorraine. A Raisin in the Sun *and* The Sign in Sidney Brustein's Window. Ed. Robert Nemeroff. New York: NAL, 1987.

Harshbarger, Karl. *The Burning Jungle: An Analysis of Arthur Miller's* Death of a Salesman. Washington: UP of America, 1979.

Hayashi, Tetsumaro, ed. *Arthur Miller and Tennessee Williams: Research Opportunities and Dissertations Abstracts*. Jefferson: McFarland, 1983.

———. "Arthur Miller: The Dimension of His Art and a Checklist of His Published Works." *Serif* 4 (1967): 26–32.

———. *An Index to Arthur Miller Criticism*. 2nd ed. Metuchen: Scarecrow, 1976.

Hayden, Delores. *Redesigning the American Dream: The Future of Housing, Work, and Family Life*. New York: Norton, 1984.

Hayman, Ronald. *Arthur Miller*. 1970. New York: Ungar, 1972.

Hegel, G. F. W. *The Philosophy of Fine Art*. Trans., with notes, F. P. B. Osmaston. 4 vols. London: Bell, 1920.

Heilman, Robert B. *The Iceman, the Arsonist, and the Troubled Agent: Tragedy and Melodrama on the Modern Stage*. Seattle: U of Washington P, 1973.

———. *Tragedy and Melodrama: Versions of Experience*. Seattle: U of Washington P, 1968.

Hogan, Robert. *Arthur Miller*. Minneapolis: U of Minnesota P, 1964.

Horkheimer, Max. *Critique of Instrumental Reason*. New York: Seabury, 1974.

Huftel, Sheila. *Arthur Miller: The Burning Glass*. New York: Citadel; London: Allen, 1965.

Hurrell, John D., ed. *Two American Tragedies: Reviews and Criticism of* Death of a Salesman *and* A Streetcar Named Desire. New York: Scribner's, 1961.

Hutcheon, Linda. *A Poetics of Postmodernism: History, Theory, Fiction.* New York: Routledge, 1988.

Ingarden, Roman. *The Literary Work of Art: An Investigation on the Borderline of Ontology, Logic, and Theory of Literature.* Trans. George G. Grabowicz. Evanston: Northwestern UP, 1973.

Jackson, Esther Merle. "*Death of a Salesman*: Tragic Myth in the Modern Theatre." Bloom, *Modern Critical Views* 27–38.

Jensen, George H. *Arthur Miller: A Bibliographical Checklist.* Columbia: Faust, 1976.

Kallen, Horace M. *Individualism: An American Way of Life.* New York: Liveright, 1933.

Kaufmann, Walter. *Tragedy and Philosophy.* Garden City: Doubleday, 1968.

Kazan, Elia. *A Life.* New York: Knopf, 1988.

King, Bruce, ed. *Contemporary American Theatre.* New York: St. Martin's, 1991.

Kolin, Philip C., ed. *American Playwrights since 1945: A Guide to Scholarship, Criticism and Performance.* Westport: Greenwood, 1989.

Koon, Helene Wickham, ed. *Twentieth Century Interpretations of* Death of a Salesman: *A Collection of Critical Essays.* Englewood Cliffs: Prentice, 1983.

Krieger, Murray. *The Tragic Vision: The Confrontation of Extremity.* Baltimore: Johns Hopkins UP, 1973.

Lacan, Jacques. *The Language of the Self: The Function of Language in Psychoanalysis.* Trans. and ed. Anthony Wilden. Baltimore: Johns Hopkins UP, 1968.

Lasch, Christopher. *The Culture of Narcissism.* New York: Norton, 1979.

———. *Haven in a Heartless World: The Family Besieged.* New York: Norton, 1977.

Leaska, Mitchell A. *The Voice of Tragedy.* New York: Speller, 1963.

Leech, Clifford. *Tragedy.* London: Methuen, 1969.

Lentricchia, Frank. *Criticism and Social Change.* Chicago: U of Chicago P, 1983.

Lewis, Allan. *American Plays and Playwrights of the Contemporary Theatre.* Rev. ed. New York: Crown, 1970.

———. *The Contemporary Theatre: The Significant Playwrights of Our Time.* New York: Crown, 1962.

Luepnitz, Deborah Anna. *The Family Interpreted: Feminist Theory in Clinical Practice.* New York: Basic, 1988.

Lukács, Georg. *The Theory of the Novel.* Trans. Anna Bostock. Cambridge: MIT, 1978.

Lumley, Frederick. *New Trends in Twentieth-Century Drama.* Liverpool: Tinling 1972.

Lyotard, Jean-François. *The Postmodern Condition: A Report on Knowledge.* Paris: Minuit, 1979.

Mailer, Norman. "The White Negro." *Advertisements for Myself.* New York: Putnam, 1959. 311–46.

Mamet, David. *Glengarry Glen Ross*. New York: Grove, 1984.

Mander, John. *The Writer and Commitment*. London: Secker; Philadelphia: DuFour, 1962.

Manocchio, Tony, and William Petitt. "The Loman Family." *Families under Stress: A Psychological Interpretation*. Boston: Routledge, 1975. 129–68.

Manske, Dwain E. "A Study of the Changing Family Role in the Early Published and Unpublished Works of Arthur Miller, to Which Is Appended a Catalogue of the Arthur Miller Collection at the University of Texas at Austin." Diss. U of Texas, Austin, 1970.

Martin, Robert A., ed. *Arthur Miller: New Perspectives*. Englewood Cliffs: Prentice, 1982.

———. "Bibliography of Works (1936–1977) by Arthur Miller." Miller, *Theatre Essays* 379–92.

———, ed. Death of a Salesman: *The End of the American Dream*. New York: Twayne, forthcoming.

Martine, James J., ed. *Critical Essays on Arthur Miller*. Boston: Hall, 1979.

McGoldrick, Monica, and Randy Gerson. *Genograms in Family Assessment*. New York: Norton, 1985.

McLuhan, Marshall, and Quentin Fiore. *War and Peace in the Global Village*. New York: McGraw, 1968.

Milhous, Judith, and Robert D. Hume. *Producible Interpretation: Eight English Plays, 1675–1707*. Carbondale: Southern Illinois UP, 1985.

Meserve, Walter J., ed. *The Merrill Studies in* Death of a Salesman. Columbus: Merrill, 1972.

Mielziner, Jo. *Designing for the Theatre: A Memoir and a Portfolio*. New York: Bramhall, 1965.

Miller, Arthur. *Arthur Miller's Collected Plays*. Vol. 1. New York: Viking, 1957. Vol. 2. New York: Viking; London: Secker, 1981.

———. *Broken Glass*. New York: Penguin, 1994.

———. *Death of a Salesman*. 1949. New York: Viking Penguin, 1976.

———. *Everybody Wins*. New York: Grove, 1990.

———. "The Family in Modern Drama." *Modern Drama: Essays in Criticism*. Ed. Travis Bogard and William I. Oliver. New York: Oxford UP, 1965. 219–33.

———. Introduction. *Arthur Miller's Collected Plays* 1: 3–55.

———. *The Last Yankee*. New York: Penguin, 1994.

———. *The Ride Down Mt. Morgan*. New York: Penguin, 1991.

———. Salesman *in Beijing*. Photographs Inge Morath. New York: Viking, 1984.

———. *The Theater Essays of Arthur Miller*. Ed. Robert A. Martin. 1978. London: Secker, 1979.

———. *Timebends: A Life*. New York: Grove, 1987.

———. "Tragedy and the Common Man." *Miller, Theater Essays* 3–7. Weales, Salesman: *Text and Criticism* 143–47.

Moss, Leonard. *Arthur Miller*. 1967. Rev. ed. New York: Twayne, 1980.

Mottram, Eric. "Arthur Miller: The Development of a Political Dramatist in America." Corrigan, *Critical Essays* 23–57.

Murphy, Brenda. *American Realism and American Drama, 1880–1940.* Cambridge: Cambridge UP, 1987.

Murray, Edward. *Arthur Miller: Dramatist.* New York: Ungar, 1967.

———. *The Cinematic Imagination: Writers and the Motion Pictures.* New York: Ungar, 1972.

Nehamas, Alexander. *Nietzsche: Life as Literature.* Cambridge: Harvard UP, 1985.

Nelson, Benjamin. *Arthur Miller: Portrait of a Playwright.* London: Owen; New York: McKay, 1970.

Nelson, Richard. *The Return of Pinocchio. An American Comedy and Other Plays.* New York: Performing Arts, 1986. 73–101.

Nietzsche, Friedrich. *The Birth of Tragedy. Basic Writings of Nietzsche.* Trans. and ed. Walter Kaufmann. New York: Modern Library, 1968. 3–144.

———. *Human, All Too Human.* Trans. Marion Faber. Lincoln: U of Nebraska P, 1984.

———. "On Truth and Lies in a Nonmoral Sense." *Philosophy and Truth: Selections from the Notebooks of the Early 1870's.* Trans. Daniel Breazeale. Atlantic Heights: Humanities, 1979. 79–97.

———. *Thus Spoke Zarathustra.* Trans. and ed. Walter Kaufmann. New York: Viking, 1966.

———. *The Will to Power.* Trans. Walter Kaufmann. New York: Vintage, 1968.

Noonan, Peggy. *What I Saw at the Revolution: A Political Life in the Reagan Era.* New York: Random, 1990.

Olson, Elder. *Tragedy and the Theory of Drama.* Detroit: Wayne State UP, 1966.

O'Neill, Eugene. *The Emperor Jones, Anna Christie, The Hairy Ape.* New York: Vintage, 1972.

———. *The Iceman Cometh.* New York: Random, 1946.

———. *Marco Millions. Eugene O'Neill: Complete Plays, 1920–1931.* Ed. Travis Bogard. New York: Library of America, 1988. 385–467.

Orr, John. *Tragic Drama and Modern Society: Studies and Literary Theory of Drama from 1870 to the Present.* Totowa: Barnes, 1981.

Overland, Orm. "The Action and Its Significance: Arthur Miller's Struggle with Dramatic Form." *Modern Drama* 18.1 (1975): 1–14.

Panikkar, N. Bhaskara. *Individual Morality and Social Happiness in Arthur Miller.* New Delhi: Milind, 1982; Atlantic Highlands: Humanities, 1982.

Parker, Dorothy, ed. *Essays on Modern American Drama: Williams, Miller, Albee, and Shepard.* Toronto: U of Toronto P, 1987.

Parker, Richard. "America the Beautiful." *The Myth of the Middle Class.* New York: Harper, 1974. 3–17.

Parrot, Harold F. "Rate Sportsmanship First in Eagle Teams at A & S's Luncheon." *Brooklyn Daily Eagle* 10 Jan. 1932: 4C.

Partridge, C. J. *Arthur Miller.* 1970. New York: Ungar, 1972.

Plato. *The Republic*. Trans. B. Jowett. New York: Dial, 1936.

Porter, Thomas E. *Myth and Modern American Drama*. Detroit: Wayne State UP, 1969.

Prince, Gerald. "Introduction to the Study of the Narratee." *Reader-Response Criticism from Formalism to Post-structuralism*. Ed. Jane P. Tompkins. Baltimore: Johns Hopkins UP, 1980. 7–25.

Rahv, Philip. *Literature and the Sixth Sense*. Boston: Houghton, 1969.

Raphael, D. D. *The Paradox of Tragedy*. Bloomington: Indiana UP, 1961.

Raucher, Alan R. *Public Relations and Business, 1900–1929*. Baltimore: Johns Hopkins UP, 1968.

Riesman, David. *Individualism Reconsidered, and Other Essays*. Glencoe: Free, 1954.

Riesman, David, with Reuel Denney and Nathan Glazer. *The Lonely Crowd: A Study of the Changing American Character*. New Haven: Yale UP, 1950.

Ritzdorf, Marsha. "Challenging the Exclusionary Impact of Family Definitions in American Municipal Zoning Ordinances." *Journal of Urban Affairs* 7.1 (1985): 15–25.

Rose, Stephen J. *The American Profile Poster*. New York: Pantheon, 1986.

Roudané, Matthew C., ed. *American Dramatists: Contemporary Authors Bibliographical Series*. Vol. 3. Detroit: Gale, 1989.

———. *Conversations with Arthur Miller*. Jackson: UP of Mississippi, 1987.

———, ed. *Public Issues, Private Tensions: Contemporary American Drama*. New York: AMS, 1993.

Rubin, Gayle. "The Traffic in Women: Notes on the 'Political Economy' of Sex." *Toward an Anthropology of Women*. Ed. Rayna R. Reiter. New York: Monthly Review, 1975. 157–210.

Sartre, Jean-Paul. *Being and Nothingness: An Essay on Phenomenological Ontology*. Trans. Hazel E. Barnes. New York: Philosophical Library, 1956.

Savran, David. *Communists, Cowboys, and Queers: The Politics of Masculinity in the Work of Arthur Miller and Tennessee Williams*. Minneapolis: U of Minnesota P, 1992.

Scanlan, Tom. *Family, Drama, and American Dreams*. Westport: Greenwood, 1978.

Schlueter, June. "Arthur Miller." Roudané, *American Dramatists* 189–270.

———, ed. *Feminist Rereadings of Modern American Drama*. Rutherford: Fairleigh Dickinson UP, 1989.

Schlueter, June, and James K. Flanagan. *Arthur Miller*. New York: Ungar, 1987.

Schopenhauer, Arthur. *The World as Will and Representation*. Trans. E. F. J. Payne. 2 vols. New York: Dover, 1966.

Schroeder, Patricia R. *The Presence of the Past in Modern American Drama*. Rutherford: Fairleigh Dickinson UP, 1989.

Schumach, Murray. "Arthur Miller Grew in Brooklyn." Roudané, *Conversations* 6–9.

Seivers, David W. *Freud on Broadway: A History of Psychoanalysis and the American Drama*. New York: Hermitage, 1955.

Sewall, Richard B. *The Vision of Tragedy*. Rev. ed. New York: Paragon, 1990.

Sharpe, Robert B. *Irony in the Drama: An Essay on Impersonation, Shock, and Catharsis*. 1959. Chapel Hill: U of North Carolina P, 1967.

Shorter, Edward. *The Making of the Modern Family*. New York: Basic, 1975.

Silverman, Kaja. *The Subject of Semiotics*. New York: Oxford UP, 1983.

Sophocles. *The Women of Trachis*. Trans. Michael Jameson. *The Complete Greek Tragedies*. Vol. 2. Cambridge: Harvard UP, 1978.

Stanton, Kay. "Women and the American Dream of *Death of a Salesman*." Schlueter, *Feminist Rereadings* 67–102.

Steiner, George. *The Death of Tragedy*. New York: Hill, 1961.

Strindberg, August. *A Dream Play and Four Chamber Plays*. Trans. and introd. Walter Johnson. Seattle: U of Washington P, 1973.

Styan, John L. *Modern Drama in Theory and Practice*. Vol. 1. *Realism and Naturalism*. Vol. 2. *Symbolism, Surrealism, and the Absurd*. Vol. 3. *Expressionism and Epic Theatre*. London: Cambridge UP, 1981.

Thom, Gary. *The Human Nature of Discontent: Alienation, Anomie, Ambivalence*. Totowa: Rowman, 1983.

Tompkins, Jane. " 'Indians': Textualism, Morality, and the Problem of History." *Critical Inquiry* 13 (1986): 101–19.

Ungar, Harriet. "The Writings of and about Arthur Miller: A Checklist, 1936–77." *Bulletin of the New York Public Library* 74 (1970): 107–34.

Vernant, Jean-Pierre. *The Origins of Greek Thought*. Ithaca: Cornell UP, 1982.

Vogel, Dan. *The Three Masks of American Tragedy*. Baton Rouge: Louisiana State UP, 1974.

von Szeliski, John. *Tragedy and Fear: Why Modern Tragic Drama Fails*. Chapel Hill: U of North Carolina P, 1971.

Walden, Daniel. "Miller's Roots and His Moral Dilemma; or, Continuity from Brooklyn to *Salesman*." Martine, *Critical Essays* 189–96.

Weales, Gerald, ed. *Arthur Miller: Death of a Salesman: Text and Criticism*. Viking Critical Library Series, 1967; Harmondsworth, Eng.: Penguin, 1977.

———, ed. The Crucible: *Text and Criticism*. 1971. Harmondsworth, Eng.: Penguin, 1977.

———. *The Jumping-Off Place: American Drama in the 1960s*. New York: Macmillan; London: Macmillan, 1969.

Weber, Max. *The Protestant Ethic and the Spirit of Capitalism*. Trans. Talcott Parsons. New York: Scribner's, 1958.

Welland, Dennis. *Arthur Miller*. Edinburgh: Oliver; New York: Grove, 1961.

———. *Miller: A Study of His Plays*. London: Methuen, 1979.

———. *Miller: The Playwright*. London: Methuen, 1983.

Wellwarth, George. *Modern Drama and the Death of God*. Madison: U of Wisconsin P, 1986.

White, Sidney H. *Guide to Arthur Miller*. Columbus: Merrill, 1970.

Wilden, Anthony. "Lacan and the Discourse of the Other." Lacan, *Language of the Self* 157–312.

Williams, Raymond. *Drama from Ibsen to Brecht.* New York: Oxford UP, 1953.

———. *Modern Tragedy.* Stanford: Stanford UP; London: Chatto, 1966.

———. "The Realism of Arthur Miller." *Arthur Miller: A Collection of Critical Essays.* Ed. Robert W. Corrigan. Englewood Cliffs: Prentice, 1969. 69–80.

Williams, Tennessee. *The Glass Menagerie.* New York: New Directions, 1945.

Wilson, Robert Neal. *The Writer as Social Seer.* Chapel Hill: U of North Carolina P, 1979.

Winkler, John. "The Ephebes' Song: *Tragoidia* and the *Polis.*" *Representations* 11 (1985): 26–62.

Wylie, Philip. "Common Women." *Generation of Vipers.* New York: Farrar, 1942. 184–204.

Zeitlin, Froma. "Playing the Other: Theater, Theatricality, and the Feminine in Greek Drama." *Representations* 11 (1985): 63–94.

Audiovisual Aids

Arthur Miller Speaking on and Reading from The Crucible *[and]* Death of a Salesman. Recording. Spoken Arts 704, 1956.

Death of a Salesman. Film. Dir. Stanley Kramer. With Fredric March and Mildred Dunnock. 1951. 16 mm, 115 min., b & w. Distr. rental agencies throughout the U.S.

Death of a Salesman. Made-for-television production. Dir. Volker Schlondorff. With Dustin Hoffman, Colleen Dewhurst, John Malkovich, Charles Dunning, and Stephen Lang. 1985. Distr. Lorimar Home Video.

Death of a Salesman. Recording. Dir. Elia Kazan. With Thomas Mitchell, Mildred Dunnock, Arthur Kennedy et al. [1950]. Decca DXA-102 (DL 9006-DL 9007), 1950.

Death of a Salesman. Recording. Dir. Ulu Grosbard. With Lee J. Cobb and Mildred Dunnock. Caedmon TRS 310, 1966.

The Life and Times of Rosie the Riveter. Videocassette. Prod. and dir. Connie Fields. 1987. Distr. Direct Cinema.

Private Conversations on the Set of Death of a Salesman. Videotape. Dir. Christian Blackwood. 1986. 82 min., color. Distr. Karl-Lorimar Home Video, Castle Hill Prods. Offers a unique perspective of the 1985 Schlondorff revival and reveals the complexity of moving from text to context, from script to spectacle.

INDEX

Modern Language Association of America
Approaches to Teaching World Literature
Joseph Gibaldi, series editor

Medieval English Drama. Ed. Richard K. Emmerson. 1990.

Melville's Moby-Dick. Ed. Martin Bickman. 1985.

Metaphysical Poets. Ed. Sidney Gottlieb. 1990.

Miller's Death of a Salesman. Ed. Matthew C. Roudané. 1995.

Milton's Paradise Lost. Ed. Galbraith M. Crump. 1986.

Molière's Tartuffe *and Other Plays*. Ed. James F. Gaines and
    Michael S. Koppisch. 1995.

Momaday's The Way to Rainy Mountain. Ed. Kenneth M. Roemer. 1988.

Montaigne's Essays. Ed. Patrick Henry. 1994.

Novels of Toni Morrison. Ed. Nellie Y. McKay and Kathryn Earle. 1997.

Murasaki Shikibu's The Tale of Genji. Ed. Edward Kamens. 1993.

Pope's Poetry. Ed. Wallace Jackson and R. Paul Yoder. 1993.

Shakespeare's King Lear. Ed. Robert H. Ray. 1986.

Shakespeare's The Tempest *and Other Late Romances*. Ed. Maurice Hunt. 1992.

Shelley's Frankenstein. Ed. Stephen C. Behrendt. 1990.

Shelley's Poetry. Ed. Spencer Hall. 1990.

Sir Gawain and the Green Knight. Ed. Miriam Youngerman Miller and
    Jane Chance. 1986.

Spenser's Faerie Queene. Ed. David Lee Miller and Alexander Dunlop. 1994.

Sterne's Tristram Shandy. Ed. Melvyn New. 1989.

Swift's Gulliver's Travels. Ed. Edward J. Rielly. 1988.

Thoreau's Walden *and Other Works*. Ed. Richard J. Schneider. 1996.

Voltaire's Candide. Ed. Renée Waldinger. 1987.

Whitman's Leaves of Grass. Ed. Donald D. Kummings. 1990.

Wordsworth's Poetry. Ed. Spencer Hall, with Jonathan Ramsey. 1986.

Wright's Native Son. Ed. James A. Miller. 1997.